GW00673121

Ecrins Massif, Cerces and Queyras *Selected Climbs*

Ecrins Massif, Cerces and Queyras

SELECTED CLIMBS
By John Brailsford

General Editor: Les Swindin

ALPINE CLUB . LONDON
2002

Ecrins Massif, Cerces and Queyras *Selected Climbs*

First published in Britain by the
Alpine Club 55 Charlotte Road London EC2A 3QF

Copyright © 2002 by the Alpine Club
Replaces Ecrins Massif 1987

Produced by the Alpine Club Editorial and Production Board

Sketch maps and topos drawn by Rod Powis

Cover photographs
Front La Meije N face *Jean-Louis Francou*
Back Climbing on the SW face of the Aiguille de Sialouze
Neil McAdie
Typeset in Plantin from the General Editor's word processor by
Tony Welch, Forest View Consultancy, Gloucester

Black and white and colour reproductions by
Bordercolour, Carlisle

Printed through Colorcraft Ltd, Hong Kong
Printed in China

British Library cataloguing in Publication Data. A catalogue
record for this book is available from the British Library
ISBN 0-900523-63-8

Contents

List of photographs

Rock Climbing

All uncredited photos are by *Jean-Louis Francou*

General Editor's preface

The previous volume of selected climbs in the Ecrins Massif, published in 1987, was the first in a new series of guide books published by the Alpine Club. This volume is the first of these to be updated and to take into account the ever changing Alpine environment as well as the developing ability of climbers on both rock and ice. Over the intervening years the series has developed in layout and features in a way that we hope has improved the ease of use. These changes have been incorporated into this volume.

The author, John Brailsford, has been involved with guide book writing for longer than he probably cares to remember. He is, of course, a very well respected figure in mountaineering circles, not only as a climber and as a guide but also as a developer of climbing techniques and equipment. He has spent many years climbing in the region, which is now his home, developing friendships with many people in the local climbing community and acquiring an intimate knowledge of the region. All this experience is invaluable in the guide book writing process.

The Ecrins Massif has a character of its own and people visiting for the first time might be in for a shock if they expect to see terrain similar to other Alpine regions. That said, it is extremely popular, especially amongst the French, and is usually very busy in July and Aug. Most of the mountains are of modest altitude and the weather in the area is generally better than in the mountains further north. Briançon claims to have 300 sunny days per year, perhaps this has an influence on the snow cover. Although plenty of snow falls in winter, the warmer climate ensures that it disappears relatively early in the summer leaving barren mountain sides much in evidence. As a consequence there are relatively few easy 'snow plods' and much more emphasis on rock ridges and faces. The selection of routes described takes account of this pattern with fewer climb in the lower grades of difficulty than is usual.

Whilst the major part of the guide book is devoted to the

description of mountain routes, There are two sections in it which are new and reflect the developments that have taken place over recent years. The first of these is a section on winter ice climbing. This region has an abundance of easily accessible, low altitude ice climbs, the winter equivalent of sport rock climbing but without the bolts. To say that the region is a Mecca for ice climbing enthusiasts would not be inaccurate. In fact, each winter an international meet in organised for just this purpose. Similarly there are enormous opportunities for sport rock climbing on quite easily accessible crags. Although this is not new, it has developed at a tremendous rate over the last decade. We trust that the selection of climbs described in both sections will offer something for climbers of all abilities.

As usual I would like to point out that the Alpine Club welcomes any comments about the routes described and any suggestions of other routes that deserve inclusion in future volumes. If you care to comment, it would be useful to us if information about when the route was climbed and the conditions that were encountered were given.

Finally my thanks once again to Alan Lyall for his proof reading of the text, a far from easy task. In addition I would like to thank John Slee-Smith and Peter Hodgkiss of the AC Guide Books Editorial and Production Board for getting the book into print and Rod Powis for his work on the sketch maps.

Author's preface

Since 1987 there has been a series of quantum leaps in every aspect of mountain activity in and surrounding the Ecrins National Park, the central core of which is the Massif des Ecrins. In addition to the almost feverish human activity, there have been radical changes in climate, with resultant modifications to the mountains themselves. Rapidly retreating glaciers have altered some of the hut approach routes. During the season, June to Sept, rapid melt also involves change in the path line. There are more predictable changes in the configuration of alpine style climbs. Some celebrated ice routes, such as the Couloir Chaud on the Pelvoux, have all but disappeared by mid-summer and are only possible in the early season or winter. By complete contrast, the abundance of early season snow has, on occasion, given snow gully approaches to classic valley rock around Ailefroide - a factor which has taken many visitors by surprise and which is universal throughout the region.

These changes have been taken into account in updating the section dealing with alpine style mountaineering and advice has been sought from a great many local guides from all around the Massif. In company with Murray Hamilton, another British guides living permanently in the region, we have been personally, deeply involved in noting and recording all the current and recent activity. It is still, however, essential to make personal judgement of conditions on the spot since the influence of the Mediterranean climate is as changing as it is profound.

Over the last five years there has been abundant winter and spring snow which, when allied to higher temperatures in summer months, has given rise to increased stonefall. Awareness of this factor is urged in relation to early season (ie May and June) mixed climbing and on rock climbs on the fringes of the main alpine region. It is suggested that local advice be sought relating to these issues when you arrive. Bureaux des Guides are the most reliable source of such help. Every sector has such a Bureau and, since hut bookings may be made at these offices, it is no difficult task to kill the two birds....

On the human activity front, development has taken place at an unprecedented level. Ice climbing may be said to have been reborn in the context of the new approach to waterfall, mixed ice-rock and 'cigar' style, technical challenges. The selection we give of the major areas of such development is witness both to the volume and distribution of this aspect of winter activity. The purely technical levels attained by the leaders in the field match those anywhere else in the world.

Access to these centres varies considerably. Some areas such as the Fournel valley above l'Argentière la Bessée have an access road which is cleared by the commune and relates to the International Ice Meet held there every Jan. Other sectors may only be approached on snow shoes or ski. Generally speaking there is no access by mechanical uplift via the ski resorts, except at la Grave. The options for roadside ice climbing are too many to list.

Rock climbing is now irreversibly divided into two distinct categories. Sport climbing abounds - there are even artificial walls in Argentière, Villeneuve and Montgenèvre. Both in the granitic valleys such as la Bérarde and Ailefroide and on the limestone blocks, such as Montbrison and the Massif des Cerces, equipped climbs of 450m are not uncommon and 600m climbs both equipped and classic are included in this guide. Climbing at higher altitude is subject to constraints agreed by the National Park and other bodies such as the Guides, but it is only prudent to add that some inroads of great significance have been made. These new, equipped climbs are to be found on the Aiguille de Sialouze, Aiguille Dibona, la Meije (S face) and the Contrefort des Bans. Climbs on the N face of the Pic Sans Nom such as 'Aurore Nucleaire' and 'Magic Stone' leave the climber with the option of retreating from the top of the rock section by a series of rappels (*in situ*) or continuing in traditional fashion to the summit of the mountain.

We do not wish to become involved with the debate surrounding these developments. It is the sole intention of this new volume to inform.

A serious, cautionary note must be included. Firstly, climbers will be wise to respect the environment in which they operate both in relation to nature and to the vagaries of alpine tempest. Secondly, there is no knowing whether the equipment in place is sound, and skill and speed in multi-abseil descents is essential, with care taken in relation to testing the anchor points placed for rappel purposes. Finally, there are some of the most gifted alpinists, rock and ice climbers in the world operating and living in the region. The standard of climbing is consequently high. *In situ* equipment does not mean that it is possible to cheat up routes. If climbers cannot climb the grade then it is more than likely that they will not complete the route. That said, there is some extraordinary climbing to be had at all times of the year, on ice or rock, and there remains the classic repertoire of climbs for which the Massif des Ecrins is justly famous, be they of the stature of the Gervasutti route on the Ailefroide NW face or the Voie Normale on the Pic de Neige Cordier and the Barre des Ecrins itself at 4,102m.

Skiing divides into three major categories, alpine (or piste), ski-mountaineering and Nordic. Most of the important resorts, together with those of the Queyras, offer off piste skiing, adjacent to the treated and groomed facility, which benefits from the lift system. In recent years, many British and other visitors have found their ski legs at these resorts, tested their equipment and acclimatised before setting out on their tours. Journeys in the Massif des Ecrins itself tend to be steep and committing but the author also recommends both the Massif des Cerces and the Queyras Regional Park as offering excellent ski-mountaineering at all levels.

Addendum

The winter of 2000/2001 was exceptional by any standards in the Hautes Alpes. Widespread, high volume precipitation fell at relatively mild temperatures. This gave less powder and more 'sticky' snow, which compacted quickly and was not blown off by the wind. As a result there was a continual winter cover of 3-4m at 1,600m (ski-resort level) and much more at higher altitudes. As late as April there was 14m depth at the Glacier Blanc hut with depths of 16-20m in certain areas.

Ski mountaineering continued into late June and the N and NW facing flanks remained encased. Rimayes, couloirs and crevasses were well filled, offering more straightforward climbing than in recent seasons.

There is a considerable body of opinion among local experts that if this pattern of heavy precipitation continues, there may be a marked improvement in travel and climbing conditions relating to snow/ice and glacier traverses. There is no suggestion of rejuvenation of the glaciers. It should also be noted that similar levels of snowfall were recorded in the late 1970s and in 1996. The 2001 level only affects the high altitude surfaces, covering the early season in particular. Three examples are: the Couloir Chaud had a recorded ascent on June 6th; all climbs from the Glacier Noir had rimayes fully filled with snow: the ordinary route on the Barre des Ecrins has been skied and climbed directly between the two sérac barriers.

The author has consulted many local guides and other professionals concerned with observation of conditions at altitude and suggests the following, should such conditions recur in future:

Early season climbs are likely to be more easily accessible on N and NW faces.

Do not attempt climbs which are recommended for the early season later than early July, unless there are conditions of snow/ice in their favour.

Alpinists make their choice of climbs and take account the nature of the snow cover on the day. Judgement of conditions is a major criterion for the individual to accept (when making decisions whether to climb or not).

If there is any doubt regarding the condition of the intended climb, then it is recommended that the visitor seeks the advice of a local Guide. There is no guarantee that hut guardians have the necessary expertise.

Credits

The author is indebted to many friends and colleagues in France. Without their professional advice, experience and cross checking, the work would lack authenticity. Days shared climbing have enhanced the job of producing this work which is, hopefully, balanced in terms of the grade, style and geographic distribution of climbs. Prominent among these are: Guy Martin, Murray Hamilton, Carol Nash, Terry Lowry, Marcel and Robin

Molinatti, Jean-Pierre and Jean-Louis Flandin, Jean Durand, Bruno Soleymieux, Seb Constant, Gérard Fiaschi and Lionel Alphand. Guillaume Christian created the Fournel topos. Jean-Louis Francou has provided most of the photographs, producing them in digitised form. All other photographs are credited.

Club Alpin Français, Briançon section, allowed me access to their original archive material and their kind support for my overall philosophy in producing the guide is much appreciated.

Thanks go to *Montagne Magazine* for permission to use their sketch map showing the distribution of climbs in the Fournel valley. For those not mentioned, I apologise for my omission but I value their moral support along the journey to fruition.

British support comes from members of the Alpine Club, former Vice President, Lindsay Griffin and the General Editor, Les Swindin.

Lyn Noble, who has partnered many climbs since our early visits in the 1960's, sharing cold bivouacs and inspirational moments alike, to him I owe special gratitude for 40 years of climbing friendship. Eric Jones and Jeremy Trumper came to share our visit to the Sirac (in 1999) and check out this neglected corner.

It is worth contemplating upon this unselfish goodwill within our alpine climbing fraternity, without which our world would be much poorer. It has been my priviledge to enjoy such goodwill.

John Brailsford

l'Argentière la Bessée, France

General Information

USING THIS GUIDE

Route Numbers

In this guide book we use the system whereby each mountain is given a unique numerical identity with the various routes on the mountain being differentiated by a unique letter. Thus the Barre des Ecrins is numbered **37** and the N Face and W Ridge Route is identified by number **37a**. The letter 'a', as in this case, is usually but not exclusively used to identify the 'ordinary' route of ascent of the particular mountain.

   In the section of the book describing 'valley' rock climbs, the routes are listed numerically but are identified as rock climbs by the inclusion of the letter '**r**'. Thus the Fissure on the Fissure Buttress at Ailefroide is numbered **r1**. A similar identification system is used for ice climbs, using a prefix letter '**i**' and for *via ferrata*, using the prefix '**vf**', in the appropriate sections.

Mountain Route Introductions

The route introduction, found in italics, gives a brief overview of the route and sometimes includes important information, both historical and practical, that would not normally be appropriate in the route description that follows. Quite often the height of the route is given in the introduction. Unless otherwise stated, this is the vertical interval from the base (perhaps the rimaye) to the top of the route. The actual climbing involved may be much greater.

Mountain Route Descriptions

Route descriptions vary considerably in detail from short explanations to detailed accounts. As the majority of the routes in the Ecrins region are of a mountaineering nature, topo diagrams have not been used. In the vast majority of cases the line of a route can be seen by consulting the appropriate photograph(s). Common British usage in naming routes and features has mostly been maintained. The terms L and R or Lwards and Rwards are always used with reference to the direction of movement of the climber. Occasionally, with features such as couloirs and glaciers the orographical reference to L or R bank is applied when viewed in the direction of flow (ie looking downwards). At the end of the route description is the total time proposed for the ascent. This will give a good indication as to the time needed for a rope of two climbing competently at the standard and experiencing no delays due to route finding and extended rests, other parties, weather etc. However these figures give no more than an indication; the timing of routes is an inexact science.

The Alps are in a constant state of flux. Glacial recession, warm winters with less that 'normal' amounts of snow, hot summers, rockfall/landslides, all can dramatically alter the character of a route. Although every effort has been made to ensure accuracy, absolute accuracy can never be guaranteed. It may be that the changing conditions have affected the route, or the route itself has had very few ascents, or even the author, the people he has has consulted and his correspondents have simply got it wrong. Unlike a pure rock climbing guide to a crag which will describe a route line with some intimacy, alpine route descriptions give direction, allowing parties to use their experience, route finding abilities and, most of all, sound judgement to follow the correct course. The basic information is all there, but when using this guide responsible mountaineers at whatever standard will assess the current conditions and employ common sense.

First Ascent

Brief details of first ascentionists have been included both to supplement information on the climb and so that the history is not lost. The climbers involved in the first ascent are listed in alphabetical order, irrespective of the roles played by the various members during the course of the ascent. In the case of older routes the guides names are listed after those of the clients.

First Winter Ascent

The first winter ascent (FWA) of a route, where known and considered relevant or historically significant, has been recorded as it is believed that its inclusion will supplement the information on the climb. As noted elsewhere, the UIAA recommendation, which is now widely accepted, is that the dates for winter ascents should fall between 21st Dec and 20th March.

Valley Base

This gives an indication of the most popular and most convenient valley base from which to attempt the climb. However, it is not suggested that the climb cannot be done from a different location if so desired.

Grade

The overall grade of the climb is indicated in the margin below the route number. In this guide, unless the route in question is fairly short and purely a rock climb, the well known and convenient French Adjectival Grade is used. In order of increasing difficulty: F (facile or easy: eg Routes 29a and 52a), PD (peu difficile or not very difficult: eg Route 46a), AD (assez difficile or quite difficult: eg Routes 28a and 49a), D (difficile or difficult: eg Routes 13k and 40f), TD très difficile or very difficult: eg Routes 13e and 37c) and ED (extrêmement difficile or extremely difficult: eg Routes 40e and 43d). Further refinement is possible by adding a plus or minus sign to the grades of TD and below but the ED grade is open-ended in a numerical fashion ie ED1, ED2 etc. The overall grade reflects not only the technical difficulty of the route but also its seriousness and the commitment needed to complete it. Length, altitude and objective danger play an important part in this grading and certain climbs, while they may not be technically demanding by modern standards, receive a high overall grade due to their inherent seriousness. This will generally be discovered in the introduction to the route.

Climbs have been graded for a completely free ascent unless otherwise stated. A number of ice/mixed routes described in this book are generally only feasible in winter/spring and their overall grade reflects the added problems with climbing at this time of year.

Technical difficulties on rock, on mountain routes, are graded according to the UIAA system. This numerical system uses Roman numerals ie I, II, III etc and is open-ended. Further refinement is acheived by adding a plus or minus sign. For most routes climbed for the first time prior to c1980 the upper grade tended to be given as VI however difficult the climbing and whether the crux pitch(es) was climbed free or was 'frigged'. In this guide book, where the information is known, any pitch graded VI is now also graded using the French rock climbing grades. This uses Arabic numerals and is refined by the addition of a letter 'a', 'b' or 'c'. Thus a grade VI pitch might now be indicated as 6a or 6b (or even 7a) when climbed free. A table of grading comparisons is printed at the end of the General Information section but should only be used as a general indication.

Rock climbs on mountain crags with first ascents dated post c1980 are treated in the same way as the valley rock climbs described towards the end of the guide book, the French numerical grading system being used.

Aid climbing is graded A0, A1, A2 etc. A0, a popular alpine grade, occurs when a bombproof piton/bolt/nut is used as a handhold to aid progress. On A1 and above climbers will need to stand in slings/étriers and use progressively sophisticated gear (hooks, copperheads etc) with prospects of increasingly long falls should a piece fail.

With climbs that involve technical difficulties on snow and ice the grading system is less precise due to the variable conditions from season to season and from year to year. On routes involving hanging glaciers or ice slopes with sérac formations there are constant changes in the difficulties and objective dangers. Glacier approaches can and have become extremely tortuous in recent dry summers and formerly classic snow arêtes can be exposed crumbling shale by mid-season. The average angle of a mixed/ice face is sometimes quoted and the angles of some ice pitches are given as an indication of the difficulties.

Photograph Numbers

If a particular route is marked on any of the photographs assembled in the back of this guide then the number of that photograph appears inside a shaded rectangle in the margin. Some routes may be visible and marked on more than one photograph. If this is the case, the photograph which best shows the route has its number displayed in the shaded rectangle whilst the other number(s) is shown below this in a small font size. A short-dashed line indicates that this section of the route is not visble on the photograph. On some photographs the lines of routes referred to in the text but not described in detail have been added as long-dashed lines. On a few mountain crags (notably the Aig Dibona and the Sialouze) some modern, bolt equipped routes have been described. These line are shown with a dot and dash line.

Topo Numbers

There are a few topos for ice climbs in the Fournel valley. The appropriate topo number is shown in the margin alongside the route details in an open rectangle.

Abbreviations

These are used for points of the compass (N, S, E, and W), left (L), right (R), hours (hr), minutes (min), circa (c) and metres/kilometres (m/km). Others that are frequently used: CAF (French Alpine Club), Pt (Pointe) as used on the map for a summit. Pt is also used for a spot height marked on the relevant map. The abreviation 'var' or 'alt' appears on some photographs indicating a variation or alternative line of ascent. The letter P is used to signify a pitch in a rock climb. Abreviations, which are obvious, are used for the months of the year.

Glossary of terms

Some words have been left untranslated where there is no exact English equivalent:

Brèche: a notch in a ridge, a gap or depression between two points.

Col: a pass or saddle.

Couloir: roughly the same as a gully, but more open, or sometimes a big feature in a mountain face.

Diédre: an open corner, often with a crack at the back, a V-groove (literally a dihedral).

Névé: hard snow turning into ice.

Rappel: to rope down: to abseil.

Rimaye: a large terminal crevasse where the glacier separates from the snow or rock slopes of a mountain, a bergschrund.

Rognon: a rock island in a glacier or ice-fall.

Sérac: an ice cliff.

Voie: (as used in route names) Route

USING HUTS

The network of mountain huts allows time to be spent in the heart of the range close to the proposed ascents and without the burden of a heavy rucksack. Several routes can sometimes be accomplished from a single hut base before returning to the valley. Although relatively inexpensive, hut fees can be significantly reduced on production of a reciprocal rights card (such as those from national clubs such as the Alpine Club, Austrian and Swiss Alpine Clubs etc). BMC members are not entitled to a reduction in fees unless they can produce a UIAA reciprocal rights card. These are available from the BMC.

In many of the huts in the region it is necessary to pre-book bed space even for small parties. This is particularly so in the height of the season (most of July and Aug) when it may be necessary to give several days notice of a visit. If unsure, aim to get there early. Most of the huts are now on a telephone link and their numbers are noted in the huts section. Unfortunately not all hut guardians and their staff speak English. If you have a problem communicating by telephone the local Tourist Office will usually make a booking on your behalf or you can ask campsite or hotel staff to do the same.

On arrival at a hut the first priority, whether a reservation has been made or not, should be to report to the guardian (after changing boots for hut slippers). Tell the guardian your proposed route for the following day and what time you wish to rise (although you will often find that there is a 'standard' time to rise). To minimise early morning disturbance you will probably be given a room with others who wish to depart at the same time. It is possible that very late arrivals may find their reserved bed space has been allocated to someone else. Inform the guardian if you expect to be late. Most importantly, please remember to telephone and cancel if you know you are not going to be able to take up your booking.

Most huts offer a restauraunt service and you should book meals when you reserve your places. French huts normally make provision for visitors who wish to self-cater as long as a stove and cooking utensils have been brought. Sometimes gas cookers are provided but there may be a heavy demand for their use.

Despite the benefits of hut facilities, during the high season noise, overcrowding and increasing costs have led a number of parties to camp or bivouac nearby. Discreet wild camping is tolerated in the mountains but not in the close viscinity of huts.

Whether camping, bivouacking, staying in huts or travelling through the mountains there is no excuse for not taking all refuse back down to the valley for proper disposal or recycling. Huts provide plasic bags for the purpose.

WHEN TO CLIMB

The alpine summer season may extend from mid-June to late Sept, although at the beginning of this period there can still be copious amounts of spring snow, whilst towards the end of the season the nights can be cold and a heavy snowfall is possible.

Alpine huts do not usually open until their approaches are largely clear of the spring snows. They tend to close by mid-Sept when most holiday makers have gone home (15th June - 15th Sept is often the normal period for wardened huts, apart from the ski-touring season in spring). July and Aug are the busy months with the peak period generally the last two weeks of July and the first two in Aug. Climbers looking for tranquility on other than the more esoteric routes should come outside these times. Summers, especially in more recent years, have been hot and characterised by unsettled weather with violent thunderstorms. More stable conditions tend to occur in late spring - an ideal time for ice/mixed climbs on faces that can become barren in the summer - and in Sept/Oct, when the colours can be brilliant, the atmosphere free from haze and the mountains almost empty.

Winter climbing as opposed to ski-mountaineering is not practised here to anything like the extent it is in the Mont Blanc Massif. The same cannot be said about lower altitude ice climbing. The lack of téléphérique systems giving access to high mountain winter venues leads to long, complicated and often avalanche-prone approaches. Although the accepted period for a winter ascent to be valid is from 21st Dec to 20th March inclusive, ascents outside this period can be equally, if not sometimes more demanding.

April, May and early June are usually popular with ski-touring/mountaineering parties and some huts can be extremely busy during this time, especially the Ecrins, Glacier Blanc and Alpes huts.

MAPS

Users of this guide book are recommended to use the excellent TOP 25 series 1:25000 scale maps published by the Institut Géographique National (IGN) as:

3436 ET Meije. Pelvoux

3336 ET Les Deux Alpes Olan. Muzelle

3437 ET Orcières-Merlette Sirac. Moure Froid

3437 OT Champsaur Vieux Chaillol (for the GR54 only)

These are available in GPS compatible form ie they have grid lines.

Detail of maps which relate to each of the sections described are listed in that section.

An alternative is the 1:50000 IGN maps published by Didier and Richard. This may be used but many of the spot heights and features mentioned in the route descriptions are not marked (or vary) on these maps. A series '900' has been issued (summer 1999) by IGN, which caters for special interests. Amongst these are: 909 - Climbing sites, 903 - Long Distance Footpaths (GRs), 906 - Long distance mountain bike (VTT) routes.

OTHER GUIDE BOOKS

All the books listed below are in current use and readily available.

Mountaineering

Labande F *Guide du Haut-Dauphiné*
Vol 1 (2000) ISBN 2 909907 15 5
Vol 2 (1998) ISBN 2-909907-24-4
Vol 3 (1998) ISBN 2-909907-22-8
Publisher: Editions de l'Envol

Sommets des Ecrins Chevaillot, Grobel and Minelli (1997)
Publisher: Glénat ISBN 2-7234-2007-8

Le Massif des Ecrins - vu du ciel Poulet and Sombardier (1992)
Publisher: Glénat ISBN 2-7234-1459-0

Le Massif des Ecrins - Les 100 Plus Belles Courses Randonnées
Gaston Rébuffat Publisher: Denoël, Paris. New version published but it is far from reliable. This is a book for inspiration only.

Rock Climbing

Oisans Moderne: Oisans Sauvage J-M Cambon (1995)
ISBN 2 9502597-2-3
Escalades en Valgaudemar R Karle Private publication
Escalades à Ailefroide PH Paillasson and J-M Cambon (1998)
Dépôt légal: 514
Escalades du Briançonnais S Péguy and J-J Roland Publisher:
Aphrys The original guide to the Briançon and Durance
climbing developments which may repay the search for unbolted
climbs, many of which are seldom done today. Available for
study only at the CAF Briançon office
Haute Romanche: Montagnes Sauvages B Soleymieux (1992). A
topo guide ISBN 2-9507195-0-3 Publisher: La Pierre Farabo.
Covers la Grave area.

Ice Climbing

Cascade de Glace J-M Asselin and G Perroux (1984)
ISBN 2.86519-042.0 - now very dated.
Les Cascades de glace R Balestra (1996) Private publication
Cascade et Glace R Boris and P Turin (2000) Dépôt légal 728
Covers Briançon, Argentière and Embrun
Cascades de Glaces - Oisans au Six Vallées F Damilano F and G
Perroux (1992) Dépôt légal: 789

Further reference

Descriptions of the latest modern rock climbing routes in the
region are available at huts, Bureaux des Guides and the CAF
office in Briançon (open 4pm to 7pm weekdays). Local
publications are updated at reasonable intervals.
Oisans Nouveau - Oisans Sauvage (East) J-M Cambon (2000)
ISBN: 2-9502597-6-6. Well produced but with little new route
information. A companion volume is in preparation

Les Plus Belles Escalade Calcaires des Hautes Alpes J-P Bizet,
P Giraud and J-J Rolland (2000) Private publication. Some good
coverage but inconsistent diagram quality
Grimpeur dans la Haut Val Durance Y, M, and J-J Rolland (2000)
Dépôt Légal 114. Extensive and deals with crags. Diagrams are
only adequate

Projected new editions

New climbs in Cerces, Montbrison, Queyras and Durance valley.
J-J Rolland and Philippe Giraud
Ice F Damilano and G Perroux

Walking

Tour de l'Oisans - Hautes Alpes - Isère, GR 54 Topo guide R Canac
Publisher: Parc National des Ecrins
Tour de Queyras A Castle Publisher: Cicerone Press
Ecrins Park, Dauphiné Alps RG Collomb Publisher: West Col
The Tour of the Oisans Harper Publisher: Cicerone Press
50 Randonées autour de Briançon R Kehrès (1995)
ISBN 2-910929-01-9

Local walking guides are available at all the Syndicat d'Initiative
and Tourist Offices in the region.

Walking and Ski-touring

Massif des Ecrins et Haut Dauphiné, Randonées pédestre et à skis
O Gumuchian and L Martin Publisher: Didier Richard,
Grenoble
Massif du Queyras et Haut Ubaye, Randonées pédestre et à skis
J Cadier and RH Gros Publisher: Didier Richard, Grenoble
Grande Traverse M and N Parker (1986) ISBN 0-906371-81-3
Publisher: Diadem (walk/ski touring)

Massifs des Ecrins and Haute Dauphiné Randonées and ski
O Gumuchian and L Martin (1981) ISBN 2-7038-007-X
Ski de Randonnée Isère ISBN 2-88086-226-4
Ski de Randonnée Hautes Alpes ISBN 2-88086-256-6 Both
published by Editions Olizane SA
Ecrins Nord V Shahshahani ISBN 2-912063 Publisher Volopress.
A must for serious skiers. A companion volume is in preparation.
Névache, Vallée de la Clarée - Itinéraires skieurs J-G Ravary (1998)
ISBN 2-909051-03-X

Also published by the Alpine Club is the Alpine Journal, an
annual compilation of information and articles on mountains
and mountaineering worldwide. Pertinent to this and other
guide-books is the section headed 'Area Notes' which gives
further information about route descriptions where conditions
have changed.

EQUIPMENT

Many of the standard routes on the snowy peaks will require
little more than a single rope, an axe and crampons plus the
ability to judge snow conditions and extricate a member of the
party from a crevasse. On middle grade climbs where lengthy
rappels are not anticipated most parties will nowadays use a
single 10mm or possibly 11mm rope, carry a small selection of
wires and hexentrics and several long slings for spikes and flakes.
A couple of ice screws may also prove useful, even for glacier
travel. On the harder routes a double rope, full set of rock and ice
gear (quick-draws, Friends and rock pitons) and possibly
bivouac equipment will be needed. There are many manuals on
the craft of alpinism for the less experienced and by the time
parties are attempting routes in the upper grades, they should
have gathered all the requisite know-how to judge for themselves
exactly what gear will be needed.

WEATHER FORECASTS

A good weather forecast is available at the Bureaux des Guides
or, in la Bérarde, at the rescue post adjacent to the CAF centre.

There is a national service with a local (Briançon) centre, accessible by telephone under 'Météo France' 04 92 68 04 04: the region is classed 'Alpes du Sud'. This service is very reliable and strongly recommended.

The internet site www.meteo.fr/e_index.html provides a three day forecast using symbols that are easily understood. Click on *'en France'* and then you can choose the region or the town (eg Briançon).

RESCUE AND INSURANCE

In an emergency it is usual to contact the nearest guarded hut. Alternatively, call any gendarmerie or any of the following rescue posts. A mobile phone is now widely used by alpinists but it is not always successful eg in deep valleys such as Ailefroide.

La Grave: The post serves la Meije, le Pavé, Pic Gaspard and the Planchard cirque. The actual helicopter service is based in Briançon. Briançon serves Massif des Ecrins, Pelvoux and S side of les Bans, N side of la Meije and Râteau and le Sirac.

Tel: 04 92 21 10 42 (Gendarmerie)

Tel: 04 92 22 22 22 (CRS)

La Bérarde: Serves Sorreiller (Dibona), Ailefroide, les Bans, Vallon des Etages and the Western area. Tel: 04 76 80 54 83 (Bureau des Guides)

Tel: 04 76 79 51 00 (PGHM)

The cost of rescues and hospitalisation can be very high. The basic helicopter 'lift' off the mountain is free but if any searching is involved, helicopter time is charged for. If a guide becomes involved on the mountain or crag, it depends how much he is involved and also whether his client charges for the disruption. It will be a very minor incident when some form of charge will not be made. Climbers are strongly urged to insure themselves adequately. The BMC offers good cover for rescue but this should be reinforced by British climbers' obtaining form No E111 from their Post Office or local Department of Social

Security. This form must be up to date, contrary to the belief in UK that the form E111 is 'for life'. The French system does not recognise forms more than five years old. Because of the complexity and cost of rescue it is prudent to leave details of any intended expedition with a responsible person, camp office or the Bureau des Guides.

Other emergency telephone numbers are as follows:

Fire Brigade/accident (Pompiers)   18
Police   17
Other emergency service   15

These are free, national services.

MEDICAL SERVICES

Hospitals are at Grenoble, Briançon and Gap.

There is a new ambulance service to Briançon from Vallouise (tel: 04 92 23 42 48) and, in an emergency other than a mountain rescue, the Fire Brigade (Pompiers) Tel: 18, may be called from Argentière la Bessée into the Vallouise area. Generally, the Bureaux des Guides and Syndicats d'Initiative are most helpful and supportive. There is a European emergency telephone number (112).

Ambulance services are privately run.

Doctors are available at: Briançon, Serre Chevalier, Argentière-la-Bessée, Vallouise, la Grave, le Bourg d'Oisans, la Mure, St Bonnet, St Firmin, Gap and Corps,

Dentists are available at: Briançon, le Bourg d'Oisans, Grenoble and Gap.

Pharmacies are located at: all the main centres and towns but no in Ailefroide or la Bérarde.

INDEXES

At the back of the book, just before the photographs and topos, are two indexes: a tabulated list of routes and general index in conventional form. The tabulated list includes the valley base from which the route is normally attempted, the style of the climb (rock, ice, mixed etc), an indication of the route length and the overall grade. This should assist parties at a particular base to choose a route according to conditions, weather and ability.

VALLEY BASES

Each of the valley bases are easily accessible by car, at least in the summer season. Apart from la Grave and Vallouise they are inaccessible in winter.

La Grave lies on the N side of the range, high up the Romanche valley, at 1,480m. It is easily accessible being on the main Grenoble-le Bourg d'Oisans - Col du Lautaret - Briançon trunk route (N91). In the village are a number of hotels and pensions, dortoirs, food and equipment shops, a post office and a Bureau des Guides and much enlarged and modern camping facilities, controlled by the commune. Specialised information regarding the climbing, skiing and ice in this sector, may be discussed with local guide, Bruno Soleymieux at 'La Pierre Farabo', an excellent restaurant/snack bar.

La Bérarde lies at 1,720m at the road head in the Vénéon Valley, which runs W from almost the centre of the range. There is a bus service from le Bourg d'Oisans, which is reached in its turn (bus) from Grenoble or Briançon by the N91. The road from le Bourg d'Oisans to la Bérarde is narrow and in places steep. It has been considerably improved in the lower section in recent years. The village is small, but has hotels, restaurants, food and equipment shops and guides. There is a new campsite to replace and extend the old one, with good, modern facilities.

A CAF centre offers *dortoir* or single room accommodation and excellent meals at, for its situation, reasonable cost and there are other dortoirs in the village.

Mail may be left either at the camp site or the Syndicat d'Initiative, which also controls camping within the confines of the commune. La Bérarde is fast developing as a first-class high mountain centre. The Gendarmerie now have a permanent rescue base with helicopters on the spot.

Ailefroide lies at the head of the Gyronde (or Vallouise) valley at 1,500m. It can be reached by a bus or taxi from Argentière la Bessée via Vallouise. The road and bus continue a little further up the valley to Cézanne (or Pré de Mme Carle), situated at 1,874m: this is a group of two or three buildings including a restaurant and a chalet-hotel (reduction for CAF members) and a new National Park office and ugly, extended car parking. The site heaves with visitors throughout July and August. Camping is forbidden.

Ailefroide itself has 3 hotels and shops selling a good selection of food and equipment. A newly extended camp site, office and buildings provide excellent services for campers including toilet facilities, hot showers and post service. There is also a Bureau des Guides and several public telephones. Self catering facilities, suitable for small groups or families, may be found at the Clouzis hotel/restaurant. A gîte, run by the Albrand/ Giraud families, is to be found just beyond the main village, facing the *école d'escalade*.

Vallouise, which is lower in the Gyronde valley (c1,160m) compared with Ailefroide but offers similar facilities with shops, hotels and restaurants, dortoirs and camping. It has the advantage of being rather less crowded than Ailefroide in the high season.

Valjoffrey and Valgaudemar, in the W of the region, are the starting points for some of the climbs included in this guide. They offer very little in the way of tourist facilities in the upper part of the two valleys and are not suitable for long stays. The lower parts of these valleys are much more tourist friendly.

BANKS

There are banks at Briançon, Argentière la Bessée, Vallouise, le Bourg d'Oisans, la Grave, Gap, St Bonnet en Champsaur but not in Ailefroide or la Bérarde. They are usually open on Sat and close on Mon but this varies with the bank and it is worth checking locally. Credit cards are the safest form of cash transactions and cash machines abound in the main towns and some larger villages.

TRANSPORT

Most vistors to the region will approach via Grenoble and most, at least in summer are likely to be travelling by car. Grenoble is easily accessible by the French motorways (Autoroutes) from the Channel ports. Grenoble itself can be avoided by the motorway standard ring-road. From Grenoble, the whole of the Ecrins/ Cerces/Queyras region is open via well signposted 'N' roads. There is no motorway as yet. Access to most centres (see details above in Valley Bases) is via the N85 (to Vizille) and then the N91 (towards Briançon). Beyond Briançon the N94 heads S through l'Argentière la Bessée for access to the Queyras.

Valjouffrey (refuge Fond Turbat) and Valgaudemar are reached by following N85 (to Vizille) and then towards Gap - 'Route Napoléon'. Turn off at la Mure, on the D526, for Valjouffrey and just beyond Corps for Valgaudemar (D985a). The road between la Chapelle and the Hotel Giobnerney is closed in winter.

Visitors travelling by rail might use Eurostar to Paris and then a TGV (Train Grand Vitesse) to reach Grenoble. From there use a bus to Bourg d' Oisans, La Grave, la Bérarde and Gap.

A winter rail service links Paris with Milan by TGV. It stops at Oulx which is just 16km from Montgenèvre on the French-Italian border, giving access to the Durance valley. Links by bus and mini-bus run in winter to Briançon but as yet, there is no regular service in summer. It is anticipated that such liaison will improve as the rail service becomes established. An overnight train (with couchettes) between Paris and l'Argentière la Bessée/ les Ecrins continues to offer direct access to the SE sector of the region. This train stops at all stations from Gap, thus giving access to the Queyras. A bus service runs regularly from Eygliers/ Mont Dauphin to the villages of Ceillac, Aiguilles and Abries. It is wise to book seats in advance. Buses also run to Vallouise and Ailefroide and relate to train arrivals.

Travelling to the region by air is not particularly convenient. Flights to Turin give quick access from the major airports of Britain. In winter only, the ski charter flight, transfer buses may offer links to the resorts around Briançon. Similarly for flights to Geneva. Car hire is the only other means of transfer available. Flights to Nice, Lyon (Satolas) and Grenoble are frequent but also involve private car hire or similar.

Coaches, which are relatively cheap, run from London Victoria to Grenoble. However onward travel to climbing centres by rail or bus has to be arranged.

The general consensus on travel is that private transport provides maximum flexibility in every sense. If visitors wish to move around the region there is no really practical, alternative and the western flank of the massif is very poorly served by public transport.

MOUNTAIN GUIDES

There are two means of obtaining a Guide. The traditional Bureau des Guides still flourishes in every community but the services now reflect the growing need for group tuition and expeditions. The quality of guiding is high but in the Dauphiné, little (good) English is spoken. The British Mountain Guides can be contacted either through the BMC in Manchester or direct via the Guides' office: B M Guides, Capel Curig, Gwynedd LL24 0ET. Tel: 01690 720 386 or Fax: 01690 720 248. E-mail futurmedia@infinet.u-net.com or ml.tb@virgin.net. website: http://www.bmg.org.uk. Many guides now have their own personal e-mail address and website, details of which may be obtained from the Capel Curig office.

Details of tariffs and types of services are also available. The British guides enjoy excellent relations with their Dauphiné colleagues and are affiliated to the International Union of Guide (UIAGM).

WALKING IN THE REGION

It is perhaps true to say that there are ten serious mountain walkers for every single alpinist in the Ecrins massif. The region is rich in wild, unspoiled hill country which would delight any lover of open spaces.

The most celebrated hill walk must be the 'Tour de l'Oisans' coded as the GR54 with its link route into the Queyras region, the GR541. There is a Topo-Guide, published in 1981, written by Roger Canac, the French Guides' former president, for the National Park and costing c8€. See also *Tour of the Oisans* by Harper. The visiting climber would also find the booklet valuable since it offers detail of access to huts and means of linking valley to valley. Alternative walks radiating from the route add to its value. The black and white maps contained in Canac's guide are adequate but it is strongly recommended that the IGN 1:25000 TOP 25 series is used. Three such maps cover the entire tour and are listed under the Maps heading, page 26.

Tour de Queyras (GR58) is contained in Castle's book of that name and covered by the following maps:

3537 ET   Guillestre Ceillac

3537 OT   Viso St Véran

3536 OT   Briançon

National Park information bureaux and local 'Syndicats d'Initiative' carry much useful information.

The Didier and Richard 1:50000 map 'Ecrins, Haut-Dauphiné' No 6 and 'Queyras and Haute Ubaye' No 10 give a wealth of path and hut site detail as well as ski-touring routes.

Walking potential varies:

La Bérarde is the most sparse, being virtually the hub of the massif. Walks to huts or glaciers are about the extent of village based outings. However, down the Vénéon valley and around Bourg d'Oisans, the countryside opens out to offer many opportunities.

Briançon, Vallouise and the Durance valley abound with exhilarating offerings. The hanging valleys above l'Argentière la Bessée and the Durance river, such as Val Fournel and

Fressinières are delightful and of good motoring access to the starting points of walks.

The Queyras Park E of the Durance is well worth visiting. The highest centre of population in Europe is the village of St Véran, which is occupied throughout the year and serves as a ski resort in winter.

The Massif des Cerces S of the Col du Galibier and sandwiched between the Guisane river and the Italian border, is a limestone massif of charm and variety. It is accessible via the Clarée valley from Briançon or points along the Serre Chevalier-Col du Lautaret road (RN91).

To the W, Valjouffrey gives access to the Olan group whilst Valgaudemar serves the SW sector of the park, including le Sirac Gap is a good base from which to enter the Dévoluy and Pic de Bure sector. This last area is least known to British visitors.

For the more adventurous, a tour of the high cols must offer some of the finest high level travelling in Europe. Huts (CAF and private), gîtes d'etape, as well as hotel accommodation are all available, offering good value for money at all levels. Guides' offices as well as the normal tourist agencies offer advice and will also offer conducted tours throughout the season. CAF and National Park offices issue an annual list of huts with details of the guardians and their phone numbers, so that advanced bookings may be made.

MOUNTAIN BIKING

The author would be remiss if he omitted to include a note on this most popular and fast growing sport. Mountain bikes (VTT to the French) are banned from within the Park official boundary. However, the surrounding country offers challenging and exciting adventure, with routes attaining 3,000m. CAF have a great involvement and have elected officers to overlook the sport. Rules are not written but it is expected that riders in the region will, first and foremost, have good mountain knowledge and experience and use sound common sense values as their

guide to behaviour. Above all, the bike gives way to walkers!
There is a very good series of guide books available locally and
many Communes offer their own, local publications.

WINTER ACTIVITIES

Piste skiing is the major winter sport, apart from alpinism,
which dominates the whole region. Serre Chevalier,
Montgenèvre, les Deux Alpes, Alpe d'Huez and other major,
relatively recently developed stations such as Puy St Vincent,
Risoul/Vars and Orcières-Merlette are well known to British
skiers seeking piste facilities. All ski resorts have a free shuttle
service (ski pass needed) between villages.

Nordic skiing (ski de fond) is very popular, especially in
Valgaudemar, the Queyras, Clarée valley and Vallouise/Puy St
Vincent centres. The long, relatively flat valleys of the Massif des
Ecrins are ideally suited to this branch of ski sport. Equipment
hire, tuition and guides are available at all main centres and costs
are most reasonable. The region is far from crowded. Once away
from the pistes, the mountaineer will find solitude and beauty in
abundance.

   More serious ski touring/mountaineering is not carried out
in the true winter season as the best conditions are found in the
period April-mid June; but at any time, the main massif is not a
place for the novice. Ample choice for day outings exists to suit
all levels of ability.

Ski mountaineering: It is not the purpose of this guide to
provide 'in depth' detail of ski mountaineering itineraries. Suffice
to say that there exists an abundance of ski touring and ski
mountaineering. Pleasure may also be derived from the
dreaming and planning...

   Normally the season runs from the end of March into June.
It is interesting to note that over the last five years or so, late
snowfall has been significant, prolonging the season.

   Classic tours in the main massif are well documented
elsewhere and the Didier Richard and IGN maps carry well

marked itineraries. What is less well known is the wealth of potential outside the main Massif des Ecrins. The tours of Cerces, Queyras and Viso are all possible on ski and broadly follow the summer routes.

Day tours and short journeys have been well documented and the source material is to be found in the bibliography above. The volume by Kehrès (Briançonnais) is particularly recommended, offering a wide range of outings which are effectively described and illustrated. The Soleymieux book, *Haute Romanch* contains information around la Grave and the Meije group. It is again worth noting that there is a bus link between St Christophe (Vénéon valley) and the téléphérique at Venosc, which rises to les Deux Alpes (Girose glacier and Mont de Lans glacier). This link opens up the Vallon de la Meije - Vallon de la Selle circuit, as well as providing for those who have left a vehicl on one side of the massif or the other and are involved in longer trips or ice climbing. Huts need to be booked in advance.

GITES D'ETAP

These institutions offer accommodation varying from dortoir to 'bed and breakfast' and include rural apartments for letting. They are organised by regions. The addresses for the region are:

Relais départemental des gites de France (Haute-Alpes), 1er, ru Capitaine de Bresson, 05000 GAP Tel 04 92 51 31 45

Relais départemental des gîtes de France (Isère), Maison du Tourisme - 14, rue de la Republique, 38000 or 38019 GRENOBLE CEDEX Tel 04 76 54 34 36 TELEX 980 718

Dortoirs, with meals available, run by local people (who speak fluent English) in the summer season:

La Bérarde: Christiane Amevet Tel 04 76 79 54 20

La Grave: Bruno Soleymieux (Guide) Tel 04 76 79 90 03

Ailefroide: Gîtes d'étape Albrand Tel 04 92 23 32 03, Hotel/ restaurant, self cater appartments 'Les Clouzis' Tel 04 92 23 52 90 and 04 92 23 32 07

GRADING COMPARISONS

French	French	UIAA	British	British	USA	Australia
1		I	M		5.1	4
2		II	D		5.2	6
2+					5.3	
3-		III	VD		5.4	8
3		III+			5.5	10
3+		IV	HVD		5.6	12
4	4a	IV+ / V-	S	4a	5.7	14
4+	4b / 4c	V	HS		5.8	16
5	5a / 5b	V+	VS	4b / 4c	5.9	
5+	5c	VI-	HVS	5a	5.10a	18
6a		VI	E1	5b	5.10b	19
6a+		VI+			5.10c	20
6b		VII-	E2		5.10d	
6b+		VII		5c	5.11a	21
6c		VII+	E3		5.11b	22
6c+		VIII-	E4		5.11c	23
7a		VIII		6a	5.11d	
7a+		VIII+			5.12a	24

The grading comparison table above can at best be approximate. It has never proved simple to equate differing rock types or climbing styles between different countries. However, hopefully it should be of assistance to visiting climbers unused to the French numerical grading system, which is used in this guide book and is becoming the system of choice throughout the Alpine regions.

Remember that the French 'technical' grades evolved as a means of assessing the difficulty of France's developing sport climbing, which primarily took place on steep limestone. Unlike the British technical grade, but in common with most other systems currently in use (eg American YDS etc) the French grade reflects the overall difficulty of the pitch (or section) rather than its hardest individual move.

HUTS

Access routes to all the huts useful to the expeditions in this
guide book are well used, clearly marked tracks. The Aigle hut is
the exception, where the Tabuchet glacier and other factors
complicate the route. The recommended 1:25000 maps clearly
indicate the position and the winter and summer approaches for
each hut. The following list indicates the capacity and responsible agencies only. National Park waymarking facilitates route
finding further. The huts are grouped for ease of reference.

La Grave

H1 Adèle Planchard Hut 3,169m (STD). *This is a newish hut, with 64
places. It is guarded in spring from early Apr to early May and during
July and August. The hut is open in winter (25 places). There are no
cooking facilities.* Tel: 04 76 79 92 14. **5-5½hr** from Pied du Col

H2 Aigle Hut 3,450m (CAF Briançon). *The hut is situated NE of the
Pic Centrale de la Meije. It is wooden, has room for 20, mattresses and
blankets, a stove, cooking pots and water. The route to it from la Grave
involves a good deal of glacier, some of which is crevassed. The hut is
not easy to find in bad visibility. It is guarded in the summer seasons.
(See Photo 16, taken in 1998 which indicates a fall in snow level of
some 15-20m in 10 years! An older photo may be found in Rébuffat,
Page 146). The president of CAF Briançon dreams of carrying this
ancient edifice to the valley and constructing a modern refuge in its
place - who knows?* Tel: 04 76 79 94 74

From Pied du Col, which is approached in a few minutes
by car from la Grave. Leave the car at the obvious bridge, due S
of the hamlet of Pied to Col at 1,662m. Cross the Romanche
and follow a good track into the valley below the Bec glacier.
Gain the ridge separating the Bec and Tarbuchet glaciers at a
point 200m S of the Col du Bec (paint marks). The ridge above
rises a little more steeply: follow it for c200m until a ledge leads
R (fixed cable) on to the Tarbuchet glacier. Follow the R bank of
the glacier to reach the hut. **5½-6hr**: 2½hr for descent

Another approach that can be used early in the season is to follow Route 12a to the top of the Enfetchores and then traverse the Meije glacier to the Passage du Serret. Follow this on to the Tabuchet glacier and cross this to the hut.

It is worth noting that there is a new camp site and Gîte facilities just beyond the car park area at the start of the Pied du Col 'walk in', beside a small, artificial lake. The unmade road which used to lead towards the Pavé and Alpe huts is now closed to vehicles.

H3   Alpe Hut 2,077m (CAF Briançon): *86 places. It is guarded end-Mar to mid-May and in summer. It is a popular stopping place for tourists. The most modern hut in Hautes Alpes - with showers!* Tel: 04 76 79 94 66. **1½hr** from Pied du Col

H4   Chancel Hut 2,506m (CAF Briançon): *40 places. An old hut of wood and stone construction which is guarded at weekends in winter and during the summer period at all times. It is easily accessible from the mid-station of the Meije télécabine. It is easily accessible from the Col de Ruillans by ski and is often opened in good ski conditions.* Tel: 04 76 90 84 38. **1hr** from the mid-station, 3hr from la Grave

H5   Pavé Hut 2,841m (CAF Briançon): *26 places. It is a metal, workmans hut. Guarded in summer, it is cramped but serves well as a high access for climbs about the upper Cavales glacier and the Couloir du Diable. Open in winter.*

The hut is often used as a rest stop by parties crossing between the Romanche valley and la Bérarde. Mid-day groups can give a wrong impression of the number of overnight hut users. Tel: 04 92 24 88 03. **4hr** from Pied du Col

Note: Téléphérique, la Grave

This facility runs from the last week of June up to the first week of Sept. A special, 'alpinist' cabin leaves at 8am (normal time for the public is 10am). It drops off at the first station to give access to the Brèche de la Meije via the Enfetchores and the Col de Ruillans, well placed for the Girose glacier and all climbs thereabouts. The lift takes c30min from bottom to top. The whole of the ski season is served.

La Bérarde

La Bérarde Centre 1,740m (CAF Isère): *172 places. It offers dortoir or small room accommodation, restaurant services and showers. It is relatively new and well appointed, being used as a base for a variety of training courses. It may be booked in advance by writing to the Director of the Centre. For those wishing to move straight into the mountains and not to camp, the centre is excellent value.*
Tel: 04 76 79 53 83

H6 Chatelleret Hut 2,232m (CAF Isère): *70 places. Guarded from early Apr to mid-May and in summer. It is much frequented. A winter section is open with one dormitory available.* Tel: 04 76 79 08 27. **2hr** from la Bérarde

H7 Alpe du Pin Hut 1,805m (State owned): *30 places. There is water beside the hut. No resident guardian. The hut is available between May and end-Oct with the key held by M. Claude Turc, Bar 'La Cordée' in St Christophe. Reservations can be made via 'La Cordée'* Tel: 04 76 79 52 37. **1½hr** from St Christophe en Oisans

H8 Lavey Hut 1,797m (CAF Isère): 70 places. *It has a guardian in summer and on demand in Spring. There is a spring close to the hut.* Tel: 04 76 80 50 52. **1½hr** from Champhorent

H9 Muzelle Hut 2,115m (Venosc Commune): *50 places. The hut is on the GR54 and is guarded in summer. Groups should contact the guardian in advance. The keys are available out of season from M. Durdan at the Amis de la Montagne hotel in Vénosc (Tel 04 76 11 10 10). Start from Bourg d'Arud. There is ample space for bivouacs.* Tel: 04 76 79 02 01. **3hr** from l'Bourg d'Arud

H10 Pilatte Hut 2,577m (CAF Isère): *100 places. This well appointed hut is guarded from early Apr to mid-May and throughout the summer. The old wooden hut provides winter accommodation for 20.* Tel: 04 76 79 08 26. **3½hr** from la Bérarde

H11   Promontoire Hut 3,082m (CAF Isère): *36 places. It is guarded in summer. In winter, there is accommodation for 18. It is always overbooked in summer - make your reservation in good time!*, Tel: 04 76 80 51 67. **5hr** from la Bérarde

Note that the hut can be reached from la Grave via route 12a. This puts the car in place for the traverse of the Meije.

H12   Selle Hut 2,673m (STD): *79 places. It is guarded, on demand in Spring, and in season. Cooking facilities are available. In winter only the old section is open with room for 32 (no cooking facilities).* Tel: 04 76 79 56 56. **3hr** from St Christophe en Oisans

H13   Soreiller (Dibona) Hut 2,719m (STD): *110 places. Guarded throughout the summer. Open but not guarded in winter/spring.* Tel: 04 76 79 08 32. **3hr** from les Etages

H14   Temple-Ecrins Hut 2,410m (CAF Isère): *103 places. It is the least attractive of the huts in the region, being little more than a draughty, concrete barrack. Guarded in summer with a winter provision for 10.* Tel: 04 76 79 08 28. **2½hr** from la Bérarde

Ailefroide-Vallouise

H15   Bans Hut 2,083 (State owned but CAF Briançon administered): *30 places. It is guarded in summer and is used as a restaurant by many walkers throughout the day. There is water just beside the hut door. The winter access is dangerous due to severe avalanche occurrence. There is a local bus service (Cars Engilberge) from Vallouise serving the point of departure to the Bans hut which operates during July and Aug. This leaves Vallouise daily at 7.00am for Entre-les-Aygues.* Tel: 04 92 23 39 48. **1½hr** from Entre les Aygues

H16   Ecrins Hut 3,175m (CAF Briançon): *120 places. Formerly the Caron Hut, it is guarded throughout the summer season and from late Apr to early June. It is wise to avoid the hut between the end of July and the middle of Aug. Bivouac sites are sparse and often taken up by the army! Booking absolutely essential and large parties need to book* *well in advance (month!).* Tel: 04 92 23 46 66. **4-4½hr** from Pré du Mme Carle

H17   Glacier Blanc Hut 2,542m (State owned but CAF Briançon administered): *135 places. Guarded from early Apr to mid-May and from the end of June to mid-Sept and at major holidays. It is one of the most popular huts in France. The winter accommodation provides 30 places. Advance booking essential.* Tel: 04 92 23 50 24. *1½-2hr from Pré du Mme Carle*

H18   Pelvoux Hut 2,700m (CAF Briançon): *58 places. Formerly the Lemercier Hut, it is guarded in summer with 12 places available in winter, when it is difficult to reach. There are numerous bivouac places and water is tapped just by the hut entrance. Advance booking essential.* Tel: 04 92 23 39 47. **3-3½hr** from Ailefroide

H19   Sélé Hut 2,511m (CAF Briançon): *76 places. This is one of the most modern huts in the Massif. Its design is unusual and the facilities are first class.* Tel: 04 92 23 39 49. **3½hr** from Ailefroide

Note: the old bivouac hut on the Col de la Temple no longer exists. It was flattened by the weight of snow in the late 1970s. The ruin forms a useful wind-break.

Other centres

H20   Fond Turbat Hut 2,169m (CAF Isère): *30 places. This modern hut is guarded in summer. The old hut offers spartan winter accommodation for 12, but the access is avalanche prone in spring. Approached from Valjouffrey in the W of the region.* Tel: 04 76 30 29 23. **3hr** from le Désert en Valjouffrey

H21   Pigeonier (Rouies) Hut 2,423m (CAF Gap): *60 places. This is a newly renovated hut, approached from the end of the motorable road in Valgaudemar. The is guarded in summer.* Tel: 04 92 55 27 82. **2hr** from Gioberney

At the road-head, the Hotel-Chalet Gioberney offers dortoir facilities only a little more expensive than CAF rates.

H22 Vallonpierre Hut 2,271m (State owned but run by CAF Gap): *35 places. This stone built hut, situated on the N side of the small lake, serves the Sirac and GR54 -Tour de l'Oisans. Easily approached from the Gioberney hotel via the GR54. It is wise to book in high season as space is limited.* Tel: 04 92 55 27 81. **2½hr** from Gioberney on GR54

H23 Olan Hut 2,344m (CAF Gap): *54 places. Approach from la Chapelle en Valgaudemar. Follow the road to Gioberney, crossing the Séveraisse torrent. A little further, the path to the hut leads off to the left.* Tel: 04 92 55 30 88. **3hr** from la Chapelle en Valgaudemar

The hut may be reached from the Fond Turbat hut via the Col Turbat in c3hr

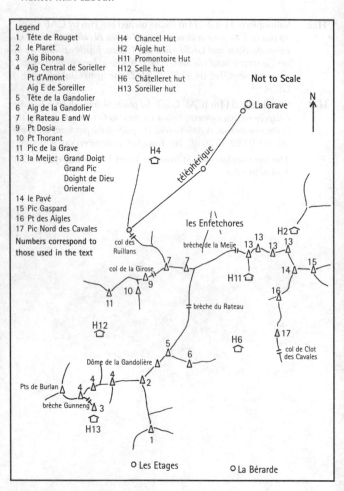

Legend
1 Tête de Rouget
2 le Plaret
3 Aig Bibona
4 Aig Central de Sorieller
  Pt d'Amont
  Aig E de Soreiller
5 Tête de la Gandolier
6 Aig de la Gandolier
7 le Rateau E and W
9 Pt Dosia
10 Pt Thorant
11 Pic de la Grave
13 la Meije: Grand Doigt
           Grand Pic
           Doight de Dieu
           Orientale
14 le Pavé
15 Pic Gaspard
16 Pt des Aigles
17 Pic Nord des Cavales

Numbers correspond to
those used in the text

H4 Chancel Hut
H2 Aigle hut
H11 Promontoire Hut
H12 Selle hut
H6 Châtelleret hut
H13 Soreiller hut

Not to Scale

N

La Grave

téléphérique

H4

les Enfetchores

H2

col des
Ruillans

brèche de la Meije

13 13 13 13

H11

15

col de la Girose

7 7

14

9

16

10

brèche du Rateau

11

H12

H6

17

col de Clot
des Cavales

5

6

Dôme de la Gandolière

4 4 4

2

Pts de Burlan

4

brèche Gunneng

3

H13

1

Les Etages

La Bérarde

North-West Sector

This sector is located between the Romanche valley in the N, in which la Grave is the main valley base, and the Vénéon valley in the S where la Bérarde is the major valley base. The Meije, which is the E-most mountain in the group and which lies immediately S of la Grave (and N of la Bérarde), is one of the two principal peaks in the whole of the region and of great interest to the alpine historian. An important access route into the heart of these mountains is the Selle valley. This valley, down which the Diable river flows, runs into the Vénéon valley at St Christophe-en-Oisans. See Map 3436 ET

Tête de Rouget 3,418m

E Boileau de Castelnau with P Gaspard snr and jnr, 23 July 1877

This is a fine, rocky peak located NW of la Bérarde. Its W face, on which there are a number of climbs, is prominent in the view from the Soreiller hut. Of particular interest, as far as this guide book is concerned, are the routes on the impossing S face and those on the W ridge.

1a
PD+
1

VOIE DES PLAQUES

A Leroux and C Rodier, 26 July 1928
Valley base: La Bérarde

A classic climb on the S flank and SW ridge. It is an interesting and fairly exposed climb with no great difficulties and on very good rock.

From the Soreiller hut, cross in the direction of the Tête du Rouget over boulder strewn ground and névé. Well before reaching the foot of the couloir issuing from the Brèche du Rouget, veer off towards the R. Join the snow/scree slope that rises towards two brèches, separated by a gendarme, at the foot of the SW ridge. Go up these slopes over broken rocks to the L-hand brèche. 1½hr

After going over a few easy rocks, reach a long inclined slab (30°) adjacent to the SW ridge. Go up this slab, then follow small easy couloirs along the SW ridge itself to a small shelf situated above the cliffs of the S face. Head L and climb a small chimney, then the slabs bearing R. Go directly upwards via a very open dièdre (III) and continue straight ahead over steep, smooth rocks in order to reach a stony terrace (it is also possible to head gently R and follow the edge above the cliffs of the S face). From the terrace, move R to an ill-defined couloir (one move of III). This couloir becomes less steep. Follow the ridge on the L (the R bank of this couloir) and thus attain the summit (the couloir itself may also be climbed). 2½hr: **4hr** total

Descent: Either by the same climb (if gear has been L at the brèche) or, by preference, by the N ridge as follows: (First ascent party: F)

Descend the N ridge, either by its crest or by its W flank, and reach the Brèche du Rouget. Descend to the W via the rock face close to the R bank of the couloir issuing from the brèche, one rappel in the lower section may be useful. 1hr: **5-6hr** in all

1b
TD-
1

EPERON GIROD

P Girod and Mlle F Carrel, 15 Oct 1955
Valley base: La Bérarde

The first route to be created on the S face of the Rouget. It follows the spur forming the L bank of the big couloir which separates the true S face from SSW face. The bottom of the spur is 150m above the cirque of scree and névé at the foot of the face. The rock is excellent. The first ascent party climbed from the foot of the face but time can be saved, by parties approaching from the Soreiller hut, by starting the climb at the foot of the spur itself, thus avoiding the less interesting lower wall. The first part of the climb follows the R flank of the spur then it is followed more or less on the crest. It isn't always easy to find the exact line. Sustained climbing, which never exceeds V+. The climb is not equipped.

Approach via the brèche at the base of the SW ridge, as for Route 1a and, on the E flank of the gap, make three rappels on the L bank of the couloir leading towards the foot of the S face (stonefall possible). These lead to the point where the ground levels out, roughly level with the base of a big couloir which separates this part of the face from the larger pillar on the R which provides the line of the route. Traverse across easy ground to reach the spur.

Climb easily to the first step and overcome it by slanting gently L. The second step is climbed direct. From the foot of the third step, climb a corner on the R leading to a slab on the L flank of a dièdre. Climb the dièdre and leave it by moving R (IV+/V) then return to the arête by a ledge and a crack. For the fourth step go L and climb a small overhang (poorish rock) and then a slab to rejoin the arête at a brèche. The fifth step overhangs slightly; climb it directly (IV+) to arrive on a platform on the R and then climb an overhanging block before going R by a slab and a narrow ledge.

Return to the arête. Follow it to a balcony at the foot of a slab which is bypassed on the R and followed by a chimney. The arête leads to the foot of a first, sharp, yellow gendarme. Traverse R to a large shoulder on a secondary spur of the S face at the foot of a 50m high gendarme. Turn R and climb 30m straight up (IV+) and then traverse R towards a dièdre. Climb this for 2-3m and then its R, overhanging flank (V+: exposed) to a good stance. Climb a dièdre and then move R (IV) to reach a platform below the crest and a second slender gendarme. Climb a flake forming a dièdre and finish on the R (IV+) then an arête before a traverse across unstable flakes leads to a brèche at the foot of a third gendarme. Climb this on the crest at first, stride across a gap and then climb a cracked slab. Descend to a 'V' brèche at the foot of a square gendarme with two levels. Climb the R flank of the gendarme by slabs and short traverses (IV) and reach the top of the first level. A sharp ridge and a short traverse lead to the top of the gendarme. Descend to the next brèche, the source of the deep couloir separating the ridge from the S face. Climb by couloirs and easy ledges for 80m on the R flank of a squat tower (Tour Christine) then reach the E ridge some 100m from the summit.

1c
ED1

LE TRESOR DE RACKHAM LE ROUGET

J-M Cambon, P Chapoutot and J Saez, 23, 24 and 30 July 1993
Valley base: La Bérarde

This is the only long climb on the face which is equipped with bolts but a few nuts may be useful for the top pitches. It is possible to descend the climb by rappel although consensus is that the 'Voie des Plaques' in descent is preferable.

Slant L on poor rock, then straight up to climb a line of little roofs c15m above the ledge (5). The rock now becomes excellent. Slant up L and traverse horizonally L to above the roofs, then straight up to a stance (5+). Move R (bolts *in situ*) and make a long run out, slanting R to a small ledge (6a/b: finishing 6c). Continue Rwards to a hidden dièdre closed by a bulge (6c). Two easier pitches lead to beneath another bulge. Climb this by a little loop L then R (6a) and reach the edge of a little cirque. Climb on the L side of it on a sharply defined rib (6a/b: small stance on a little shoulder). Continue R to reach fine, grey slabs on the other side of a trench (2 pitches 5, 5+). Two easy rope lengths lead exactly to the summit.

1d
TD

SOUTH FACE DIRECT

J-P Bourley and P Chapoutot, 25 July 1976
Valley base: La Bérarde

A fine climb on excellent rock. The approach from the Soreiller hut allows the original easy section to be avoided. Technical difficulties up to 6a: 470m of climbing.

Approach and rappel as for Route 1b to the point where the ground levels out. Keeping fairly high, traverse R along a horizontal ledge to the foot of the big couloir. 2hr

Follow Route 1c to the top of the first pitch above the lower, easy section (5+). An overhanging crack (V) and a dièdre (IV/IV+) lead to a platform. Climb an open, vertical dièdre to a spacious ledge on the L (sustained: V+/6a). Climb another dièdre, which butts up against overhangs, to mid-height then traverse R (IV/V). Move R for 8-10m and climb a dièdre which borders the L side of a pillar (IV+: a move of V). Continue by another cracked dièdre (IV) and yet another, open dièdre on the L which is followed to an obvious hole (IV+). Pass R of the hole (IV+). The climbing now becomes easier. Continue to move up and Rwards and reach a dièdre which ends beneath overhangs. Pass them on the R side (IV). A last pitch (IV/IV+) leads to the 'Voie des Plaques' not far from the summit. 5hr: **c8hr** in all

1e
D-

SOUTH PILLAR AND SOUTH-WEST RIDGE

R Chèze, H Jullian, J Martin, G Oury, A Peltier and J Sapin,
25 July 1963
Valley base: La Bérarde

A classic climb on good rock which is equipped with pitons.

From the Soreiller hut follow Route 1a to the inclined slab. Climb the slab then, slightly higher, reach the base of the SW pillar by a lengthy traverse L along easy ledges. Start up the pillar by climbing a small couloir which merges into the pillar. Climb a series of slabs and grooves Lwards for 30m (III). Above, climb a system of ledges inclined at 45° (IV) and move Rwards to a stance. Make a short, horizontal traverse R (IV: exposed) then climb a 15m vertical wall (IV: good stance). Climb a detached block Rwards and, keeping R, arrive at a vertical cracked wall. Climb this (V) and exit L to a good belay. Above and R, climb a little rib (IV) which marks the end of the pillar and leads to a fine arête separating the S and W faces. Climb this arête (III: sustained) and turn several overhangs by the S face to join the 'Voie des Plaques' c80m from the summit. Follow it to the top. **4½-5hr** in all

Le Plaret 3,564m

H Cordier, J Anderegg and A Maurer, 7 June1877

This is the highest summit in the Massif du Soreiller, a group of mountains, interconnected by a long, high ridge, situated above the Soreiller hut on its N side. Access to the N side of the le Plaret is via the Selle valley.

2a
TD

NORTH FACE

M Laloue and P Paquet, 29 July 1949
Valley base: La Bérarde

The N face of the Plaret, 500m high, comprises two distinct sections. The lower, of whitish boiler plate slabs comprises on the L, a poorly marked spur, supporting the séracs of a little hanging glacier. The upper section (200m), of reddish rock, forms a vertical wall, split for the whole of its height by a large chimney leaning from R to L, not well defined and dominated in the middle by a big rocky overhang supporting a little ice gully descending from the summit. The route is sustained in the upper section. It is best climbed in a dry season as in a poor year the iced up rock becomes unclimbable. Similarly the chimney can be difficult to climb. The route has had very few ascents to date.

From the Selle Hut, descend the approach path a little and then cross the Selle glacier towards the branch below the N face which, in the middle, at mid-height, is split by a rocky rognon. Climb either R (crevassed) or, for preference, L of the rognon, moving by steep slopes, then trend bit by bit towards the R to reach, in its E corner, the upper snow plateau at the foot of the face. 2hr
Climb the rimaye and then the rock spur supporting the hanging glacier more or less in the middle. Follow a poorly defined ledge for c12m Rwards on slabs, then climb a chimney (III) finishing at a little brèche. Continue up the spur by easy rocks. Slant gradually R and by an ascending traverse gain the middle of the face, passing beneath a bulge of slabs at the base of the reddish steeper section. Reach the base of the big diagonal

chimney by steep, overlapping slabs with few holds (IV), and by icy slabs (take a pendule from a piton to get across the main one). 2½hr

The bottom of the chimney forms a 15m, overhanging wall. Turn this on the L by a steep dièdre (V+), then go back R by a horizontal traverse, (IV+) to reach the chimney. This section can be avoided by using a little ascending ledge on the L (situated R of the steep dièdre: bad rock) and climb the bulge and a detached flake on the L (V+: very exposed). Climb a dièdre (V) for 15m to reach a little stance on the R. Go back to the chimney and climb a crack on its R (IV). Climb the rib which is on its L, to gain easier rocks leading to the big rocky overhang (III). Turn this on the L, climbing a steep wall amongst slabs (IV) to reach an ascending ledge, trending L, which is followed to its E extremity (good resting place). Above is an overhanging wall at the base of which an easy ledge leads L. Do not follow this, but slant easily R, traversing a rocky bulge dominated by the wall (IV).

The difficulties are over. Move R over broken rocks to gain the R bank of the snowy summit couloir and climb this to the summit. 4½ hr: **7hr** from the foot of the face

2b DESCENT BY THE EAST FLANK

F

6

First ascent party
Valley base: La Bérarde

This is the ordinary route from the Châtelleret hut (or la Bérarde).

Descend the S ridge on easy rocks to the upper Plaret glacier, on its L bank. Follow this side of the glacier to some big zones of slabs which are traversed obliquely down and R towards a rocky spur which forms a loose rocky apron of the E ridge of the Pic Gény. Go down rocks, then scree on the L bank of a little rocky, cradle-like hollow enclosed on the R by the spur and join an open couloir. Follow this to reach a path leading down the L bank of the Torrent du Plaret and follow this to the valley bottom. **3½hr** in total to la Bérarde

Aiguille Dibona 3,131m

A Dibona and G Mayer, 27 June 1913

More commonly refered to simply as the Dibona, this remarkable rock peak lies just outside the back door of the Soreiller hut.
It is a mecca for rock climbers whether they prefer to utilise
traditional methods or enjoy modern sports climbing. The rock
is excellent and the approaches to the routes are short, once the
1,000m of climbing to the hut are over. Because of its height, the
Dibona does attract bad weather quite quickly so that climbers
attempting a long route on it should be on the lookout for such
an eventuality and be prepared to 'bale out'.

3a
AD

3

BOELL ROUTE

J Boell, A Chevalier and A le Ray, 4 Sept 1922
Valley base: La Bérarde

*A very good climb of modest difficulty on excellent rock which utilises
parts of the E, S and W faces as well as the SW ridge. The route is not
easy to follow in the upper section and today the mountain is so criss-
crossed by climbs that it is easy to stray off route at various points.*

From the Soreiller hut, go NE by snow slopes or scree at the
base of the E face to reach the start of a large terrace system
which cuts this face at one third height (30min). Follow these
terraces S (there are alternative lines) and a little before they
break up climb 40m up easy rock and a dièdre-chimney, in a
general line obliquely L. Then turn L and descend 20m. Gain a
second system of ledges which are followed Swards to their
extremity below a big couloir-chimney, which ends on the SE
arête. Climb this couloir and at the point where it steepens
(overhang) make a delicate traverse on a flake (III) which leads
Lwards to the ridge. Several easier m follow to a large 'beak' at
the start of a ledge which cuts the S face of the Aiguille at about
mid-height (the Vire Boell). Follow this L and go down a slab for
3m to get into a long, enclosed couloir which loses itself in the W
face. Climb this for two thirds of its height (III) and then traverse

horizontally R by slabs to reach the foot of a short chimney
which leads to a characteristic shoulder of the S face.

Traverse R (E face) by a steep slab passing the foot of a
dièdre which must not be taken. Turn an angle on the R and
then climb grooved cracks for 12m to a terrace (IV). Move back
L (III: delicate) to the second of two grooves above the dièdre
and climb by oblique cracks for c100m (III with a move of IV).
These lead to large ascending ledges just below the S arête
(junction with the S Face Direct). Follow the ledges for 30m;
return for a moment to the ridge by a vertical flake. Use the
ledges on the E face to reach the summit. **3½hr** from the hut

3b
TD
2

EAST FACE DIRECT

M Laloue and A Madier, 11 Aug 1939
Valley base: La Bérarde

The route is varied, sustained and classic in style.

From the Soreiller hut follow the path to the foot of the E face
(10min). Start directly below the summit in a poorly defined
couloir. Climb 30m, then up cracks in a slab, bearing Rwards
(IV), to reach the R extremity of a long grassy ledge just at the
foot of a characteristic black dièdre 90m from the start. Climb
the dièdre, often damp (V) and go up, moving R a little, for 25m
passing a bulge (IV). Arrive at the lower terraces of the Boell
route (Route 3a). Follow this route up the 40m of easy rock and
the chimney-dièdre, on a line generally slanting Lwards from the
point of arrival on the terraces. The main section of the E face,
which is 175m high, starts here. 1-1½hr.

Climb straight up by slabs directly below the dièdre-
chimney for 25m (IV-) to reach a platform. Above, the big
dièdre-chimney marks the line of ascent for a while. From the
platform climb a few m utilising flakes on the R of the dièdre
(IV), then move 5m R and climb towards a roof some 8m higher.
Now move L below the roof (piton) to get back into the dièdre.
Climb the dièdre for 30m, sometimes by its L side, to a stance on
the L (IV+/V). Climb a slab of 4m (V) on the R of the dièdre,

level with the stance, and traverse horizontally R, turning an angle (V-) to reach a big ledge. Follow this ledge, slanting up R, for 15m. Climb up L by steep rocks (III) before moving Rwards again for 20m (easy). Now climb 10m to reach the bottom of an overhanging wall. This point can also be reached by climbing the dièdre-chimney from the stance below the 4m slab. Continue up the dièdre and then move R to reach the overhanging wall (V). Climb the wall (V) and reach an earthy terrace. Climb a crack (III) then another 20m by broken blocks to a big terrace leaning gently L. Now slant R, by a ledge and groove for 20m; above is another ledge which is bigger, directly below the summit. A little wall above the ledge leads L to a tiny shelf at the foot of the final, smooth and vertical slabs (IV- from the terrace). Climb directly (V+ then V-) to reach the summit. **3-5hr** from the foot of the face

3c
TD+
2

MARTINE IS ON THE ROCK

D Bancillon and E Allene, 1988
Valley base: La Bérarde

A fine, modern route with quite varied climbing. Technical difficulties up to 6b/c (5+ obl): totally equipped. Escape options exists from the Vire Boell (rappel down the S face) and the climb itself is equipped for descent.

Start 15m R of the commemorative plaque below a small overhang.

P1 5+: P2 6a and 5: P3 6b/c: P4 5+ and 5: P5 4: P6 6b and 5: P7 easy: P8 6a: P9 5 and 6a: P10 5: P11 6a: P12 5+: P13 3 and 4: P14 4+ **5-7hr**

Descent via Route 3h is the easiest.

3d
TD
3

SOUTH FACE DIRECT

A Madier and M Fourastier, 1 Sept 1937
Valley base: La Bérarde

This is the best traditional style rock climb on the Aiguille and one of

*the best routes in the Ecrins Massif. Perfect rock, which is sustained
and steep. The most conspicuous feature of this face is a great dièdre
slanting slightly R to L. This gives the line of the first half of the route.*

From the Soreiller hut gain, by a path, the foot of the face
vertically below the opening of the great dièdre. Follow cracks in
the slabs until you are a few m from the opening of a tunnel
which gives access to the dièdre. By a slab (IV+) enter the tunnel
and climb it; continue up the long channelled groove which
follows (IV) to the foot of an overhang (usually wet). From there
traverse L on slabs for 15m (V) until beneath some grooves
which slant slightly R. Climb these (IV+ to begin with) and a
line of cracks slanting obliquely R for 15m. Traverse R towards a
slab which leads to the bottom of a big groove; belay above a
darkish overhang. Climb the groove, by its L edge at first, for
25m (V/V+: sustained) and then move R by climbing an
overhang on good holds (IV: exposed) to reach a narrow ledge. A
more direct line follows the groove to its end (V+). Leave the
ledge moving Lward (IV+/V: exposed) to join a ramp of easy
slabs culminating in an overhanging wall which is climbed
directly (IV+). Above, climb a 40m chimney and then less steep
ground to the 3m slab at the end of a wide, horizontal ledge
(Vire Boell of Route 3a: this route can be followed to avoid the
Fissure Madier which follows). 2hr

Go to the R (E) end of this ledge to reach a crack leading
to a large overhang. Climb the crack for 10m (V) then traverse L
under the overhang. Climb it (IV+) and then the long crack
(Fissure Madier) which follows (20m: V+ to VI-, depending on
the amount of aid used, then IV). A dièdre leads to the characteristic shoulder of the Boell route. The climb can be finished by
following the Boell route. Alternatively, and more in keeping,
climb a small groove leading to a grooved slab. Climb this
(Stofer grooves: a good pitch, IV+ then IV) and an overhang
(IV). Above, on the R, rejoin the Boell route on the E face.

Another possibility is to finish by the last section of the
Livanos route. From the top of the Stofer grooves, traverse L for

3m (Livanos traverse: V) and climb a deep crack which leads to a large terrase on the W face. Above, climb a 5m slab (V) then a crack on the R (IV) to gain a level section on the crest of the S arête. Follow the arête and, when it steepens, go on the E side (to join the Boell route) by ledges that are followed for 30m. A vertical step and ledges lead to the summit. 2-3hr: **4-5hr** from the foot of the face

Another variation to this route avoids the difficulties in the lower part of the route associated with the great dièdre. This is the Berthet variation which leaves the the Direct route just below the black (wet) overhang. Climb a crack slanting R for c12m (delicate and exposed). Above are a series of slabs cut by cracks. Climb straight up these to reach the E edge of the Vire Boell (IV/IV+).

3e
TD+
3

VISITE OBLIGATOIRE

P Junique, L Belluard and W Legrand, 1988
Valley base: La Bérarde

This climb is entirely equipped and is considered to be the best of the modern style climbing. There is a choice of start on either side of the overhangs on the L of the Dièdre Anglais (see Route 3f). 5+obl

P1 6a - either way!: P2 6a/5+: P3 5+: P4 6a - belay level with the roof: P5 5+/6a: P6 5+/6a: P7 4/5: P8 6a (belay on the shoulder of the Boell route): P9 6a: P10 5+. **5-6hr**

Note. A line of equipped rappels descends from one rope length above the Boell ledge on the S face. The first section lies R of 'Visite', it then joins with the top of P4 of the climb and continues by this line to the foot of the face.

3f
TD+
3

VOIE DES SAVOYARDS

P Chapoutot and B Wyns, 6 Sept 1967
By the Dièdre Anglais: C Jones and D Wigget, 27 July 1967
Valley base: La Bérarde

This is a classic, sustained and exposed climb, with good stances and excellent rock. Technical difficulties up to 6a.

From the Soreiller hut take the path to the start of the line of the S Face Direct route (3d).

Start on the big face well L of the great dièdre, directly below the steep section of the SW ridge, by easy slopes to the foot of a chimney. Climb the chimney (V) and exit on the R. Continue, moving a little R, following a flake (IV/V), then slant up R for 10m and go straight up to a comfortable ledge (IV/V: sustained: 40m). This point may also be reached by the 'Dièdre Anglais' as follows: Start at the foot of the S Face Direct route and take a dièdre parallel to that climb. Exit L at the comfortable ledge after five rope-lengths (V+ and 6a: sustained).

Move up slabs Lwards (V to 6a depending on the line taken) to the foot of a dièdre climbing towards the big, horizontal overhang. Climb the dièdre (V then IV+) to a terrace. Step L, climb to below the overhang and traverse horizontally L for 15m; bypass a red block, making use of some flakes, make a move L and climb the overhang by a gymnastic move (V and V+ from the terrace: very sustained and exposed). Above the overhang climb a dièdre-chimney cut by overhangs (2 rope-lengths: a slab (IV) and less steep ground, then a nice 12m crack (V-), followed by a chimney (IV)). There is a good terrace before the last overhang of the dièdre. Climb a system of grooves and cracks (III and IV+) to enter a big hollow where the couloir-chimney of the Boell route is joined. Climb this and continue to where the SW ridge loses itself in the W face. Slant up Lwards for 20m, passing a big flake (IV-) to reach a terrace and the foot of a vertical crack which goes up to the summit ridge. Climb this crack for 10-12m (V), go obliquely L (V-), pass a small overhang on its R side and traverse 5m horizontally R by an almost vertical, smooth slab (6a) to a crack which leads to an excellent stance behind a big block (V+: 40m from the terrace). A fine, vertical dièdre (V) leads to the summit ridge from which the top is easily gained. **6-8hr** from the hut

3g WEST FACE - MADIER ROUTE

TD
4

M Laloue and A Madier, 9 Aug 1939
Valley base: La Bérarde

This is a classic climb with a short pitch requiring aid. Two equipped climbs exist on this face but they do not enjoy popularity.

Leave the Soreiller hut heading W, skirting the foot of the S face of the Aiguille. Traverse L and round over the lowest rocks of the SW ridge by an easy gully. Walk up scree or snow slopes to the tongue of rock which juts out from the W face. Dodge L round this, and return R over easy ground, making for the Brèche des Clochetons situated L of the twin peaked Clochetons Gunneng at the foot of the N ridge of the Aiguille. The col between the Clochetons Gunneng and the Aig Dibona is the Brèche Gunneng. Descend R a little, before reaching this brèche, to the foot of the W face.

Start up easy rocks just L of the centre of the face. Climb a short wall (V-: or use combined tactics) then slant R and up a shallow chimney (III) to a little platform. On the R a crack (IV) leads to a large terrace. Move to its R-hand (S) end and climb a dièdre ending with a flake which leads to a poor stance under an overhang (IV+). Move L (IV) and up a dièdre to an overhang (V). Now go R along a ledge and up a long crack (V-) to beneath an oblique overhang. Traverse L under this overhang (A0/V, 5 pitons) and climb up the L edge of the slab above (V) to a point above a recess. Continue towards the R by a black and lichenous, grooved slab (IV+), followed by a short overhanging chimney (IV+). Now take a wide crack to a ledge beneath the summit (some rotten rocks). Climb a short, vertical dièdre (V) to the summit ridge. **3-4hr**

3h DESCENT VIA NORTH RIDGE

PD
4

First ascent party
Valley base: La Bérarde

This is also the line of the Ordinary Route.

From just below the summit, down the N ridge, are two fixed rappel points allowing two 25m rappels. By this means reach the obvious wide ledge system leading from the Brèche Gunneng (the col at the foot of the N ridge) to the easy scree slopes below the W flank. The well marked route to the hut may be névé early in the season.

In ascent, skirt round the W side of the mountain and then traverse E to the Brèche Gunneng at the foot of the N ridge. From the brèche climb straight up via a 20m dièdre on the W flank of the ridge (III+) leading to the crest at the level of a large block. Continue up slabs (III) to the summit. **1½hr** from the Soreiller hut

Massif du Soreiller

East summit: F Gardiner and C and L Pilkington, 24 July 1878
Point d'Amont: Mme B Leirens with J and P Turc, Aug 1924

Essentially this is a long ridge on the N side of the Vénéon valley, running E-W from the Col Oriental du Soreiller, W of le Plaret, to the Pts de Burlan. Of particular interest, as far as this guide is concerned are the Aig E du Soreiller and the Pt d'Amont. These two summits present an imposing wall on their N side overlooking the Vallon du Diable, with two magnificent ridges and one face route of character. The two summits are joined by an arête which may be traversed (Route 4d). The climbs are best descended Swards towards the Soreiller hut and thence to les Etages.

Pointe d'Amont 3,338m

This summit is linked to the Aig Dibona by a ridge running, via the Aig Central du Soreiller (3,338m), roughly S from its summit. Its N flank, overlooking the E Diable glacier, is particularly impressive.

4a NORTH RIDGE

A Migot, P and R Tézenas du Montcel, 29-30 Aug 1932
Valley base: La Bérarde

A fine, long route, the only true classic past and present on this N (Selle) flank of the Massif du Soreiller.

From the Selle hut descend the approach path for a little way and then cross the stream in the valley bottom where convenient. Pass below the base of the ridge descending from Pt 3,361m and get on to the E branch of the Diable glacier. Cross it heading W to reach the N ridge of the Pt d'Amont to just beneath Pt 2,844m. Climb the crest of the arête to the foot of a large step. On the L flank of the step, climb a slab, twin cracks then a second slab. Now climb easy chimneys and a *râteau de chèvre* (flake come ledge) to reach a 40m long ledge. From its L-hand end, climb the face Rwards, first by steep rock (1 move IV) and then by easier terraces. Follow another well marked ledge Rward until close to the arête. Climb steep, cracked rock for 15m just L of the crest (IV). Climb a scoop Lwards (IV+) then flakes for 5m (V) to reach a good terrace below the top of the step, this in turn is reached by taking the ridge itself (III). Follow a shattered ridge up to a big gendarme and pass it on the R (W), descending some 30m. Climb a second step by slabs and chimneys then take the arête to the summit. 3hr: **c5hr** from the hut

Descent: By the SW ridge which links the Pt d'Amont to the Aig Centrale du Soreiller. From the summit follow the ridge to a brèche between the two peaks either by the ridge crest or rocks on its S flank. From the brèche, climb (or rappel) down cracks, make a traverse R to reach a suspended patch of névé. Descend a chimney on the L to another, lower névé, which is circumnavigated and then follow a couloir to join the route to the Soreiller hut. PD

To the L of this route is a line climbed by S Coupé and J Merle, 16 Aug 1952 (see Photo 5).

Aiguille Orientale du Soreiller 3,380m

A relatively undistinguished summit due E of the Pt d'Amont. Its main features of interest are the pillar projecting into the upper part of the E Diable glacier and the face immediately W of the pillar.

4b
TD
5

NORTH FACE

N Candau and A Joubert, 7 July 1968
Valley base: La Bérarde

This mixed route climbs the face which dominates the E Branch of the Diable glacier R (W) of the previous route. The route is not often climbed.

Approach as for Route 4a from the Selle hut to reach the E branch of the Diable glacier. Climb it to the foot of the N ridge and then move up Rwards to the foot of the face (1½hr). Attain a constriction where there is a 6m slab and climb this from R to L (V/V+). Continue by a zone of broken rock for some 200m (lll and IV) and reach a suspended patch of névé, which is crossed from L to R in the direction of a chimney/dièdre. Start this by a vertical flake (V/V+) then follow the dièdre for some 200m (delicate and exposed: lll and IV). The dièdre loses itself amongst slabs; a rope move Rwards leads to a ledge, which is not too obvious, and follow it for 50m (IV/IV+) to the level of a gendarme. Climb straight up (IV/IV+: thrutchy). Continue Rwards to a brèche some 100m W of the summit (lll/lll+: poor rock) and follow the ridge to the top. **6hr**

Descent: Scramble down towards the col E du Sorreiller and instead of climbing down the steep (but easy) step to the col, leave the ridge on its S side and reach the couloir below the col by a ledge which descends to it at mid-height. Continue to the screes (snow) and the Soreiller hut. 1-1½hr

4c

NORTH RIDGE

TD

5

P Girod and M Puissant, 31 Aug 1957
Valley base: La Bérarde

The ridge, which projects into the upper part of the E Diable glacier, lies parallel with and R of the couloir which descends from the Col E du Sorreiller. It is a long and serious climb which offers some superb positions and views. Pitons, wedges and Friends should be carried. To date there have only been a few ascents. 530m

Follow Route 4a from the Selle hut on to E branch of the Diable glacier. Climb it to the foot of the ridge, which form a steep wall. 1½hr

Start on the W flank where the wall changes orientation. Climb towards and then up a 30m chimney (mediocre rock). Pass an overhang then flakes towards the R (IV/V) and reach a terrace. Climb 30m (IV) towards a vertical wall then take this first on the R, then L (IV/IV+) and finally direct (A1 for 5m) to a small stance on a detached flake.

Climb a less steep section, dominated by a smooth rock pinnacle, by its R flank then ascend a step, which ends this section, to a small brèche (IV/IV+). Climb Rwards via delicate, broken flakes to a dièdre in a zone of red slabs (IV/IV+). Good, grey rock leads to a large pinnacle. Traverse Lward, crossing a small dièdre, to reach the foot of a large, grey gendarme L of the crest of the ridge. The face of the gendarme is seamed by two cracks, climb the R-hand one to a brèche (V).

Continue to another brèche from where a big gendarme can be seen higher up. Climb for 2 rope lengths on the L flank of the ridge (blocks, then a slab) and continue on the crest to a cleavage at the base of a red step. Climb a slab on the R flank, a dièdre, then on the L side, a smooth, brown slab followed by a section of unstable grey rocks and flakes (IV+). Go back to the crest of the ridge and then take its R flank to a terrace below the big gendarme. Avoid this by the wall on its L flank (60m: IV) and again follow the ridge for 3 rope lengths to reach the summit ridge a little E of the top. **8½hr** from the foot of the ridge

Descend as for Route 4b

Voie des Savoyards on the Aiguille Dibona (Route 3f) Guy Muhlemann climbing Simon Richardson

4d   SOREILLER RIDGE TRAVERSE

AD-

5

Valley base: La Bérarde

A fine route of no great difficulty, best started from the Soreiller hut. It is usual to make the traverse in an anti-clockwise direction. There are two possible routes to the Aig E du Soreiller; via its S ridge and via the Col E du Soreiller. The first is slightly more difficult.

From the Soreiller hut head across scree slope to turn the foot of the S ridge of the Aig E du Soreiller. Climb up W of the ridge on scree and then snow on the E Soreiller glacier, making directly for the obvious Col E du Soreiller. Climb to the col by a fairly steep, rocky couloir. From the col, turn W and climb an easy step in the ridge ahead (poor rock). Avoid a second step on the L and continue to the summit of the Aig E du Soreiller be easy ledges just off the crest. Join the crest shortly before reaching the summit. 3hr from the hut

   To climb the S ridge, get on to the ridge from its W side between the first and second shoulders. Climb a 6m chimney and then continue for a long way up the ridge to the top of the third and much higher shoulder. Cross a patch of névé to the foot of a red tower. Climb up stepped rocks to its R to just below a vast overhang forming the head of the tower. Traverse L for c5m, crossing the ridge, and climb a 4m slab on the W flank back on to the crest. Follow this to the top of the tower. Follow the horizontal section of ridge and cross a small brèche to reach the foot of the final step. Follow the crest, at times just on the E side, climbing over gendarmes (III) to the last of these. Turn this on the W flank and gain the summit. 4hr from the hut

   Descend the ridge heading W to a dramatic steepening. Rappel 20m, then follow the exposed ridge, on excellent rock, crossing a large flake *à cheval*, to reach a platform overlooking the N face. Climb a narrow crack to regain the crest and then, after some exposed moves descend carefully into a brèche just before a gendarme characterised by a rock finger c5m long. Make a short rappel down the couloir on the S side and continue c10m below the crest, on stony ground with the possibility of

Climbing the Pic du Glacier Blanc S ridge (Route 28a) Wil Hurford climbing   *Photographer unknown* névé, to reach the Pt d'Amont. Climb up to the summit on the S flank (excellent rock), getting on to the crest just below the summit. A 8-10m wall with fairly few holds leads to the top (III). 3-4hr

Descend the SW ridge on the S flank to the brèche between the Pt d'Amont and the Aig Central du Soreiller. Follow the NE ridge of the latter easily to the summit (1hr). Alternatively descend as for Route 4a to the Selle hut.

Now turn S and follow the ridge down, at first on the crest and then on the E flank via grooved slabs and cracks (rappel a short section of III). Reach an easier section and descend easy chimneys to reach névé slopes below. Go down these, slanting R, to where a rocky couloir leads down L towards the hut. 1½hr: **c10-12hr** in all

Tête de la Gandolière 3,542m

W Coolidge and F Gardiner with C Almer snr and jnr, 29 July 1880

The most significant peak on the long ridge running NW from the summit of le Plaret which forms the watershed between the Selle and Etançons valleys. The latter valley descends S to join the Vénéon valley at la Bérarde.

5a
AD

TRAVERSE BY THE DOME DE LA GANDOLIERE

A Colomb, F Germain, R Mallet and L Rey, 13 Aug 1942
Valley base: La Bérarde

This is a pleasant ridge traverse, on a comparatively low peak, so that it can reasonably be completed from la Bérarde in the day. The technical difficulties are not great, the rock is good enough and the positions are often airy.

Start from la Bérarde, along the path to the Chatelleret hut (a potential starting point), cross a bridge (Passerelle du Plaret Gény) over the Etançons stream close to Pt 1,979m (a snow bridge remains until well into the season). Now walk up an ill-defined path on the R bank to Pt 2,039m. Climb more steeply up a zigzag path until in sight of the Plaret stream. Join the path which climbs direct from the Chatelleret hut at the Plaret stream itself (Pt 2,306m). This is much used. Climb a little further up the R bank of the Plaret stream to where the path turns off L. Leave this path and turn a little cliff by a vegetated ledge on the L before climbing again to the upper valley of the Plaret stream, which is shut in by the cliffs below the Plaret glacier. Walk up vegetated and stony slopes towards the outflow of a splayed couloir situated on the extreme L of a broad rock barrier. Some easy rocks lead up to its R bank. Cross the couloir and go up its L bank and up a scree cone to a wide stretch of easy slabs. Cross these, slanting up R, to the L bank of the Plaret glacier. c3hr

Continue up the L bank of the glacier towards the NW and then W to a snow slope below the brèche at Pt 3,411m, situated between le Plaret and Pt 3,438m. Climb the slope for c100m and continue up a stretch of white slabs to reach the brèche. Turn R (NW) and follow the easy ridge to the summit of Pt 3,438m. 1½hr

From this summit follow the ridge to start with and then take to the easy ledges on the S side, so avoiding several slender gendarmes, to reach a deep and narrow, V-shaped brèche. Continue up on the S side of the ridge. Turn the first gendarme on the R, climb the second by its S face and third via a ledge on its N side to reach a narrow brèche nicked out of its ridge. Continue along the crest of the very jagged, airy ridge to the foot of a red tower. Turn this on the S side to the next brèche and then move on to the N side and climb it to the top of a 60m step. Continue along the horizontal, mixed snow and rock ridge to the summit of the Dôme de la Gandolière (3,495m). 1½hr

Now descend the narrow, rocky E ridge to the brèche between the Dôme and Tête de la Gandolière. Climb the SW ridge of the latter, on the crest at first and then turning a gendarme by its S face across a black slab. Now stay exactly on the crest which bristles with sharp points, turning only the last two along a ledge on the N side. A chimney leads direct to the summit. 45min: 7-8hr from la Bérarde

From the top, descend the E ridge for 70m, then turn L on to the NE face and descend direct towards a hanging snow slope. Turn this on either side and descend to the Gandolière glacier, crossing the rimaye on its R (E) side. Slant NE down the glacier and descend the steep slopes of its L bank on to easy slabs. Now slant down R under the lower tongue of the glacier, and descend mixed ground to the R-hand end of the big cliff under the glacier. Continue down a couloir with a little stream in it, on the N side of a rocky spur, and cross the valley to the L bank of the Gandolière stream and the well-used path which is followed to the Etançons valley. Cross the Etançons stream to the Chatelleret hut and so back to la Bérarde. 3-4hr from the top: **c11hr** for the round trip

Aiguille de la Gandolière 3,324m

Mlle J Kaiser with D and M Gaspard, 3 Aug 1901

This is a large, rocky peak which lies SSE of the Tête de la Gandolière and is separated from it by a fairly deep brèche. It has a steep and rocky N face, well to the E of which is a steep pillar which provides the line of the route described.

6a
TD
6

NORTH PILLAR
N Candau and P Brient, 20 Aug 1967
Valley base: La Bérarde

A magnificent climb of 350m, airy and a bit athletic. There are about 10 pitons in place. If the climb is continued to the summit, it produces a fine and varied climb.

From the Chatelleret hut take a good path crossing the Etançons torrent to the mouth of the Gandolière valley and climb grass and scree slopes on the L bank of the Gandolière torrent. Traverse L to reach the rock barrier supporting the Gandolière glacier. Climb the rocks at the extreme L and climb by a couloir on the N flank of the first and lowest rognon (little stream). By a succession of gullies, scree and terraces, reach a little rock beak beneath the lower tongue of the glacier. By easy slabs follow the line Lwards to the foot of the N pillar. Climb a little rimaye and start up smooth slabs trending L (III and IV) and reach a ramp climbing L to a niche where it is interrupted. Go straight up for 3m, turn an overhang on the R (V) and climb a dièdre cut by little overhangs. Exit L on to a terrace after having avoided, on the L, the biggest overhang (IV/V). Climb a succession of little walls moving gradually Rwards (IV and IV+) to a platform and reach (L) a chimney blocked by an overhang. Climb a step of red rock on the R of the chimney (rounded holds, V/V+) to gain a large, pebbly ledge which is followed R to reach the crest of the pillar. At the end of the ledge, climb a little red wall to set foot on the pillar (III). Climb R, then L in a dièdre-chimney (IV+) to reach an easy section.

Climb bulging slabs for 30m (IV/V, rounded holds). Above, make an ascending traverse L (III/IV) to reach a vertical red wall. Dodge this by the L and go back to the crest. Follow the edge and its immediate sides (III and IV) to the top of the pillar (6hr). Climb the E ridge, one delicate pitch (V), and then turn or traverse the gendarmes to the top of the Aiguille. 1½-2hr: **c8hr** total

Descend from the summit along the W ridge as far as the brèche at Pt 3,252m. Now go down the S side to the Plaret glacier to join the descent from the Plaret (Route 2b).

It is also possible to descend from the top of the N pillar without going to the summit of the Aiguille. Descend the E ridge and then a couloir of the S side. Follow easier slopes round the foot of the ridge to the rock barrier supporting the Gandolière glacier.

Le Râteau 3,809m

Miss Brevoort, W Coolidge, C Almer, P Michel jnr, P Bleuer an‹
C Roth, 11 July 1873

The Râteau, which lies W of the Brèche de la Meije, is well seen
from la Grave, its splendid N face being particularly prominent
in the view, otherwise the mountain is somewhat hidden from
view, at least from the valley. It has two principal summits
separated by a long, crenellated ridge. The E summit is 50m
higher than the W summit. The Col de la Girose forms the W
boundary of the mountain and provides a means of access to the
slopes on the S side for climbers based in la Grave. Access to the
mountain from the N has been greatly facilitated by the
construction of the téléphérique from la Grave to the Col des
Ruillans on the E edge of the Girose glacier. At least this is better
than the one time proposal to build a railway to the summit of
the Râteau! An important feature of the mountain is the long,
broken ridge leading NE from highest summit. At the foot of the
ridge, above where the ridge loses itself in the moraines below
the Râteau glacier, are the Enfetchores buttresses, the location of
a number of climbs and a route of approach to the Brèche de la
Meije.

East summit

7a
PD
7

SOUTH RIDGE - WEST FLANK

Valley base: La Bérarde

The climb is the ordinary route and offers a summer snow climb and
winter ski itinerary and is justly popular.

Follow the path from the Selle hut to reach the Selle glacier just
beyond the base of the S ridge of Pt Thorant. Cross the upper
glacier plateau heading E then bear L towards the upper section
Reach the foot of two broad couloirs emanating from the upper
part of the S ridge of the Râteau which are separated by a

rognon. In summer, take the L branch which is slightly steeper but carries more snow generally (obviously, the R branch may be followed given suitable conditions). The couloir leads to the upper section of the broad S ridge close to the foresummit. Climb this before turning W to reach the main summit. **4-5hr**

Note: It is quite feasible to climb the whole of the S ridge from the Brèche du Râteau. This route is the easiest means of ascent to the E summit and has become the normal means of ascent (F: 4hr from the Selle hut).

7b
D
7

SOUTH RIDGE AND WEST PILLAR-SILENCE DE LA MER

E Benbassath, A Brulé and B Soleymieux
Valley base: La Bérarde

The climb was created to give length and spice to the ordinary route described above. The route is equipped and a 50m rope is recommended. 300m of climbing in 11 pitches to the crest of the S ridge.

From the Selle hut start as for Route 7a. Once on the Selle glacier follow a line towards the Brèche du Râteau then swing L along the base of the rocks of the W pillar. The start is just by the highest point reached by the glacier against the face. After a dog leg R move back obliquely L (1 rope length). Continue slightly Rwards to mid-height of the face. Climb directly up, then move slightly L to continue straight up and arrive close to the crest of the pillar on the L.

P1 IV: P2 V: P3 V+: P4 IV: P5 IV: P6 IV: P7 V+: P8 V-: P9 IV+: P10 V-: P11 IV

From the crest either, continue up the S ridge to join Route 7a or, descend to the Brèche du Râteau and return to the Selle hut via the approach route.

North Face

The N face is the most impressive feature of the mountain. It is c500m high and very steep, even vertical towards the top. The main features on the face are the low profile rib leading to the E summit and the shallow couloir descending from a square brèche W of this summit. Climbs on the face are best attempted when the rock is dry.

7c
TD+
9

ARETES ROUTE

J-M Cambon and B Francou, 25 July 1979
FWA: R Molinatti, P Rizzardo and P Robach, 17 Jan 1993
Valley base: La Grave

The climb takes a line up the L bank of the couloir descending from the square brèche on the summit ridge. On the L bank of this lies a rib which is quite distinct in the upper section of the face. This is a good, sustained route, quite exposed, with difficulties up to 6a. The rock is good to very good and there is no equipment in place.

Approach as for Route 7d. Climb directly below the brèche on the summit ridge and cross the rimaye R of the gully. Thence, 50m up, steep snow leads to a comma-shaped snow feature, inclined towards the L, beyond and directly above a big, light grey dièdre. Climb a Lwards slanting crack on dark coloured rock (3 rope lengths: IV/IV+ and a move of V). Traverse R to a little chimney. Climb this (20m: V, one step of V+) and then reach and cross the median névé, slanting towards the couloir. 6hr

Climb a crack in a pillar, forming a red tower (3 rope lengths sustained at IV+/V+ and a move of 6a). Get on to a rotten ledge and traverse along a ramp for 10m (V). Return L, turning the tower (V) and reach its top. Gain the summit ridge either by a short wall or by a brèche on the L (IV/III). 6hr

Reach the E summit by the crest of the ridge in 1½hr.
c14hr in all

Descend via the ordinary route (7a).

7d **FOURASTIER-MADIER ROUTE**
ED2
9
M Fourastier and A Madier, 18-19 Aug 1938
FWA: P Chevalier and J Samet, 27-30 Dec 1975
Valley base: La Grave

This is a great climb of considerable difficulty, length and some danger.
The second ascent was made in 1953, disaster having overtaken a
previous party, probably owing to the dislodgement of loose blocks in
the upper couloir. As far as the final wall there are pitches of V and the
final wall itself has two pitches of VI (6a and 6b). The first ascent
took 20hr from the rimaye with a bivouac just under the ice slope
below the final wall, the second took 13hr.

There are three alternative starts; from the Evariste Chancel hut
(seldom used and not described); from the Col des Ruillans
(upper téléphérique station); from the middle station.

From the middle station (2,416m) attain and climb the
Râteau glacier to the start at c3,200m. c3hr

From the upper station the most logical way is to descend
the upper slopes of the Vallon glacier NNE below the pylons and
pass beneath the rocks of Pt Trifide to reach the upper plateau of
the Râteau glacier (2hr). It is also possible to reach the same
point by ascending SE on the Girose glacier to the small col
between Pointe Trifide and le Râteau W summit. From the col
descend the NE-facing ice slope (45°), with possible rappel
points on the rocks on the L, to reach the glacier. 1½-2hr

The climb follows the spur which descends directly from
the E summit. To reach the spur, climb Lwards to the first
rimaye (rock rognon) at the foot of a triangular ice slope which
forms the centre of the base of the face. Climb the rimaye on the
L and then slant up Lwards across the ice slope to the foot of the
spur. Climb a second rimaye at c3,325m, usually by climbing a
rock overhang although the method will vary according to
conditions, to reach the L of the spur. This section varies
considerably from season to season.

Climb the L flank of the spur for 70m and then return R to

the crest and follow this for 35m (steep). Continue to a tottering overhang forming a barrier on the ridge and contour it Rwards. 30m higher reach the foot of a reddish wall which is climbed on the L by a large block attached to it. Next climb a vertical wall, still keeping L (V) and continue to a verglassed couloir which is also climbed (loose). Continue via slabs and then climb a second, loose, couloir by its R bank (V). Both of the couloirs described are delicate and exposed and require care. Continue up less steep slopes but on verglassed rocks to a steep wall. A possible bivouac site is above on the L.

Move Rwards along the base of the wall (IV: poor rock) to below a large crack. Climb this vertically for 10m (IV: verglas) to a cave and then climb an overhang on its L side to reach a chimney-crack dominated by large, tottery blocks. Climb the crack (5-6m) and then traverse 2m L before moving Rwards by a short section of slabs (IV) to reach a couloir-chimney. Climb half-way up this (V) and then traverse L (VI, 6a) at the level of a pile of blocks situated on the R. Do not be tempted by a direct finish line to the summit via the couloir-chimney (the original route). Continue straight on to a vague ledge and then towards a chimney-crack which forms a cave (easily identified from la Grave).

Climb this and exit R (VI, 6b). A short, steep 20m couloir of loose and verglassed rocks leads to a brèche c15m W of the summit. **10-12hr** from the rimaye

7e
D
9

NORTH-WEST COULOIR

R Ginel and M Liotier, 31 May 1959
FWA: M Genday and M Viézat, Feb 1981
Valley base: La Grave

Possibly the easiest of the N face climbs since it avoids all the rock difficulties. It is high in ambience and best climbed at the beginning of the season. The rimayes may prove delicate.

Follow Route 7c to the foot of the spur which descends from the E summit. Climb L of the spur and follow a couloir between this and the first sérac barrier (55°-60°). Traverse L below a second barrier (exposed) and then continue directly by less steep snow which slants Rwards to the E ridge a short distance from the summit. 500m: **9-10hr**

7f
PD
8
7

SOUTH-EAST FLANK

First ascent party
C Brook with D Gaspard and J Eymard climbed the E ridge complete, 1922
Valley base: La Bérarde

It is possible to follow the whole of the E ridge from the Brèche de la Meije but the rock is poor and it takes 5hr. The ordinary route from the Promontoire hut takes the SE flank. It is a glacier climb and as such should be avoided in descent late in the day when conditions are dangerous.

From the Promontoire hut traverse horizontally to the W branch of the Etançons glacier. Pass below the Brèche de la Meije and a big rock buttress of the E ridge, then climb gently into the glacier cirque S of the E ridge. Avoid the crevasses and séracs which are on the L and above their level slant L. A first rock barrier is climbed on its L or dodged by a cone of snow immediately to its L. Above, a snow arête leads to a second rocky barrier. Either climb it or cross the snow on the L to reach the final snow slope. Climb this to the upper section of the S ridge either L or R of the cornice. Arrive at a foresummit from where the E ridge is taken to the E summit. **4hr** from the hut

Descent is either by the same route to the Promontoire hut. Alternatively, and recommended late in the day or in warm conditions, is a descent to the Chatelleret hut. However it should be noted that the descent from the Brèche du Râteau is not very pleasant when there is little snow.

To reach the Chatelleret hut follow the S ridge, keeping mostly on its W flank to avoid cornices, to the Brèche du Râteau, 3,235m. From the brèche, descend E by a little rock couloir and small glacier. Keeping L, reach the big terrace below the SW-most part of the Etançons glacier. Descend into the couloir which descends from the Brèche du Râteau and continue down its L bank, keeping well to the L, to the foot of the couloir (stonefall possible). From the mouth of the couloir reach the Chatelleret-Promontoire path which is followed to the hut. PD: **2-2½hr**

It is easy, from the Brèche du Râteau, to descend to the Selle hut but this makes a return to la Bérarde more difficult.

Enfetchores de Droite 2,989m

NE of the Râteau E summit is a long rock ridge separating the Râteau and Meije glaciers. The lower part of this ridge, which is well defined in its own right, is the Enfetchores de Droite. It is almost 300m high. At its NE foot is a massive rognon which is c150m high and on its W side, directly above the rognon is a triangular face rising to a small pinnacle, somewhat detatched from the Enfetchores itself, known as the Pointe de St Antoine.

Partially detached from the Enfetchores R is a second rock ridge (above Pt 2,364m) which loses itself in the Meije glacier. This carries a well known and easy track leading to the Brèche de la Meije and the Meije N face climbs.

On the Enfetchores R there are several climbs of varying style and difficulty. Three routes are described which may be climbed independently or as direct starts for the NE ridge of the Râteau to give 1,300m of continuous climbing.

7g
TD+

PILIER O SOL E MIO

B Soleymieux with a group from the C A B, 1983
Valley base: La Grave

A fine, direct climb on good, varied rock: equipped. Difficulties up to 6a.

Leave the col des Ruillans lift at the first station and descend S and get on to the crest of the moraine near Pt 2,371m. Climb it a short way then traverse L across the Clot des Sables and under the massive rognon. Beyond it climb the snow/scree slope to the mouth of the couloir descending from the brèche on the E side of the Pt de St Antoine. Traverse L to the foot of the spur and the start which is just L of the crest of the spur, directly beneath a series of dièdres split by overhangs. Reach the dièdres and climb them, finishing Rwards on to a platform (3 rope lengths 4+ to 5+).

It is here that Sol E Mio branches off R. Traverse R and climb to a little terrace on the crest of a rib (4). Climb straight up via a crack (4+: 1 rope length: exposed). Slant on the R and, by its edge, reach the top of the big flake, which is characteristic of the lower section of the ridge (5). Climb into the brèche between the flake and the main wall and from there climb a rope length to a Lwards slanting ledge. Go to the R end of this ledge and climb an overhang on its R (5 and 6a: crux). A final direct pitch (5) leads to the top of the spur.

Descent: From here a series of easy ledges lead R to a position above the Pt de St Antoine. Descend to the brèche and either go down the gully on snow (impractical in rock slippers) or scramble to the top of Pt de St Antoine from where a series of equipped rappels descend to the scree.

7h BRECHE DE ST ANTHOINE - GRAND COULOIR
PD
10

Valley base: La Bérarde

The gully, mentioned above as a possible descent, is often taken as a route to either the Brèche de la Meije or to the Râteau.

In good snow conditions, climb to the Brèche de St Antoine then bear E by ledges to the top of the Enfetchores R from where the W branch of the Meije glacier is reached or the continuation to the Râteau (by Route 7i).

7i VOIE CANDAU
D
10

N Candau and P Gervais, 2 July 1967
Valley base: La Grave

A long climb to the summit of the Râteau with the main difficulties in the lower part which can be climbed for their own sake. It is not equipped.

Approach as for Route 7g to the mouth of the couloir. From here, traverse L for c100m until a rock rib comes into view. Start up a 10m chimney. Slant R by ledges of light grey granite and on rounded holds. Climb towards a crack and use this (IV+) to reach a grassy ledge. Follow this ledge R. Descend slightly and traverse to the foot of a 40m dièdre which is climbed (V-). Slant slightly L then climb a vertical wall to a black flake. Climb this to reach a ledge above (V). Climb Lwards on rounded rock (IV/IV+) then return more easily R to the top of the spur. From this point it is possible to descend using the line of rappels described in Route 7g.

To continue to the summit of the Râteau, follow the ridge easily to the foot of a gendarme, turned by the L flank, and climb an exposed 30m dièdre (III) leading to the top of the gendarme. Climb a succession of pinnacles to the foot of a second step in the form of a big flake. Pass this easily on the R for 100m and regain the ridge by slabs (III: rounded holds). Now follow the crest of the ridge (III) which ends at 3,330m and gives way to snow/ice. Climb this arête for 400m to reach the E ridge and hence the E summit. **7-9hr**

West Summit 3,766m

7j
D+
8

SOUTH PILLAR (PILIER CANDAU)

N Candau, 7 Aug 1966
Valley base: La Bérarde/La Grave

The S pillar, which is located E of the Col de la Girose and rises from the upper Selle glacier to the W ridge of the Râteau. At the foot of the pillar are two prominent ribs. The climb takes the steepest and most prominent of these. The climbing is interesting, the rock excellent. The climb is equipped with traditional pitons, a small rack is useful.

From la Grave (or the Chancel hut) follow Route 8b to the Col de la Girose then descend to the foot of the snow couloir on its S side (c1½hr from the Col des Ruillans). From the Selle hut follow Route 8a to the same point. Follow the base of the W ridge to the foot of the climb. 2½hr

Start between the two ribs by a couloir. Cross the rimaye and climb almost in the bed of the couloir, then get on to the L rib at the level of the initial step (traces of yellow paint). A Lwards slanting traverse leads to above this step. By a short chimney and slabs (III), reach a small col at the foot of a first steep step on the crest of the rib (this is 3 rope lengths from the start). Follow the rib (III/IV), climb a slab (IV/IV+) and then stay on the L to reach the foot of a big, red step (III/III+). Climb an overhang by the R (V: strenuous) then, by seamed slabs go straight up the L side of the pillar and continue by grooves on the rib itself (5+/6a) which lead to the top of the step. Follow the crest easily up to another step which is climbed directly (III/III+).

Continue up to a spike from where a descent is made between two flakes. Climb a cornice, then bear R to reach the W ridge just below the final summit steps. **4-5hr** from the foot of the climb

Descent by Route 7k

7k
PD
7

WEST RIDGE

H Scott Tucker and C Turc snr and jnr, 17 July 1906
Valley base: La Bérarde/La Grave

This is the normal route from the Selle hut to the lower of the Râteau summits and is quite frequently climbed.

From the Selle hut follow Route 8a the Col de la Girose (3hr). The route may be climbed from the la Grave side via the Col des Ruillans, thence to the Col de la Girose. c1hr

On the R (E) of the col is a triangular snow slope pointing at the W summit of the Râteau. Climb this up the centre or up the ridges on either side according to conditions. Continue up snow and rocks to the first step. Either climb this direct up good rock for 25m (III+) or around it by a ledge on the S face followed by an oblique line up easier rocks. Climb the second step (III), also 25m, to the W summit. 1-1½hr: **2-2½hr** from the Col des Ruillans: **4-4½hr** from the Selle hut

Col de la Girose 3,518m

Probably Lord Methuen and General Montgomery with J Jaun and A Maurer, 1875

This is an important crossing point between the Romanche valley to the N and subsequently the Vénéon valley to the S. It can be crossed on foot in summer and on ski in winter (skiers may prefer to use the Col de la Lauze which is easier). As far as this guide book is concerned, it opens up access to climbs on the S side of the Râteau to climbers with access from la Grave. It lies between le Râteau and Pt Dosia.

8a
F
11
8

SOUTH FLANK

Valley base: La Bérarde

From the Selle hut follow the path heading NE and passing Pt 2,929m at the base of the S ridge of Pt Thorant. Get on to the Selle glacier and continue in the same direction at first before turning N up the glacier. Keep L of the rock island at Pt 3,248m, then turn a little R to reach its N side and the foot of the wide snow couloir leading to the col de la Girose. Climb the couloir to the col. **3hr**

8b
F

NORTH FLANK

Valley base: La Grave

The col is generally reached by parties approaching from the Col des Ruillans, which can be reached by lift from la Grave (so avoiding a night in a hut), or from the Chancel hut. From the latter by a path which climbs up scree slopes past some rock walls. Continue R up a rocky combe by a wide scree couloir and/ or snow slopes to the Col du Lac, the little Lac glacier being on the L. Continue up the E bank of the Girose glacier to the Col des Ruillans. From here head N up the glacier to the foot of the steepish snow slope slanting L to the col. Climb the slope to the col which is on the R at its top. **c1hr** from the Col des Ruillans

Pointe Dosia 3,611m

E Gravelotte and G Serret with C, D, M and P Gaspard and J
Turc, 20 Sept 1898

This is a minor summit just W of the Col de la Girose on the
long ridge running W from the Râteau to the Pic de la Grave.
Two climbs are described on the S flank of the mountain.

9a   **DENTS ROUGES**
D+

G Nominé and R Corompt, 4 Sept 1969
Valley base: La Bérarde/La Grave

*The longer of the two climbs here which takes a slightly more difficult
line on good rock. Not equipped*

From la Grave follow Route 8b to the Col de la Girose and then
descend the snow couloir on the S side of the col to its foot.
Continue down the Selle glacier until a traverse W across a rock
band is possible (1½hr).

From the Selle hut follow Route 8a to the L of Pt 3,248m
and continue straight ahead to the foot of the face by the two
obvious pillars. 2hr

Climb between the grey and red pillars for 1 rope length
(IV). Traverse a slab R to below a chimney and climb it for 30m
(IV+) to a grey overhang. Traverse a slab L wards and climb
grooves (IV/IV+). Slant R to join the red pillar.

Follow the crest of the pillar for 3 rope lengths to a little
brèche (III/IV+). Reach a second brèche 20m higher (IV+) and,
by the L flank, reach yet another gap. Again, follow the crest for
40m (IV/V: exposed) and reach, with ease, the teeth forming the
summit of the pillar. Rappel 20m from the last tooth which leads
to the large brèche between the pillar and the wall (junction with
the previous climb). Follow the ridge to the top (III and IV).

3-4hr climbing

Descend E ridge to the Col de la Girose.

9b PILIER GRIS

D
11
8

R Corompt and G Nominé, 3 Sept 1969
Valley base: La Bérarde/La Grave

A superb if shortish climb on very good rock. This L pillar is the slightly shorter of the two which descend directly from the summit of the Dosia but is better defined in its lower section. The route is not equipped so take a normal rack.

Reach the foot of the pillars as described for Route 9a. Start straight up the middle of the pillar (IV). Next climb a slab below an overhang, first moving R then back L (IV). Climb grooves (IV/IV+ then III) for 2 rope lengths to reach a dièdre on the L. Climb it, to finish a little R of the top of the grey pillar (IV/V)

Rappel 20m into the brèche which separates the grey pillar from the wall. Climb the crest of the red pillar which follows for 3 pitches (III/IV). Higher up on the R, link up with the finishing pillar of the 'Dents Rouges' (Route 8a) which is followed to the top. **3hr** climbing

Pointe Thorant 3,583m

O Visioz with A Turc, 5 Sept 1897

The Pt Thorant is actually a foresummit of the Pt Madeleine which borders the Girose glacier. Its S flank offers a long ridge separating the E Selle glacier from the Selle glacier. The ridge carries a zone of superb slabs on its E face. The ridge itself is split into two parts, which may be confusing until one sets foot on it.

10a VOIE DES LEZARDS

D+
11
7

J Lainez and E Arnold, 1981
Valley base: La Bérarde

A fine climb on the lower part of the S ridge. The rock is good and, although equipped, a normal rack should be carried.

The climb starts at the base of the long, S ridge which is reached from the Selle hut by following the path heading towards the

Selle glacier. The foot of the ridge is gained easily from the path.

Climb a slab up to a dièdre closed by a small roof (III/IV) and then climb the roof (IV+). Keep straight on to below a big overhang and turn it on the R (IV). Climb parallel to the ridge for 4 pitches (IV max) and rejoin the ridge by 2 rope lengths (V then IV: more delicate). Follow the crest of the ridge for 2 pitches (IV and IV+) then climb more easily on the R flank, close to the crest. **4½hr** from the foot of the ridge.

The start of the normal descent route is identified by a pierced gendarme. From the gendarme, descend the E face by rock slabs, requiring care, towards a huge, stony/snowy terrace. From its L (N) extremity a slightly difficult line leads to the glacier close to the rocky rognon. Cross the glacier E wards towards Pt 3,248m and return to the Selle hut by reversing Route 8a.

10b	**VOIE DES PLAQUES ROUGES**
D+	P Chapoutot and B Wyns, 5 Aug 1964
11	Valley base: La Bérarde

This classic climb threads its line up superb red granite, taking steep slabs adjacent to a long, red dièdre from mid-height. The climb is traditionally equipped, a small rack may be useful. In recent years the shrinking of the Selle glacier has made the start of the climb very exposed and dangerous.

Approach as for Route 9a but continue W from the foot of that route towards a rock rognon at the foot of the E face. Turn this on the R or climb it from below to start by a little, poorly defined couloir. Climb the couloir avoiding a step on its R side and an overhang by slabs on the L. The couloir becomes a chimney which widens and comes up against an overhang (niche: III/III+). Traverse L at the level of a little beak and climb a short wall (IV/IV+) then rejoin the couloir by slabs. Climb it easily by two short chimneys of 7m (III and IV). Above, the couloir becomes easy and bends L. It is here that the couloir is abandoned and the more serious climbing starts.

Traverse easily L and then climb, trending back slightly R, towards the long, red dièdre of the upper section. To reach it, climb a dièdre nestling in grey rock, then a little pillar of red and black rock to gain a belay at the foot of the big dièdre itself. Climb up Lwards, passing a slanting overhang (IV+) then straight up a fissured wall (IV/V-) to finish at a niche on the R alongside the big dièdre. A pitch slanting L, taking little walls and traverses (IV) leads to a small step at the side of a vertical crack.

Stride L across the crack, climb a little whitish wall then, moving Lwards, take a lichenous slab to a small balcony below a flake (IV/IV+). Get on to the flake by its L side (IV) and from it make a descending traverse under a red overhang. By making a large stride, reach and climb a vertical crack (V: exposed). Climb the overhang at the top of the crack (V-: exposed) and then a 50m chimney to reach the S ridge, 10m higher, by slabs (III/III+). Follow the ridge to the summit (III: then easy). **5hr** from the foot of the face

Descent: Follow the S ridge easily to the pierced gendarme referred to in Route 10a, then as for that route.

Pic de la Grave 3,669m

W Coolidge, C Almer snr and jnr and R Kaufmann, 14 July 1874

This is the last summit on the long, rocky ridge running roughly W from the Râteau, skirting the Girose glacier on its N side, before it turns to snow at the Dôme de Lauze.

11a
F+
12

NORTH FACE

First ascent party
Valley base: La Grave

The ordinary route and a very good snow climb, somewhat spoiled by the presence of ski installations.

From la Grave or from the Chancel hut, reach the Col des
Ruillans as for Route 8b. Climb the glacier following the line of
the ski-tow to reach the foot of the N side of the Pic de la Grave,
L of the sérac band which cuts the snow slope of the mountain.
It may be necessary to climb almost to the Col de la Lauze and
then contour the foot of the NW forepeak (Pt 3,645m). Cross the
rimaye (this may pose problems) and step on to the snow or ice
slope below the NE arête. Climb the slope then bear R to the col
separating the peak from the foresummit. Continue along the
NW ridge to the summit. It may be possible to start climbing on
the R of the sérac band. The slope forms a steep (40°-45°), deep
couloir between the arête descending from the foresummit and
the sérac band. The couloir is often icy but in good snow
conditions it is the favoured route. Continue above this couloir
and follow the arête to reach the forepeak easily. Then follow the
NW arête which is mainly snow to the summit. **1½-2hr** from the
Col des Ruillans

Descend the same route or the variation. In the latter case, at the
top of the couloir slant L down rocks to regain the Girose glacier.

Brèche de la Meije 3,358m

First traverse: A Moore, H Walker and E Whymper with C Almer
and M Croz, 23 June 1864

The brèche offers the quickest link between la Grave and la
Bérarde. Since the arrival of the cable car in la Grave, the easy
access to the foot of the Enfetchores (L) spur has opened up the
N face climbs on la Meije. It allows parties to descend to either
base and its significance must be fully exploited. The brèche is
easy in both directions and there is a small choice of bivouac sites
at the top of the Enfetchores rocks.

12a   NORTH-SOUTH TRAVERSE

F
10
13
15

First traverse party
Valley base: La Grave

The route is used to approach the N face routes on the Meije either from a bivouac on the Enfetchores rocks or by reversing the route as far as the Meije glacier from the Promontoire hut. It is a very good snow climb.

From the first station, follow Route 7g to the traverse below the massive rognon. Continue traversing (faint track), below the Enfetchores R, to the W edge of the Enfetchores L. Climb on to the rock spur and follow the obvious, well used zigzag route up it to reach the upper part of the Meije glacier. This is followed Rwards at first, then back L to reach the brèche. The rimaye may be tricky. 3-4hr from the station

Descend either on snow or rock, according to season and continue down and Lwards traversing beneath the SW face to reach the Promontoire hut. This is generally a well marked path. ½-1hr from the brèche: **c5hr** in all.

La Meije 3,982m

E Boileau de Castelnau with P Gaspard snr and jnr, 16 Aug 1877

This is a major alpine peak and one of the last to be climbed. Like the Râteau, there was at one time a proposal to build a railway to the summit, or at least a lift from an underground station at the Brèche de la Meije. Rather like the Matterhorn, many attempts were made before de Castelnau's party succeeded, and then not before experiencing considerable difficulties with the last few m.

The mountain, which dominates the view from la Grave, has a multiplicity of summits along its main ridge which runs E-W. At the extreme E end is the Meije Orientale 3,891m which could almost be considered a separate mountain. This is

separated from the Doigt de Dieu (also known as the Pic
Central) 3,973m by the Brèche Joseph Turc. This summit was
the first to be climbed, in the hope or expectation that it was the
highest point (Miss Brevoort and W Coolidge with C Almer snr,
U Almer and C Gertsch, 28 June 1870). W of the Doigt de Dieu
are a series of gendarmes. The first of these is known as the dent
Blanche, whilst beyond this are the third and second dents
(teeth) followed by the dent Zsigmondy. This stands directly
above the dramatic, deep, square gash in the ridge known as the
Brèche Zsigmondy. Immediately W of the brèche is the Grand
Pic de la Meije, the highest point. SW of this, and just beyond
the Brèche du Glacier Carré, are two further pinnacles; the Pic
du Glacier Carré and the Grand Doigt.

The two main faces (N and S) are equally impressive and
provide the terrain for most of the routes described.

13a
AD+/D-
15
13
16

SOUTH (PROMONTOIRE) RIDGE AND TRAVERSE

First ascent party
Traverse W-E: J Gibson, U Almer and F Boss, 3 July 1891
Valley base: La Bérarde

*One of the great expeditions of the Alps. Excellent rock, although the
climbing is rather delicate. The route described to the summit is the
ordinary route on the mountain. It is popular and often crowded.*

Start from immediately behind the Promontoire hut on the L.
Almost at once the Brèche du Crapaud is reached with the
Couloir du Crapaud dropping away R to the Etançons glacier.
Continue on the L up steep rock move R and then climb up to
join the ridge. Continue straight up the easy slabs of the
Promontoire ridge to where it suddenly steepens and becomes
impracticable. Traverse slabs L and up an easy chimney to a
large terrace. Climb the steep chimney ahead and traverse L to
reach the edge of a massive couloir (Couloir Duhamel) at a point
opposite to, and a little above, a large detached gendarme.
Descend a short steep wall into the couloir. The couloir leads to
a considerable terrace (Pyramide Duhamel 3,460m) where the
cliff opens out into a wide expanse of slabs and terraces. 2hr

Climb up Rwards above the E branch of the Etançons glacier to the foot of a steep wall. Descend R somewhat to reach the base of a short, steep slab. Climb this (III) and continue R along wide ledges to almost underneath the Carré glacier (slight icefall danger). Slant back up L along small ledges until it is possible to see the W branch of the Etançons glacier. Climb a rounded hog's back on its L (III) and move back R along a ledge. Climb two successive chimneys, neither very deep (III). Now traverse L under steep rocks to the 'pas du chat'. This pitch is a delicate L traverse across a large block overhanging the W branch of the Etançons glacier. Round the corner climb a white chimney and a steep wall and then descend a short way to a good terrace just next to the Carré glacier. 1½-2hr

Climb up on the L of the Carré glacier keeping under the rocks of the Grand Doigt, the higher of two pinnacles on the L. Pass below the Brèche du Doigt and continue along the glacier under the Pic du Glacier Carré to the Brèche du Glacier Carré at the top of the Carré glacier. ½-1hr depending on snow conditions

Climb on the R side of the ridge on easy, broken rocks to the foot of a 7m red slab on the ridge; known as the Cheval Rouge, it is bounded on the R by a steep wall. Climb the slab (III), mount the crest *à cheval* and avoid the overhang on the L (III). Go on up easy rocks to the summit. 1hr: **5-6hr** from the Promontoire hut

Descent to the Promontoire hut is made by the same route. There are some equipped rappel points.

To traverse the summit ridge, descend easy rocks towards the E and make four 40m rappels directly to the Brèche Zsigmondy. Continue along the level ridge (loose) to reach the foot of the Dent Zsigmondy (belay *à cheval*: piton). Follow the base of the Dent Zsigmondy on the N side by a 60m traverse and continue to below the brèche between the Dent Zsigmondy and the second tooth. Climb a couloir up to this brèche (from the *à cheval* stance, 110m of cables: belays on *in situ* pitons). Follow the ridge over a mixture of snow and rock over the second, third and fourth teeth to the summit of the Pic Central (Doigt de Dieu). 4hr

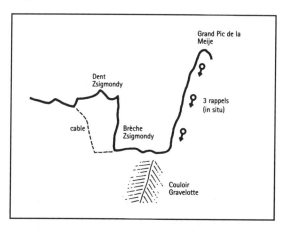

Descend (rappel) over the firm rocks on the N side of the ridge to the brèche NE of Pic Central. Climb up again for 2m and go along to the point where the ridge is left. Descend (rappel) over snowy rocks for 15m to where there is a fixed rappel point at the bottom of the rocks. Descend the snow or ice slope to the rimaye and cross it. If using a rappel for this, either 70m of rope is necessary, or find slings, normally in place, to make an intermediate rappel point. Slant down NE across the Tabuchet glacier to the Aigle Hut. 1hr: 5hr from the Grand Pic: **10-12hr** from Promontoire

South Face

This is a truly magnificent face extending for c1km from the Grand Pic to the Meije Orientale. The W boundary of the face is the Promontoire ridge descending S from the Grand Doigt. The face is effectively split into two parts by the the big couloir descending from the Brèche Zsigmondy. W of this couloir is the highest part of the entire face directly below the Grand Pic. At its base is a scree and névé covered terrace (Fauteuil des Allemands) which is supported by a rock band adjacent to the E Etançons glacier. High up on the W extremity of the face is the small but prominent Carré glacier.

The E part of the face is split at roughly mid-height by a snow covered terrace, usually referred to as the snow band. This originates in the Zsigmondy couloir and rises fairly steeply to its highest point below the third tooth of the summit ridge. From there it descends gradually before it finally merges into the E most part of the Etançons glacier. Below the snow band is a vast rock bastion, undercut by overhangs, which supports several climbs which may be continued to the summit ridge. Three climbs have been chosen to represent different generations of climber and three different styles of climb and equipment.

13b
TD+
14

DOIGT DE DIEU - SOUTH FACE DIRECT

Lower section: R Gallat nad A Santimone, July 1951
Upper section: J Walden and V Chaud, 29 July 1951
Integral: P Chapoutot and J Mercadié, 22 Aug 1968
Valley base: La Bérarde

Cut by the horizontal snow band, the climb has a mixed history. The top section, climbed by Victor Chaud is unusual. He topped out on to the summit ridge, then returned to tackle, and succeed in climbing, the overhanging finish to the Doigt itself - which today is graded 6b. This was an exceptional performance.

The rock is generally good except for 70m or so in the upper section. A full rack and several thin pegs will be useful, the gear *in situ* is traditional!

From the Promontoire hut descend to the glacier as for Route 13e and traverse to the foot of the face (1hr). Start directly below the Doigt de Dieu, R of a line of roofs and L of a little tongue of snow. Cross the rimaye to inclined slabs then climb 15m R and return by a horizontal traverse of 25m close to a large roof. Climb a steep wall (IV/IV+) then a slanting ledge Lwards. A 4m wall and then a 12m traverse L, with an overhang, lead to a vast inclined plane from which is seen a 120m, arc shaped crack marking the line of ascent.

Traverse the slab slanting L to reach the crack (IV). Climb the crack which may be wet (IV and V: a section V+). Continue in the same line (IV), passing L of a snow patch, to the foot of a steep and damp, black step bordered on the R by a chimney. Climb the wall for 30m (IV/IV+) and traverse R (IV: damp) to climb a chimney (IV and V+: exposed). Exit R below an overhanging wall and climb a slanting dièdre (IV+). This ends at the level of the snow band dividing the route into its upper and lower parts. Above is a spur which drops directly from the summit of the Doigt de Dieu. The spur forms a high, narrow, yellow-red facette flanked by two ribs. Climb easily R for 45m to contour the base of the R-hand rib (a move of V at the end). 5-6hr

Climb the black rock on the E flank of the R-hand rib to the foot of a deep chimney cut by overhangs (III/IV: verglas). L of this chimney climb a steep, cracked slab for 50m (IV+). Reach the top of the pillar and cross the brèche which separates it from the wall. Reach a small terrace above the brèche and a recess on the L (poor rock). Climb blocks and then a steep chimney slanting L (V: exposed). Return R on poor rock, then take a dièdre and tottering blocks to a good, snowy terrace reached on the R at the foot of an overhanging step.

The rock now becomes excellent. Climb a steep, verglassed chimney (IV+) and continue L for a short distance, then straight up to a platform (IV). Climb a dièdre formed by cracked blocks on the R (15m: IV/IV+) and descend to the other side of a vague spur to a narrow ledge. Follow this Rwards then continuing R on pleasant slabs (IV+). Do not climb too high but traverse horizontally R to the base of the rib which marks the E extent of the summit overhang. Pass R of the rib and follow slabs towards a verglassed, overhanging chimney. From its foot, slant R on a vertical wall (V+: exposed). Step across a little crest and reach a ledge at the top of the chimney, 12m below the summit ridge. 5-6hr: **11-13hr** in all

The Doigt de Dieu is on the L (W) but it is logical to continue Ewards to the Aigle hut. The Chaud party climbed the chimney direct (VI) and their variant, mentioned in the preamble, takes the overhangs and crack directly beneath the summit for the sake of 6m of 6b! The party reached the section by a hard traverse (6a) Lwards from the penultimate pitch to the arête.

13c
TD-
14

BASTION CENTRAL

P Chapoutot and B Wyns, to the snow band, 4, 5 July 1969
Complete: V Péguy, J Leroux and M Brissaud, 1971
Valley base: La Bérarde

The first ascent was noted for its style - only 10 pitons used. Cambon later repeated the climb (with Chapoutot), placing bolts on the stances and several elsewhere. This was condemned by many who still consider that the first ascent was a bench mark for its time and should have been left as such. However, the climb is superb, the rock excellent, the upper section above the snow band is similar in style and difficulty to the Allain climb on the S face. Reflection on the style of the first climbers puts the trend of bolting in the high mountains into an unflattering perspective. Chapoutot and Wyns' adventure epitomises the pure ethic - they must have enjoyed themselves! Approach from the hut as for previous climb.

Start between the big overhangs below the 3rd tooth on the summit ridge and the line of roofs directly below the Doigt de Dieu, by a couloir which steepens and becomes overhanging. Climb a slab on the R of the couloir for 50m (III) to a horizontal break 10m below the overhang of the dièdre. Cross the dièdre and make a 30m ascending traverse Lwards (IV/IV+) to a narrow, suspended ledge L of a niche. Follow the ledge L, climb some flakes in a corner, an overhang (V/V+: exposed) and a fine dièdre on the L (IV+). The next section is less steep and on good rock.

Climb up for 20m (snow) and tackle a zone of Lwards trending slabs (35m: III/IV). Climb slabs for 4 pitches of 35m (IV/IV+) to below some very compact rock. Slant L for 2 pitches (III and IV: a move of V) to some less steep slabs beneath a vertical pedestal. Climb to the base of this and traverse c20m R (delicate). Climb a damp dièdre to reach the bottom of a wet streak and a half-moon shaped crack formed by a flake. Traverse R to pass another flake and climb 5m to a ledge (III and IV). From there climb 30m, with a little loop Rwards (IV and V: exposed), to less steep slabs between névé on the R and a wet step on the L. A slab pitch enables the wet step to be turned. Follow a vague dièdre for 35m (IV/IV+).

Traverse L, climbing slightly, then go straight up to a large ledge (40m: IV+). Traverse L again for 30m to a wet couloir. Climb a steep, cracked, yellow wall on the R (V/V+) then a dièdre slanting R. Traverse L on slabs and ledges to reach a depression carrying blocks on the other bank of the couloir. Leave this by a descending traverse L (V) then climb easily to a flake. A crack on the R leads to the top of the bastion (IV). Follow snow and a rock boss to reach the triangular névé at the top of the large snow band. 6-7hr from the foot of the face

From here climb 40m by a chimney of blocks to a terrace below an overhang. Traverse L for 10m, turn a corner to reach and cross an inclined slab forming a ledge beneath a high overhang which ends abruptly. Reach an icy couloir on the L by a cracked, 10m slab. Climb this couloir for 30m to a terrace on the L bank. The couloir makes a R turn and widens somewhat before eventually narrowing again. Continue on the L bank to the point where it narrows. Gain its bed by a slanting crack and climb until it loses itself in the wall. Continue in the same line and by a series of little ledges and vertical walls cut by overhangs to a large terrace some 100m below the summit crest and dominated by a wall of slabs. At the R (E) corner of the terrace, climb an overhang followed by a slab. After 20m slant L towards some unstable looking blocks. Climb a chimney separating these blocks to reach a platform 50m below the ridge. From here climb two successive chimneys, traverse 15m R along a ledge and climb another chimney then return L, descending slightly (delicate) and, from a block, reach a good platform. A slab leads to an inclined platform at the foot of a 30m chimney which overhangs at the top. Climb this (Stofer chimney: IV and V). A short slab leads to the summit ridge between a secondary step and the 3rd tooth, which is on the R. 4-5hr: **11-13hr** in all

Follow the classic traverse (Route 13a) to the Aigle hut.

13d **L' EPINARD HALLUCINOGENE**
ED1
14

J Cambon and C Ferrera, 1984

Valley base: La Bérarde

The climb is equipped with bolts but a normal rack should be taken. It ends at the snow band, but it is normal practice to descend from the junction with the R-hand climb (Route 13c) by the in situ rappels. Difficulties of 6b (6a obl) and A1. Approach as for Route 13b.

Start below the first big overhangs at their R-hand end. These first pitches lead Lwards passing the first line of roofs then climbs over the second barrier and reaches the slabs which crown it. The route then follows a more or less direct line up to the top of the bastion where the top pitch of Bastion Centrale (Route 13c) is shared. This in turn gives access to the triangular névé and the summit ridge. **5-7hr** climbing

P1 2: P2 4+: P3 A1/6b: P4 6a: P5 6a: P6 3: P7 5: P8 5+: P9 6a: P10 5+: P11 5: P12 6b: P13 6b: P14 5+: P15 5: P16 5+

13e **GRAND PIC - SOUTH FACE DIRECT**
TD
15
13
14

Variant to the Glacier Carré: P Allain, J Leininger and J Vernet, 12 Sept 1934

Direct route: P Allain and J Leininger, 21 Aug 1935

Valley base: La Bérarde

This is one of the great classics of all the Alps. It enjoys good rock, safe stances and superb positions. The face is 800m high and comes quickly into condition early in the season and after poor weather, although the chimney leading to the 'Vire du Glacier Carré' can remain icy. It is possible to escape L along these ledges to the R-hand corner of the Carré glacier, as in the first ascent.

From the Promontoire hut gain the foot of the face, either by descending below the hut via the approach route and then contouring the base of the Promontoire ridge, which is safe, or by the Couloir du Crapaud (2 rappels of 40m: loose rock). There is a third option which involves following ledges leading across and downwards from behind the toilets towards the Couloir de Crapaud, which it meets some 20m above the snow. A single rappel is then sufficient. These options merit and repay a reconnaissance. 1hr

Start some way L of the lowest point of the wall. There are three chimneys, running with water, which come down from the Fauteuil des Allemands, a large bay above the initial wall formed of terraces which are frequently snow covered. Cross the rimaye below the middle one and climb steep but easy rocks L of the chimney for some m (III) and then cross the cascade to a slanting ledge which is followed Rwards. After 20m leave this ledge and climb a vertical chimney for 10m to a terrace. Move L to reach and climb a ledge leading up R. A little higher reach the lower part of the Fauteuil des Allemands. Slant up across the terraces which form the bay. Make for the rib on the R bank of the Zsigmondy couloir. 2hr

Climb a flared couloir. Above is a triangular cave with a slight hollow on its R. Pass between the two (III). Climb a little arête on the R which is above the hollow. A slab and glacis then lead to a terrace. Climb for two rope lengths obliquely R, first by a rib then by a dièdre running up the rib to reach a break below a wall. Climb the wall (V-) then return Lwards to climb a 25m crack and easy ground to a smooth inclined ledge. Climb the wall above the ledge on its L (IV+) and then cross a block covered terrace. Traverse slabs Lwards to reach a high chimney, the furthest L of two parallel chimneys easily seen from the valley and which end at the level of the Carré glacier. Climb this chimney (40m: IV+: sometimes icy at the top) to a jammed block 15m beneath a big green overhang which closes the chimney. Leave the chimney by moving L and traverse L across a 5m slab (V). Climb a steep, smooth pillar (IV+) and after 20m return R on a terrace, furnished with blocks, above the chimney. The smooth pillar can be avoided on its L (easier). Traverse R a little (IV-), then go back L easily and, by stepped terraces, reach the *Vire du Glacier Carré*. From the jammed block it is possible to climb directly in the chimney, often chocked with ice, with a hard exit on a wet overhang to arrive at the blocks. Not as good and harder! 3-4hr

From this point it is easy to escape in case of bad weather by following the ledge L to the Carré glacier to join the ordinary route (Route 13a).

From the end of the last pitch climb some m R on terraces. Next climb a small corner in a depression (delicate and overhanging: IV+) to reach the L end of a ledge called the *Vire à Bicyclette*, seen from the preceding terrace. Start moving up L, then straight up for 10m and then slanting Rwards across slabs (V) to a platform. It is possible to climb to this point directly from the *Vire à Bicyclette*. Climb an arête L of an overhanging wall (V) and follow it for 20-25m more easily (IV). Follow a ledge ascending R then climb another 40m in the direction of large overhangs (III: old pitons under the overhangs). From the belay, formed by a niche of loose rock, climb a little, then traverse horizontally R by a *râteau de chèvre* (IV+). This pitch is very exposed and the rock is a little loose but has good protection. It leads to the edge of the Zsigmondy couloir. Climb 30m up easy rocks, which are sometimes snowy, and then up a couloir, or the pillar on its L (III), to the brèche of the S arête 40m higher. From the niche of loose rock, most people go R as described; however, the original route goes directly up for some m then traverses L on exposed slabs to join a sort of steep ramp, then by slabs which end in a line of overhangs. By returning a

Barre des Ecrins summit ridge (Route 37a) Wil Hurford

little R reach a high vertical corner which is climbed with 3 pitons for protection, three times that number may be found in place! In this way emerge on easy rock and by a few pitches moving Lwards, reach the brèche mentioned earlier. This variation uses the best of the possibilities and makes a splendid climax for those able to finish the route in this fashion (V- and V+).

From the brèche climb the arête to the summit by several exposed pitches, often on unsound rock (III to IV+ with one pitch with a crack of V). 3-4hr: **11-12hr** from the Promontoire hut

From here either continue the traverse or reverse the ordinary route (13a). The latter is long and tedious. The former is better if the state of the party and the weather permits.

South-West Face

This superb, steep rock face, which forms the W flank of the Promontoire ridge and is bordered by the W ridge descending from the Grand Doigt, has four distinctive, vertical cracks in its upper part. The rock is excellent. The approach, although short, is via glaciated terrain so an axe and crampons should be taken.

13f
TD+
15
VOIE DES MARSEILLAIS
V Bourges, J Coqueuniot, J Kelle, F Labande and P Vidailhet, 27 June 1966
Valley base: La Bérarde

In its upper part, this route follows, more or less, the third crack, counting from the R of the face. It is exposed, sustained and on good rock. It is possible to reach the ordinary route (Route 13a) by traversing R towards the lower corner of the Carré glacier. The original start has become Pitch 2 (!) and the new start is harder than anything previously encountered. c450m of climbing

From the Promontoire hut climb the W branch of the Etançons glacier towards the Brèche de la Meije moving R to reach the

Just above the Brèche de Sialouze on the Aiguille de Sialouze Traverse (Route 43a) *Wil Hurford* foot of the face (½hr). Pick out a vertical, black crack which extends towards the base of the gully descending from the Pyramide Duhamel (on the Promontoire ridge). Start 20m R of the base of the black crack, by a little pillar. This pillar is R of a line of overhangs which bar direct access to the face.

Climb the steep wall (6a: exposed) to reach and climb a steep little pillar (15m, IV/IV+). Go up Rwards for 10m and the traverse R for 4m (V/V+) to gain a smooth dièdre which is climbed (V+) to a terrace on the L (IV). Make a horizontal traverse L for 20m (III) and continue to traverse for some distance, ascending slightly and crossing the black crack (a move of IV). Arrive at a zone of terraces. Climb them directly (20m), follow a little wall of 5m (IV+) and then climb some slabs trending L. Go up easily for 30m, then always straight up by slabs (IV-). Next climb obliquely R towards the bed of the couloir descending from the Pyramide Duhamel. Make a gently rising traverse L for 60m to reach the foot of a big crack. A few r beyond this crack reach the base of a little pillar to its L. 3hr

Climb a big dièdre to a terrace (40m: V and V+: sustained) Go L by a little overhanging dièdre (V: strenuous). Climb up R by slabs for 15m (IV-) to reach a little platform. From there traverse 3m L and move back to above the stance (IV+), then climb an overhang and exit on the L (V). Next reach the foot of a black chimney-crack which is climbed (lichen: V). This leads into an easy couloir which is climbed for 30m. When the couloir becomes steep and nasty, traverse R (V) and continue in this lin rising gently, for 15m (IV-). Continue straight on (III) to meet the W ridge of la Meije some 30m from the brèche of the summ edifice of the Grand Doigt. By moving R the ordinary route is joined. 5hr

From the ledges extending from the bottom of the Glacier Carré, climb a 25m chimney (a move of IV). An easy ledge rises W then another ledge goes the opposite way climbing a detache flake (III) permitting a gain of 20m in height. Follow an overhanging dièdre (V+/A1: exposed), an ill-defined chimney and a little overhang (IV). By two easy rope-lengths reach a first summit. Descend a dozen m to a little brèche and reach the second summit, very forbidding in aspect, by a little facet on the SW (15m: III) from where the Brèche du Grand Doigt is reached without difficulty and joins with the ordinary route. 3½hr: **11½hr** from the hut

13g L'HORREUR DU BIDE

ED1

15

J Cambon, G Fiaschi and S Ravel, Aug 1987
Valley base: La Bérarde

Fully equipped with bolts, this climb is now quite popular. Escape is possible in several places which tends to make the climb less serious. Difficulties up to 6c (6a obl).

Start 10m R of a black crack and 10m L of the start of the previous route. The climb traverses L after one pitch in order to pass below some small roofs, after which it climbs up to and crosses the line of the Marseillais route. After a direct line, where it comes close to the Marseillais route again close to the Duhamel couloir, where an escape is easy, it climbs towards the 1st crack (counting from the R) and to the rib to its R which borders the whole face. It follows the rib to the *pas du chat* of the ordinary route. Above it is possible to join the route described above to the Grand Doigt.

P1 6a: P2 5+: P3 6a: P4 5: P5 4, cross previous climb: P6 6a: P7: 2, close to previous route: P8 6a: P9 6a: P10 6a: P11 5+, traverse towards the rib: P12 6b: P13 6c: P14 4: P15 5+: P16 3, the *pas du chat*: P17 6a: P18 A1/5+, on the route described above to the Petit Doigt: P19 III. **7-8hr**

Descend the ordinary route or rappels to the *pas du chat* and either, follow that route or, make a series of rappels from the couloir behind the Pyramide Duhamel which may be inspected in ascent. Choice will be dictated by the traffic on either flank.

13h **WEST RIDGE**
AD
10 C Verne with M Gaspard, P Gaspard snr and jnr and B Rodier,
20 July 1885
Valley base: La Bérarde

A classic route, which despite its quality is not often followed. Good rock except for the first step.

From the Brèche de la Meije reach the foot of the first step. A ledge on the R flank is followed briefly then climb up on the flank and again move R below the step to reach a couloir descending from the brèche between this and the little step above. Climb the couloir to the arête or climb rock on its L bank. Reach the top of the second step and follow the ridge to a terrace below the big, third step. Climb a slab, which dominates the terrace, to its L edge (forming an arête:15m) then continue on the N flank of this to a terrace (lll+).

Follow the crest, or slightly on the N flank to the top of the big step. The ridge becomes level. Follow it, cross (8m rappel) a first brèche then a second at the foot of the Grand Doigt. From there traverse 15m on the R flank of the ridge which leads to the *pas du chat* of the ordinary route (Route 13a) a little higher.
4-6hr from the brèche

Note: Given good snow cover the first step may be avoided by taking to the snow on its N flank. The variant has been known and used since the first ascent but only personal judgment on the day can be relied upon.

Pic du Glacier Carré 3,862m

13i **NORTH-WEST FACE**
TD
10 P Girod and R Sandoz, 31 July 1956
Valley base: La Bérarde/La Grave

There are two parallel pillars leading to the Pic and Brèche du Glacier Carré respectively. They are separated by a steep couloir, rarely in condition, first climbed by Christophe Moulin in spring 1994 and which is as yet unrepeated.

The Girod/Sandoz climbs are typical of their creators.
Exceptional ambience and interesting mixed-style climbing with very
few pegs and no other ironwork. This climb and its partner, offer the
connoisseur classic alpinism at its best. Difficulties of V and A1: 650m

Reach the foot of the face either from the Promontoire hut, a
bivouac on top of the Enfetchore (L) or (exceptionally) the Aigle
hut. This last is often mentioned but the author suggests that the
passage of the Serret du Savon is unreliable and much time and
effort may be wasted. The start is common with the next climb
and is directly below the summit of the Pic du Glacier Carré.

Cross the rimaye and, by a brown wall, reach a large ledge.
Climb towards 3 rock points to a brèche (III/III+) then, by a
rounded spur, reach a little shoulder. Above, follow a ledge on
the L at first horizontally then it climbs. Climb a chimney on the
R of a crack and exit L and gain a brèche (IV). Climb the névé
above and the wall which dominates it, moving R (IV). An icy
couloir leads to a snowy brèche on the R-hand arête. From the
brèche, traverse L (IV: exposed) then straight up to a platform
(35m: IV and V: exposed at the top).

At the L end of the platform climb directly to the foot of a
yellow, triangular wall (platform). Climb it on the R (short
section of A1 and V) to reach a good belay on the L. Climb
straight up (short section of A1) to the edge of a fault which
leads to a brèche and continue to another, well-marked gap.
Follow snowy and verglassed rock to reach a short, grey dièdre.
Climb this (IV+) to a cirque, usually ice coated and dominated
by a black wall crowned with two rounded 'heads'. Climb
Rwards on snowy rock to a shoulder and then directly towards
the brèche between the two 'heads' to a vertical, light coloured
step. Turn the step by a large chimney on the R and reach a
shoulder above. Climb a new chimney on the L (IV) which splits
off L and leads to a terrace below a band of snow encircling the
wall like a scarf. Climb straight up to a shoulder below the final
step of the W ridge of the Pic. 3 rope lengths lead to the summit.
7-8hr climbing

Brèche du Glacier Carré 3,790m

13j
TD-
10

NORTH-WEST PILLAR

P Girod and R Sandoz, 1 Aug 1956
Valley base: La Bérarde/La Grave

This is a good, airy climb of character taking the pillar immediately W of the Z couloir. The rock is mostly excellent. The route is not equipped. Difficulties of V+: 600m

Follow the previous route up to the large ledge above the rimaye (III/III+). Climb up Lwards, to reach a wide, high chimney by a strip of snow/ice and climb the chimney (IV+) just to where it narrows and overhangs. Traverse R (IV+) to reach a ledge which is followed. Climb straight up then return L by an obvious ledge above the chimney. Follow this ledge L, cross an ice couloir (the C Moulin climb - Pinuche) and take the ledge which comes out in a couloir of vertical slabs. Reach the slabs by a detached flake and climb them for 20m (IV) to beneath a dièdre (good stance). Cross a slab R (V), then climb up R and take a chimney. Continue to the foot of a big wall and follow its base Rwards. Pass on to the W flank, climb a deep chimney (verglassed overhang) and reach a terrace on the R (cairn). Climb Rwards to a second chimney which is narrow and barred by two overhangs. Climb the first and avoid the second by a Rwards traverse below a roof (V+) to reach a platform above a deep couloir (IV) and another ledge 3m higher (IV+). Return to the chimney on the L and climb it to a small brèche. From there, climb R by a detached flake to reach and climb a rounded pillar for 30m (IV/IV+: compact). Climb over several teeth to the base of a high grey wall by a brèche marked by a snow cone. By a huge stride (more or less difficult according to the amount of snow present!) gain access to the wall. Climb the wall, slanting Rwards to a belay platform on the R edge (30m: IV/V). Go straight up for a short way, make a loop L to reach a flat area and then the top of the pillar (III/IV) crowned with snow. Above, a fine spur of very good rock then black, verglassed rock leads to the Brèche du Glacier Carré. **c7hr** climbing

North Face

The N face of the Meije is well seen from la Grave. It is steepest and highest below the Grand Pic and the Dent Zsigmondy. Further E the Tabuchet glacier rises almost to the crest of the ridge. The face is mainly rock with some icy couloirs, the most obvious of which is the Z-shaped one.

13k **Z COULOIR**

D   M Fourastier and C Rodier (guide), 13 Aug 1933

10   Valley base: La Bérarde/La Grave

The route is named after the likeness of the arrangement of its main couloirs to that of the three limbs of the letter Z written backwards. A magnificent, classic, mixed route.

Approach the Meije glacier by the Enfetchores (Route 12a) or by crossing the Brèche de la Meije from the Promontoire hut. At c3200m, above the Enfetchores, traverse the glacier in order to reach the foot of the face.

The L (E) end of the lowest limb of the Z can be plainly seen halfway up the face, under the Grand Pic, and is the point to make for. Follow the Direct Route (13l) to this point. This bottom limb is a ledge of ice rising at first gently R and sloping outwards at an angle of about 50°; an angle which increases towards the W. The ledge is about 200m long. Follow it, keeping close to the rock above it. A small rocky tongue marks the foot of the couloir which forms the middle limb of the Z. Climb this couloir for a rope-length until the ridge which forms its R bank can be reached. The ridge is easy, on fairly good rock, and leads to the upper and last limb of the Z. Here a thin layer of ice, set with fallen stones, and sloping outwards very steeply, leads almost horizontally R (W). Follow it to its W end and reach the Brèche du Glacier Carré by climbing a couloir and a snow slope. **9-11hr** from the Promontoire hut

131 DIRECT ROUTE

ED2

10

Aspirant guides R Ginel and R Renaud, 1-2 Sept 1962
FWA: C Exiga and J-C Marmier, 6-12 Feb 1973
Valley base: La Bérarde/La Grave

*One of the more difficult, classic N faces of l'Oisans. An elegant and
varied route with a particular atmosphere of its own with both rock
and ice difficulties. Excellent rock, very good belays.*

Approach via the Meije glacier above the Enfetchores (Route
12a) or reach the glacier by crossing the Brèche de la Meije from
the Promontoire hut. At c3,200m traverse it to the foot of the
face. Cross the rimaye, overhanging and difficult, at the highest
point. Climb up mixed ground, which is easier than it might
appear, as far as the start of the lower limb of the Z couloir
which is halfway up the face.

The route continues up the triangular, red wall which
dominates the lower limb of the Z couloir. Start by traversing L
into an icy couloir, the outlet of a massive, Y-shaped depression.
Go up the R bank of this couloir by rocky islands surrounded by
ice (IV/V: good stances) to just below greenish overhangs. L of a
large chimney-crack that overhangs, climb a well defined,
smooth chimney (V+/VI, 6a) bordered on the L by an almost
vertical, yellow slab. Exit R on to open slabs and climb up to a
short, yellow wall (V). Climb this via a crack (V) and continue
up mixed ground to the bifurcation in the massive depression.
Continue up the R branch via an icy couloir and a wide
chimney-crack (IV/V) to reach a brèche by a rock pinnacle
known as the *Vigie Centrale*. 6-8hr

Move up to and round an arête on the R. A little R of the
crest climb straight up to a chimney and follow this (IV) to reach
the top of the *Petite Vigie*. Under the N ridge of the Grand Doigt
climb an ill-defined dièdre on the R, which has a good crack in
its base (V), and exit R on to ice-bound rocky islands. Get into a
large chimney on the L which has a large jammed block visible
from the *Petite Vigie*. Climb it (V-) and join a terrace on the N
ridge. Follow the L flank of this arête, or follow the crest via little

overhangs (V), then, higher, traverse the arête Rwards below an overhang (poor rock). Rejoin the ridge by a dièdre (IV) or reach, on the R, icebound rock outcrops, which are climbed (compact rock: exposed) slanting L towards the N ridge. Follow the crest to the summit. 4-6hr: **12-15hr** from the Promontoire hut

There is some confusion between all the various sources of information about the route above the *Petite Vigie*. What is clear is that the prevailing conditions on the mountain govern, to a great extent, the line taken.

13m
D
10

GRAVELOTTE COULOIR

E Gravelotte, M Casimir, D Gaspard and J Turc, 24 Sept 1898
FWA: J Domer and M Janin, 3-4 Jan 1975
Valley base: La Bérarde/La Grave

The Gravelotte Couloir descends N from the Brèche Zsigmondy to the Meije glacier where it tends towards the NE. An elegant route, often rendered impossible by the rimaye.

Approach as for Routes 13j, k, and l to the foot of the N face. Cross the rimaye (difficult) and climb the L bank of the couloir until it becomes narrow. Climb the couloir to gain the brèche E of the Dent Zsigmondy, to join the traverse (Route 13a). **6-10hr** from the Promontoire hut

13n
D
10

COULOIR DES CORRIDORS

M and Mme Deschamp, M Liotier and J Véron, 26 Aug 1961
FWA: M Baumgarten and B Muller, 18-19 Jan 1976
Valley base: La Bérarde/La Grave

The Couloir des Corridors originates at the highest point of the Tabuchet glacier, at the rimaye, directly below the N face of the Doigt de Dieu (central summit), and descends to the Meije glacier. A magnificent ice route in a beautiful setting, with an average angle of 50°.

Reach the foot of the couloir as for the previous route and cross the rimaye below it (difficult). Climb the centre of the couloir, the angle of which soon reaches 50°-55°. The first and second tiers of the couloir are ascended by climbing two rognons on brittle, verglas covered rock (delicate). At the top of the couloir traverse L to gain the rimaye at the base of the Doigt de Dieu. Climb direct to the arête which is followed either on the crest, or along its R (N) flank, to gain the summit of the Doigt de Dieu. **7hr** from the foot of the climb

Descent is by the traverse of the arêtes (Route 13a).

13o MEIJE ORIENTALE - PAVE - PIC GASPARD TRAVERSE

D

16

17

18

Valley base: La Grave

This is a superb high level traverse of three great summits, spoiled somewhat by the poor quality of the rock. The purist may wish to complete a traverse (from the Promontoire hut) of the Grand Pic de la Meije to the Aigle Hut (Route 13a). The Meije Orientale may be reached from the Aigle hut by its NE ridge, (PD-: not described). However, a steeper and recommended approach may be made by its N face. J Biju-Duval, G Sourice, J-M Traynard, 6 July 1971. This is the most difficult part of the traverse. The complete traverse of the three summits is not frequently accomplished. It is much more common for it to be ended at the Pavé followed by a descent to the Pavé hut. The Pavé-Gaspard alone can be traversed by starting up Route 14a.

From the Aigle hut easily reach the foot of the face. Cross the rimaye L of the summit fall-line and R of a conspicuous rock rognon and then climb a snow slope followed by a couloir. Finally an open snow slope leads direct to the summit, 45°-50°. 2½hr

From the summit, follow the snow arête of the SE ridge to where it turns to rock. Do not continue along the rocky section but instead go down the L flank, then traverse ledges to a well-defined, little brèche on the ridge. Pass on to the S flank, go down a steep little wall and then an enclosed couloir. Traverse back to regain the ridge which is followed to the Brèche Casimir Gaspard. Continue SE along the crest towards the Pavé, moving just on to the N flank towards the top. 2½hr: PD

From the Pavé, descend the W ridge to the base of a large gendarme-tower, known as l'Ourson, which is climbed by the crest of the ridge. Two rappels on the NE face and a traverse lead quickly to the Brèche Ourson-Gaspard. Follow a rocky crest, prolonged by a ledge on the S flank and leave it before its extremity to rejoin the steep rocks of the W ridge of Pic Gaspard. Follow the ridge to the foot of the last step. Turn a gendarme on its S flank by a chimney followed by a slab. Climb a vertical, 12m chimney close to an overhanging monolith. Turn a corner to reach the little brèche on the crest beyond the monolith, follow a ledge on the S flank and then the crest of the ridge to the summit. 4-5hr: AD: **8-10hr** in all

Descend by Route 15b to the Pavé or the Alpe hut. This can be icy in late season - rappel pitons in the couloir give the line of descent.

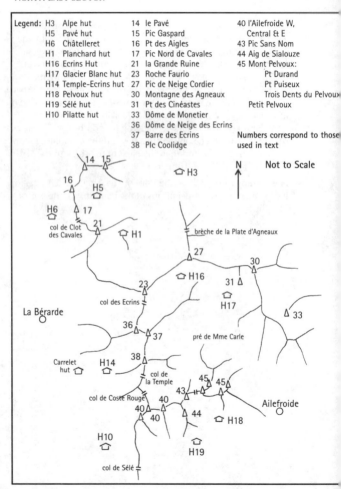

Legend:
- H3 Alpe hut
- H5 Pavé hut
- H6 Châtelleret
- H1 Planchard hut
- H16 Ecrins Hut
- H17 Glacier Blanc hut
- H14 Temple-Ecrins hut
- H18 Pelvoux hut
- H19 Sélé hut
- H10 Pilatte hut

- 14 le Pavé
- 15 Pic Gaspard
- 16 Pt des Aigles
- 17 Pic Nord de Cavales
- 21 la Grande Ruine
- 23 Roche Faurio
- 27 Pic de Neige Cordier
- 30 Montagne des Agneaux
- 31 Pt des Cinéastes
- 33 Dôme de Monetier
- 36 Dôme de Neige des Ecrins
- 37 Barre des Ecrins
- 38 Pic Coolidge

- 40 l'Ailefroide W, Central & E
- 43 Pic Sans Nom
- 44 Aig de Sialouze
- 45 Mont Pelvoux:
  - Pt Durand
  - Pt Puiseux
  - Trois Dents du Pelvoux
  - Petit Pelvoux

Numbers correspond to those used in text

N

Not to Scale

North-East Sector

This sector covers quite a large geographical area extending from the Etançons and upper Vénéon valleys in the W to the Guisane valley in the E. There are a number of access points to the mountains; from the N via Villar d'Arêne; from the E via Ailefroide, which gives access to both the Celse Nière valley and Pré de Madame Carle (Cezanne refuge); from the W via la Bérarde and the Etançons and Vénéon valleys.

The major peak in this group of mountains is undoubtedly the Barre des Ecrins, the sole 4,000m peak in the whole of the region, but not far behind in terms of the climbing potential are the Ailefroide and Pelvoux, both larger than the Ecrins if not so high. See Map 3436 ET

Le Pavé 3,823m

W Coolidge with C Almer snr and jnr, 19 July 1879

This is a significant geographical point at the head of three valleys. It lies due E of the Promontoire hut and N of the Pavé hut. From its slopes tumble the E Etançons, the Lautaret and the upper Cavales glaciers. On its E ridge, which links it with Pic Gaspard, is a prominent gendarme, l'Ourson, which forms a steep pillar on the S face of the mountain, separated from the rest of the S face by a deep couloir.

14a
PD
17
13
18

WEST FACE

First ascent party

The summit offers a fine view of the Pic Gaspard and la Meije. The route itself is pleasant enough, although much of the rock is loose. It serves as a route of descent, or for the start of the Pavé-Gaspard traverse (see Route 13m). The climb is generally difficult at the end of the season when the route from the Promontoire hut can be impassable. The couloirs can also be full of ice.

There are two approach routes.

(a) Early in the season from the Promontoire hut, descend to the Etançons glacier as for Route 13e. Cross it Ewards towards the Col du Pavé. Pass L of an ice-wall overhanging a rocky islet and slant R to avoid séracs where the glacier narrows. Turn the upper séracs on the L, slant up to the W face of le Pavé, short of the Col du Pavé. 2½hr

(b) From the Pavé hut go up scree slopes E of the lake (trace of path) to big boulders and then up to the top of the moraine. Descend a few m on to the glacier and then up it to below the S face of the Pavé. Cross the Col du Pavé by climbing a short snow/ice slope and slant up under the W face, below the rimaye, to the point where it turns downwards. 2hr

Cross the rimaye below two couloirs, the R-hand one is narrow the other wide. Climb either until level with a little gendarme on the ridge between them. Continue up the L bank of the R-hand couloir on a steep rocky slope to finish on the SW ridge above its big overhang. Go along the ridge to the top. 2hr: **4-4½hr**

In descent follow the SW ridge to a gap and descend into a rocky bay by two rappels (slings in place). From here the R-hand couloir is preferred. There are many pitons in place for rappel points.

14b   **SOUTH FACE**
TD   M Chevalier and G Rébuffat, 25 June 1944
18   By the route described (second ascent): by S Coupé and
B Salomon, 26 July 1950

The S face of the Pavé is a fine cliff some 400m high, steep and clean and its ascent provides a rock climb of considerable interest. The rock suspect in places, but the technical difficulty is not of a high order and the face is likely to be climbable when most other climbs are out of condition. With the possible exception of the first pitch, only 2 or 3 pitons are needed. There are several pitches of grade IV and four pitches of V.

From the Pavé hut go up scree slopes E of the lake (trace of path) to big boulders and then up to the top of the moraine to reach the upper Cavales glacier. Cross the glacier to the foot of the S face of the Pavé, making for the R-hand side of the face where a kind of spur is cut off from the rest of the face, on one side by a black, overhanging chimney and on the other by the couloir dropping from the Pavé-Ourson brèche. 1½hr

The lower part of the spur has a wide ramp rising from L to R. This ramp has to be reached from its L-hand extremity which, early in the season, can sometimes be done by simply stepping straight off the glacier. However the glacier level may be too low, leaving a smooth black wall which must be climbed (V: or use aid) to reach the start of the ramp. Climb straight up the ramp (III) on the R to the Pavé-Ourson couloir. Climb up the rocks on its R bank for two pitches (III/IV) to a flake. From the flake climb a steep, vertical chimney which is on the L above. Next climb a short overhanging section of poor rock before following a long but easier line Lwards on to the crest of the spur. Continue by rather loose gullies with no difficulty to the top of the spur.

The line to be followed now slants L across the face, making for the upper reaches of the big couloir which drops from just near the summit. 45m above and 25m L can be seen a L slanting dièdre. Make for this; two pitches up and then L (bits of IV) to the foot of the dièdre. Climb it. After a steep start (V-) it eases, then continue past a little spur and up the obvious easy dièdre which follows to a stance where it steepens. Move 5m L to another dièdre. Climb it for 30m and traverse out L along a ledge which has a hiatus half-way (V); the rock here is better than it looks. Climb the overhang above by a short dièdre (V) and then step R and up a chimney (IV at first) which leads to the big couloir mentioned above. Climb up on the R of this (a pitch or so of IV) to the top. 2-3hr: **5½-8hr** from the hut

The original route followed a line further L starting with a 12m traverse from the flake on the R bank of the Pavé-Ourson couloir. See the photo.

Descent is by Route 14a in reverse.

Pic Gaspard 3,883m

One of the higher mountains in the region but relatively
unfrequented. This is partly because of the difficulty of access on
the N and W sides and the fact that the easiest route is mostly on
poor rock and generally only used as a means of descent.

15a SOUTH-SOUTH-EAST RIDGE

TD   L Devies and G Gervasutti, 30-31 Aug 1935

*This is a splendid, long and exposed ridge climb, c900m high and
worthy of its creator. It has a lot of pitches of IV, one or two of V and
the difficulties of the Grey Tower, which vary with the route taken, the
original line retaining the VI grade. The route has been climbed in
3½hr by Coupé and Cornaz, climbing unroped.*

Start, either from a bivouac at the point some way up the L bank
of the Cavales stream where the combe which contains the Claire
glacier opens on the R (1½hr from the Alpe hut). The combe is
closed at its lower end by a rock wall over which tumble several
waterfalls. Leave the path a little R (E) of the R-hand most
stream, some 40m below a large shallow cave. Climb up on the L
(W) of this cave and continue up for another 70m (cables). Now
cross the stream and go up mixed ground into the combe. Climb
it to just below the Claire glacier. Traverse L to the foot of the
SSE ridge (2hr). Or, from the Pavé hut, cross the scree by a poor
track to a couloir which leads to the combe. 1-1½hr

   The ridge begins with a high, yellow step. Start up it,
rather R of the edge of the ridge, climbing up towards a dark
patch. The patch itself gives attractive climbing for 50m up steep
rock (IV+). Continue straight up to reach the crest of the ridge
half-way up the step. Continue on the exposed crest of the ridge
to the top of the step. The ridge now rises gently for a considerable distance and is garnished with many gendarmes. The last
three of these are the biggest, the first of them being climbed by
an elegant crack. Climb the next two to the foot of another high,
yellow step.

Traverse R along ledges on the E side to a big, damp, smooth chimney. Climb it and continue direct to the crest of the ridge above the step (IV). Follow the crest of the ridge to the foot of the Grey Tower, which overhangs. There seem to be three ways of tackling this:

Direct: Climb straight up the crest for 25m, over a threatening overhang (V+: 2 pitons) to a small ledge on the R (piton). Traverse 5m R (III) into a cavity with a crack at the back. Climb it for 10m and exit L (V). Continue up to the top of the tower.

Original route: Climb up for 5m and then traverse horizontally L across the W face above overhangs for 12m (VI, 6a: piton). Continue the traverse for another 5m, then climb directly upwards by a 45m chimney (IV+: 2 pitons) to the ridge.

S Coupé route: This avoids the pitch of VI by the ledges below it. No other details. It was climbed solo.

Above the tower, continue along the crest of the ridge, easy at first, then more difficult, to a little brèche before another grey step. Climb straight up this (IV) and then along the jagged ridge for a good way to the top. **10-12hr** of climbing

15b
PD
EAST FACE DESCENT
H Duhamel with P Gaspard snr and jnr and C Roderon, 6 July 1878

The rock is bad.

Seaming the E face, dropping from the SSE ridges are three couloirs. One, a snow couloir, drops from near the summit, the second only starts half-way down and the third, mixed snow and rock, starts from further R (S). Take this third couloir (the first is also possible) and descend to the rocky island on the R-hand side of the Claire glacier. Descend this (or the glacier on the L) until a ledge leads off R on to scree or snow slopes. Continue down to the combe below the glacier where the route of ascent to the SSE ridge is joined. Follow this, keeping L at the exit of the combe, to the Col du Clot des Cavales path and so the Alpe valley. **4-5hr**

It is also possible to return to the Pavé hut by contouring around the base of the ridge which separates the combe from the upper Cavales glacier. There are many grassy terraces with no defined track. However, the ground is fairly easy and there is value in staying as high as possible to avoid steeper ground at a lower level which ends in vertical cliffs.

Pointe des Aigles 3,336m

The Pointe des Aigles is a relatively unimportant point on the ridge enclosing the upper part of the Etançons valley on the E side.

16a   **WEST RIDGE**
D   P Boniface, A Colomb and F Germain, 14 Aug 1937

The ridge provides a good, medium length rock climb from the Promontoire or Chatelleret huts. The rock is good.

From the Promontoire hut, descend on to the E branch of the Etançons glacier and traverse it Ewards to a patch of scree at the foot of the ridge. 1hr

From the Chatelleret hut walk up the Etançons valley and circle round L (N) of the rock barrier directly below the Col des Chamois, thus reaching the top of the snow slopes below the W ridge. Climb these to the foot of the ridge. 1½-2hr

Climb up 10m, then R across a smooth, sloping slab (piton). Continue up steep, reddish granite to a scree covered ledge. After a few more m on smooth rocks, traverse L to the crest of the ridge, which is composed of stretches of easy slab. Start up these on the R, then cross a slab Lwards for 10m. Climb a grey slab towards a yellow overhang. Turn this on the R and continue on the crest of the ridge to a large platform forming the top of the first step (1hr). At this point two alternative starts come in from the R, one starting about 30m up from the foot of the ridge, the other from the highest point to which the snow slopes reach on the R of the ridge. Neither seems easier or more attractive than the route described.

      Continue along the ridge, climbing a narrow chimney on the R, then turning a small step on the L, to the foot of the final tower (1hr). Start the tower by slanting L up a gangway of slabs to beneath a prominent red overhang (piton). Circle round L of the overhang across some grooves and back up to a stance above it (the wider the circle the easier it is: IV+: pitons). Now continue up and climb a triangular slab on small holds (piton) and the chimney above (III: piton). Take a ledge on the L side of the ridge and climb back up to its crest on steep and unpleasantly loose rocks. Slant L up a short couloir and along a 45° ledge of unstable rock to a good ledge. Climb the cracked, grey slab above this (IV-) to the summit ridge and then follow easy rocks L to the top. 2hr: **5hr** from the Promontoire hut: **6hr** from the Chatelleret hut

16b SOUTH-EAST RIDGE DESCENT
F

L Reynier, with M Gaspard and J Turc, 29 July 1902

Start down the SE ridge by an easy gully just on its L and continue down broken rocks and ledges to the snow patch in the middle of the SE face. Turn Rwards and go down easy rocks L of the SE ridge to the Col des Chamois. Descend to the W either by the couloir or the rocks of its R bank, slant R under the W ridge and cross the glacier to the Promontoire hut. If going on down to the Chatelleret hut or la Bérarde, make a wide circle R (N) past the source of the Etançons stream to meet the path on the moraines below the Promontoire hut.
1½-**2hr** to the Chatelleret hut

From the Col des Chamois a descent on the E side to the Alpe or Pavé huts can be made with equal ease.

Pic Nord des Cavales 3,362m

Another, relatively minor summit on the E side of the Etançons valley. It is separated from the Pic Sud des Cavales by the Col du Clot des Cavales (see below). Despite its minor status it has a variety of worthwhile routes of varying grades.

17a
PD
19

SOUTH RIDGE

Mlle E Capdepon, J Capdepon and R Gley, 3 Aug 1909

The ordinary route, short and easy with pitches of III and good rock.

Start from the Col du Clot des Cavales, which is reached by Route 18a. Walk across snow on the R (E) of the S ridge to a little shoulder situated at the foot of the first step of the ridge. This is recognised by the large area of inclined slabs adjacent to the glacier. Go somewhat R to the foot of the slabs and climb them (III) to a brèche in the ridge. Follow the ridge, turning a step along a ledge on the L (or a steep little wall on the R). Go up easy slopes just L of the crest of the ridge to the foot of a dièdre with a gendarme on its R. Climb the dièdre (III), or turn it on the L by a slab (III) and join it at half-height. It leads to a little platform at a brèche. Follow the crest of the ridge over a step (III), or turn it on the L and climb a 30m chimney. Easy rocks lead to the top. 1hr from the start: **6hr** from the Alpe hut and from la Bérarde: **2-3hr** from the Pavé hut

Descend by the same route.

17b
D+
20

WEST RIDGE

G, H and M Berthet with H Turc, 16 Aug 1933

Strictly speaking this is the WSW ridge. It is a fine climb which comes quickly into condition. There is no glacier work if the climb is started at the Chatelleret hut but crampons may be useful early in the season (for the névés). Good rock after the first section. 450m

From either the Chatelleret or the Pavé huts reach the foot of the ridge using the Col du Clot des Cavales tracks (2hr). Start on the S flank of the ridge a little L of the first steep section. By eas scrambling reach the foot of this steep rock, obvious by the scars resulting from the large rockfall which took place in the late 1960's. Climb the overhang on friable rock (IV+) and then a couloir for 10m to below another overhang. Turn it on the L and straddle around the arête (IV) to reach a good platform. Go up the ridge to where it steepens and follow a ledge climbing L wards (N) for 15m. Climb cracked and grooved slabs up and towards the R (IV and IV+) and then a bulge Rwards (A1: 5 or 6 pitons), to reach the ridge which levels out. Continue easily along it to the start of the second step in the upper section.

Traverse 20m R and then climb directly up grooves in slabs for 30m (IV-). Traverse 5m L and climb a short chimney (IV-) leading on to a spacious balcony at the foot of a 10m high, rounded slab. Trend R on the crest and then return L a little to a terrace (IV). Follow the ridge more and more easily to the summit. **4-5hr**

Descend by the S ridge.

East Face

The face is easily accessible from the Pavé hut and offers a number of rock climbs of c200m in length on excellent quality rock.

17c
TD
19

VOIE TORMOZ

J-C Bécu with L Tormoz, 17 Aug 1952

This is a short, beautiful, sustained climb.

Reach the foot of the face from the Col du Clot des Cavales. Start at the low point of the face directly below the summit by trending gently R up a series of black blocks (IV). Easily reach a large landing and from there climb directly to a ledge which trends L. Climb this ledge for 20m to a widening forming a terrace. From there climb a small wall directly and gain a slab ascending R (IV) which is followed to a big flake, detached from the wall. Climb it and follow it R (IV). Climb a 10m vertical wall

(IV+: overhanging at start) to attain a little terrace at the foot of steep, unclimbable slabs. Follow a flake L for 15m (V: very exposed) to a bulge. Turn the bulge on the L and then climb R in the direction of a very steep dièdre. Struggle up the dièdre on its L side, which overhangs, and then climb direct to the summit (V). 3hr from the col: **4½hr** in all

17d   **VOIE DU GENEPI**

TD   A Guirardo, J-C Planchon, J-P and R Tomio, 19 Aug 1965

19

This route is on the L side of the face, it is steep and reaches to the summit via a big dièdre easily seen from the base of the climb. Possibly slightly under graded.

Gain the foot of the face from the Col du Clot des Cavales. Go to the base of the large inclined plane of slabs marking the start of the South Ridge (Route 17a) and continue for 30-40m R. Pick out a very smooth slab, bordered on its R by a chestnut coloured ramp, gently inclined from L to R. Climb the ramp and steep groove above it (V) to a comfortable cave. Leave the cave on the L and climb the L flank of a characteristic pillar made of flakes (60m: III). Climb c6m above the pillar (V) to a piton and then descend R to reach a little ramp (IV). Go up this (V: exposed) and belay on the top of a flake. Traverse R for 3m (V) then climb well to the R (V+: delicate) to reach a ramp-dièdre. Climb it for several m (IV) and leave it without going R, to reach a first and then second terrace at the foot of a vertical wall directly below the summit. Go L of the terrace and climb a steep wall (8m: V). Traverse L to reach a huge detached flake, climb it and find a stance above (V). Reach the foot of the final dièdre directly, or make a turning movement R to reach the same point (V: exposed). Climb the dièdre for 2 rope lengths (V then IV) to the summit. **4-5hr** climbing

Col du Clot des Cavales 3,159m

This col is the easiest crossing point of the long ridge between la Meije and the Grande Ruine which separates the valleys of the Romanche (la Grave) and the Vénéon (la Bérarde). It has been known and used for a long time and is easy, although it does involve some glacier crossing.

18a
F
20

EAST-WEST TRAVERSE

The route is well marked and is clearly shown on the map. It is described from la Grave to la Bérarde.

From le Pied du Col, E of la Grave in the upper Romanche valley, follow the path towards the Alpe hut. Cross the Romanche river by a bridge just S of the automatic meteo station and walk up the L bank of the river and then the L bank of the Clot des Cavales stream. This stream can be approached from the Alpe hut. Continue on to the large moraine on the L bank of the Clot des Cavales glacier and then zigzag up more moraine or snow slopes to the foot of a large rock island. Turn this on the L on to the glacier and cross it S to the col. 5-6hr

Start the descent from the col at a point a little R (N) of the true col, down a little rock couloir (wire cables). Follow the R bank of the snow couloir dropping from the col, which is steep towards the bottom, and go straight on down scree or snow slopes to the floor of the upper combe. Now turn rather to the L, towards the W ridge of the Bonnet des Cavales, to avoid cliffs straight ahead. Continue down by a gully. Slant down L across the W ridge of the Bonnet des Cavales, then zigzag down across the stream coming from the Grande Ruine glacier and on down some rocks. More zigzags lead down to the path in the valley where the Chatelleret path is joined, the hut being a short way along on the R. Follow the path down L to la Bérarde. 3hr from the col: **c10hr** from la Grave

Col du Diable 3,565m

The col lies between the Grande Ruine and the Roche Méane.
Notable only for the couloir on its N side.

19a
D/D+
21
20

NORTH COULOIR

A Migot and L Neltner, 25 June 1932
FWA: C Caillat, P Coda, P Monin amd B Muller,
29-30 Dec 1973

*This is a long ice climb (c450m) of uniform steepness which is best
tackled from the Pavé hut. It has had at least one ski descent.*

From the Pavé hut ascend the path towards the Col du Clot des
Cavales and, after crossing the first section of mixed ground,
traverse horizontally Lwards to the foot of the couloir. This
method of approach has little objective danger. 2hr

There are normally two large rimayes which are generally
passed on the R close to the rock. Under snowy conditions the
couloir can be climbed direct with very little risk from stonefall.
However, in drier conditions it is better to stay on the R side of
the couloir close to the rock and, at the narrows, traverse R to
reach the rocky rib. Climb this for 3 or 4 pitches (III and IV)
then regain the ice. Continue up to the col, again keeping close
to the side to obtain protection from stonefall. **4-6hr** for the
couloir

It is now possible to reach the summit of the Grande Ruine via
Route 21a, or descend to the Adèle Planchard hut.

Tour Carrée de Roche Méane 3,675m

Roche Méane is the name applied to the group of minor
summits on the ridge E of the Col du Diable and lying N of the
Adèle Planchard hut (Crête du Roche Méane). It is also the
name of the highest of these summits (3,712m). The second
highest point is the Tour Carrée.

20a
AD
22

SOUTH FACE

E Gravelotte with D, J and M Gaspard, 24 July 1897

This is a short climb from the Planchard hut with an approach from there of only 40min. There are many possible variations in the upper section and the rock is good.

From the Planchard hut gain the upper Agneaux glacier. Go up it, turning the rock spur on the L (W). Climb obliquely R to reach the foot of a vast rocky inclined plane below the Brèche Romantique which is the lowest point of the ridge between the Roche Méane and the Tour Carrée.

Cross the rimaye and then climb this inclined plane of slabs of more than 100m height, keeping as close as possible to the R edge. At the top get into a short, wide chimney crowned by an overhang which must be surmounted (III) to reach the R edge, constituting the upper edge of the plane. Follow this narrow ridge above a deep couloir. When it steepens and becomes lost in the face, traverse R to reach the bed of the couloir which is climbed to the Brèche Romantique (3,618m). From the brèche, traverse E on the S face, pass the foot of a chimney (Cheminée Choisy), then a very deep chimney-couloir (Cheminée Savoye) to reach a large, comfortable ledge which is followed. Above the ledge is a little couloir which ends in a crack (Couloir du Mauvais Pas). Go up by this couloir to the final ridge (a pitch of IV consisting of an open crack in a wide dièdre, followed by a slab). Reach the summit by the ridge. **3hr** in all

In descent, rappel the Mauvais Pas and possibly the inclined plane section.

La Grande Ruine 3,765m

This is the mountain lying W of the Col du Diable. On the N flank is the Col des Cavales glacier and on the E flank is the Grande Ruine glacier. It has two summits; Pic Maître 3,728m, the N most and the higher Pointe Brevoort. The two peaks are separated by the Brèche Giraud-Lezin.

Pointe Brevoort

21a EAST RIDGE

F

20

Miss Brevoort and W Coolidge with C Almer snr, P-M Almer jnr, P Bleuer and C Roth, 19 July 1873

This is the original route, a short snow plod ending with a few easy rocks and good views.

Start from the Adèle Planchard hut by heading WSW across the upper Agneaux glacier towards the foot of the SE ridge of Pointe Brevoort. Well short of this point, strike up the glacier as if going to the Col du Diable and curve up L to join the E ridge. Follow it up easy rocks to the summit. **2½hr**

Descend by the same route.

Pic Maître

21b WEST PILLAR AND WEST-NORTH-WEST RIDGE

TD

20

Guides M Brun and A Thevenon, 19-20 Sept 1964

The climb threads successively by the SW face, not far from the W Pillar, then the W Pillar and finally by the WNW ridge, which was first climbed in 1937 by M Fourastier with E Frendo. It is a good climb and the lower section is on very good rock. 600m

From the Chatelleret hut follow the path towards the Col du Clot des Cavales. At the point where the path crosses the rock coming down from the Bonnet des Cavales (zigzags), leave it and, by grass and stony slopes, move R wards below a rocky barrier. Follow the L bank of a well defined couloir with a little stream in it. By this line reach the R bank of the Grande Ruine glacier. From the top of the moraine go L (N), turn the last rock below the Pic Maître and reach the foot of the W Pillar. There is no track. 2½hr

Start by a couloir-dièdre between the W Pillar and a little pillar on the R. Climb up its middle for 2 rope-lengths then traverse towards the small, R-hand pillar by a little crack (IV).

Reach the top of the pillar (2hr: a big ledge offering a bivouac site). Move L on slabs and reach a detached flake (IV) and then make a horizontal move (V+) to reach the middle of a very steep couloir-dièdre. Climb it (V: sustained) to the overhangs which bar the SW face. Traverse horizontally L and then step up 1m of conglomerate rock to a niche (V/V+: sustained). Move L from the niche on a good ledge (III) to the foot of a dièdre easily seen from the foot of the face, then, always keeping L, descend towards the W Pillar by steep slabs (V). These slabs are cut by two cracks. Climb the first, leave it at mid-height for its companion on the L and continue until a very small ledge can be reached (IV/V). Follow this towards the pillar (V: good stance). From this point traverse R, climb the crest of the pillar avoiding an overhang on the L (V/VI, 6a). From here reach a snowy platform at the top of the second step in the WNW ridge. Climb another step by the crest of the ridge (IV) and continue to the summit. **12-14hr** from the foot of the face

Descend to the Planchard hut or return to the Etançons valley as follows: Go down the S ridge to the Brèche Giraud-Lézin. Descend the upper Agneaux glacier, passing below the Col du Diable. Slant down and R to a brèche at the foot of the SE ridge of Pointe Brevoort and N of Pt 3,389m. Go down slightly to the other side of the brèche and contour around the Casse Désert glacier until below the Col de la Casse Désert. Climb the rimaye and go up the L bank of the couloir by snow or scree to the col (1hr from the summit). This col can be reached from the Planchard hut in 1½hr. Go down the couloir, cross the rimaye on the R and gain the Grande Ruine glacier. Turn the SW ridge of the Pointe Brevoort and cross the Grande Ruine glacier to the path of ascent.

21c
D+
21

NORTH FACE - VOIE DIAGONALE

A and M Verney, 2 July 1978

The route is only feasible under good snow conditions, usually encountered between late spring and early July. The climb is steepest in its mid-section (60°). 500m from the rimaye.

Approach either from the Alpe or Pavé huts as for the Couloir de Diable. Start on the R of a rocky hogs back directly below the summit of the Pic Maître. The rimaye, followed by a narrowing between two rock barriers leads to the lower (suspended) snowfield which is climbed obliquely R (45°). Climb up then slant L via narrow couloirs (60°: exposed) to reach the foot of the second suspended snowfield. Slant R wards (45°) to a point 50m below a brèche in the WNW ridge at the foot of the fourth step in the ridge. Reach this brèche by a gully and follow the ridge to the summit.

Pic Bourcet 3,715m and Tour Choisy 3,671m

From the Grande Ruine the long ridge bordering the E side of the Etançons valley descends to the Col de la Casse Désert 3,483m before rising again steeply to the Tour Choisy then more gently to Pic Bourcet.

22a
D
22
20

TOUR CHOISY EAST FACE AND TRAVERSE TO PIC BOURCET

To the Tour Choisy: J Fournier and H Paillon, 30 Aug 1927
Traverse to the Pic Bourcet: A and J Boell, M Fleming and A Le Ray, 20 Aug 1933

The expedition has two parts; the E face of the Tour Choisy, which is a fine little rock in its own right and the airy traverse on to the Pic Bourcet, which extends it into a medium length expedition. The second part is AD.

Start from the Adèle Planchard hut heading WSW across the upper Agneaux glacier and then up some steep slopes to the brèche at the foot of the SE ridge of Pointe Brevoort, N of Pt 3,389m. Cross the brèche and the Casse Désert glacier to the foot of the Col de la Casse Désert (1hr). Slant L and up a sloping scree terrace and broken rocks to the foot of the E face of the Tour Choisy, immediately below the summit couloir.

Start straight up, then turn a steep wall on the R (III) and return L to the beginning of a ledge, which slants up from R to L to a square brèche on the ESE ridge. Climb up along this ledge, climbing *en route* a short overhanging chimney (IV) and a steep wall, to near the square brèche. Traverse R across the E face to the summit couloir and up this to the top. 2hr: 3hr from the hut

If not continuing to the Pic Bourcet, descend as follows: Go back down the summit couloir and then make a series of 30m rappels down the very steep slabs slightly L (N) to the rimaye under the Col de la Casse Désert (or hard L to the col itself). Pitons are used for these rappels.

From the top of the Tour Choisy, descend S to the brèche between the Tour Choisy and the Cornes du Bourcet by two rappels each of 25m; the first down a chimney opening towards the L, the second down vertical slabs directly above the brèche. From the brèche climb the Cornes du Bourcet and then follow the NE ridge of the Pic Bourcet to its summit. 3hr: **6hr** from the hut

22b
D
22

EAST FLANK DESCENT

J Boell and A and R Jamet, 1932

The descent route from Pic Bourcet.

Go back down the last step of the NE ridge and from its foot strike off R, slanting down and across the E flank along a series of ledges to a shoulder on the ESE ridge of the Tour Choisy. From here pass under the E face and retrace the route of ascent across the Casse Désert glacier and down the upper Agneaux glacier to the Adèle Planchard hut. **2-2½hr** from the summit

Roche Faurio 3,730m

T Cox, F Gardiner, R and W Pendlebury plus guides, 21 June 1873

An important summit topographically with fine views of the Ecrins. The long ridge running generally E from its summit, above the N bank of the Glacier Blanc, culminates in the

Montagne des Agneaux. Its appearance from the SE is of an attractive snowy mountain but from most other viewpoints it is much more austere. Its rocky N flank for example, lies above the uninviting slopes of the Tombe Murée glacier. Access to the mountain can be made from la Bérarde via Route 34a but it is more common to approach from Pré de Madame Carle.

23a   **SOUTH-EAST FLANK**
F
23
First ascent party

The ordinary route, mostly snow. Popular with skiers in spring.

From the Ecrins hut descend to the Glacier Blanc and climb it on its L bank to the foot of the snowy SE side of the Roche Faurio. Climb a snow slope which emerges on to a small plateau. Continue L wards (W) and, by a short slope, join the S ridge at mid-height (this arête links the Col des Ecrins and the summit). Follow the crest (cornices) and easy rock to the summit. As an alternative to joining the ridge halfway up, follow the snow slopes of the SE face and join it much higher. **2-2½hr**

Brèche de la Tombe Murée 3,630m

Sited between the Roche Faurio and the Pointe Xavier Blanc, it has easy snow slopes on its S flank. The interest lies in the steep, icy couloir of its N flank.

24a   **NORTH COULOIR**
TD+
24
B Croutaz, R Duplat and C Eberhard, 24 May 1947
FWA: J-J Lainez and J Ménégoz, 9-10 Mar 1975

This is one of the steeper ice routes of the massif, comparable with the Couloir Chaud, and is 400m long.

From the Alpe hut (or, for preference, from a bivouac higher up the Romanche valley beyond the turn off to the Adèle Planchard hut) follow the path and then the moraine on the L bank of the Plate des Agneaux glacier (alternative bivouac) and get on to the glacier. Cross it towards a big snow couloir R of the rock buttress bounding the L bank of the Roche Faurio glacier. Climb this couloir on its R bank (sérac and stonefall danger) then Rwards to join a rocky spine separating the couloir from the Tombe Murée glacier (bivouac). Descend to this glacier by an easy couloir above the séracs and climb towards the couloir which leads to the Brèche de la Tombe Murée. 5-5½hr from the Alpe hut

Climb the rimaye, then start on the R bank of the bay c100m before the couloir, usually on bare water-ice. Once in the couloir proper, climb almost vertically up snowy rocks on the R bank (2 pitches of IV). Above, a less steep slope leads to the brèche. In a good year the gully may be climbed directly on ice. **6-10hr** from the rimaye

To descend traverse the snowy ridge Rwards to join the easy ordinary route to the Roche Faurio and descend quickly to the Glacier Blanc and Ecrins hut.

It is possible to reach the Romanche valley by descending towards the Glacier Blanc, passing beneath the SE ridges of Pointe Xavier Blanc and Pointe Louise and then climbing diagonally up and R (N) to reach the Col de Roche Faurio and the glacier of that name. This is descended to the Plate des Agneaux glacier (reversing Route 26a). This may only be achieved with good snow conditions.

Pointe Louise 3,668m

It is an attractive rock peak, at least when viewed from the SE, situated on the N side of the Glacier Blanc and with very easy access from the Ecrins hut. Its rocky NW flank, like the N flank of the Roche Faurio, dominates the Tombe Murée glacier. A couloir on this flank provides the setting for a winter route.

25a
AD
23

SOUTH-EAST RIDGE

J-C Brunel and A Vincent with E Martin and J Piagay,
3 Sept 1952

A good climb which has become a classic. Good rock. It is frequently climbed.

From the Ecrins hut descend to the glacier and go up its L bank to below the Col de la Roche Faurio. Slant up obliquely to reach the foot of the ridge. ½hr

At the base of the ridge is a whitish feature in the shape of an arc. Go up R of this feature and then join the crest of the ridge slanting towards the L over grey slabs above the first step in the ridge. Follow the crest for 150m going over steps and small gendarmes (a few pitches of III) in order to reach the base of the central step. Now traverse R along a ledge for 30m and climb directly up a series of piled up boiler plate slabs for 60m. Next traverse L (III) and reach the ridge by a short dièdre. Alternatively, instead of traversing R, climb straight up along the crest of a ridge, traversing 2m L at the top and return R above this in order to reach a terrace (all of III and a pitch of IV). From this point reach the top of the step (exposed: a delicate pitch: III+). Continue along the ridge, which becomes less steep, to the summit. c2½hr: **3-3½hr** in all

Descend W from the summit by the very easy snow slopes and continue down the subsidiary glacier to the Ecrins and Glacier Blanc huts. 1hr

25b
TD+

NORTH-WEST FACE (LOUISE FINE)
R Borgis, S Constant and M Boothe, 11 March 1995

This is a modern winter climb in an open couloir which is sustained, uniform but not extreme. It contains several vertical pitches. Carry ice gear, a few thin pitons and some small wedges. There is no equipment in situ.

Approach and start as for Route 24a to the Tombe Murée glacier. Below and L of two obvious gendarmes on the NE ridge is a big wall. The couloir climbs L of both the wall and the gendarmes, starting at c2,850m. Climb directly. The line taken may vary slightly according to conditions but it is always obvious and logical. The two hardest sections are on arrival at the foot of the big wall and at its mid-height. Allow **6-8hr** climbing time

Descent: 50m L of the point of arrival on the ridge make a rappel of 50m on the Glacier Blanc flank leading to a snow couloir which slants L. This in turn leads easily, in c10 mins, to the col de Roche Faurio. Descend N by reversing Route 26a or by easy snow slopes on the S side to the Ecrins/Glacier Blanc huts.

Col de la Roche Faurio 3,376m

H Pendlebury, C Taylor and G Spechtenhauser, 1 July 1874

Of little or even no use as a crossing point of the ridge. Its only significance is that it is the lowest point along the ridge above the upper plateau of the Glacier Blanc on its N side. Its S slopes are quite benign and contrast well with those to the N.

26a
AD
24

NORTH FLANK DIRECT

First ascent party
Route described: A Giraud, L Neltner and H Salin, 21 May 1934

It is one of the best and most interesting of the easier grade glacier routes in the massif, but it is only possible given excellent snow cover. There is danger of stonefall after daybreak.

From the Alpe hut follow the path to Pt 2,315m (1½hr). Continue straight up the moraine then cross the Plate des Agneaux glacier to reach the foot of the Roche Faurio glacier. 30min

Climb straight up the lower tongue of the glacier and then the centre of the couloir, sometimes on snow, sometimes on ice. Continue to the col, avoiding a small gully by keeping R. 4hr: **6hr** from the Alpe hut

Pass through the gap and descend to the Ecrins hut without any difficulty.

Pic de Neige Cordier 3,613m

P Guillemin, E Pic and P Estienne, 3 Aug 1877

Its summit provides an exceedingly fine viewpoint which is frequently visited in spring (skiers) and in summer. It is a prominent point on the long ridge between the Roche Faurio and the Montagne des Agneaux, where the ridge forms an angle. From the summit a long ridge runs N.

27a **SOUTH-WEST FLANK AND RIDGE**

F First ascent party

25

A very straightforward, safe climb. It is very popular and an early start is repaid both as a means of avoiding other parties and obtaining good snow conditions on the S facing slopes of the climb.

From the back of the Ecrins hut, climb NE on a long, upwards traverse towards the Col Emile Pic. Pass above the first rocky outcrops, below the second (small) and below the SE spur of the Roche Emile Pic before climbing directly towards the col. The rimaye is usually crossed from L to R, the final line being a short gully which emerges into an obvious deep hollow (1hr). Make an ascending traverse L, then go R to reach a brèche where crampons may be left. Take to the rocks on the L flank of the SW ridge and follow the well marked, zigzag line to the summit. 45min: **c2hr** in all

Descent is by the same route to the Ecrins hut. The descent to the Glacier Blanc hut may be shortened by descending the SE ridge to the Brèche Cordier and then descending parallel to the S ridge of the Pic du Glacier Blanc to join the well marked hut path at the base of the rognon below the ridge. 2hr to the Glacier Blanc hut

27b **NORTH-SOUTH TRAVERSE**

PD P d'Aiguebell and L Faure, 6 July 1896

26

A classic climb principally on snow with over 1,500m of climbing from the Alpe hut via the Brèche de Plate des Agneaux and the N ridge.

Descent is by the SW ridge. It is a popular excursion undertaken in spring by ski-tourers. In summer it is best climbed early in the season when the best snow conditions are available.

From the Alpe hut follow the Col d'Arsine path until under the last slopes of the col. From these go S towards the lateral moraine of the Arsine glacier on the L bank. Follow this until below the NE ridge of the Pic d'Arsine and until in view of the Brèche de la Plate des Agneaux. This is gained without difficulty via the E couloir of the brèche. Depending on conditions (stonefall), reach the brèche using crampons or by staying more or less on the rocks of the L side of the couloir (3½hr). It is also possible to reach this brèche by climbing the small Rif de la Planche glacier staying as much as possible on the L bank, then crossing the Pic d'Arsine from N to S. From the brèche follow the N ridge to the summit. 1½hr

From the summit of Pic de Neige Cordier reverse Route 27a.
c6hr in all to the Ecrins hut

Pic du Glacier Blanc 3,525m

A minor summit which could be considered to be a subsidiary 'top' on the SE ridge of the Pic de Neige Cordier.

28a
AD

SOUTH RIDGE
H Salin and J Vernet, Sept 1936

A fine, introductory route which is on generally good rock.

From the Ecrins hut traverse more or less horizontally NE on snow slopes to a small col at the foot of the ridge under a steep step (20-30min). This point is also attainable from the Glacier Blanc hut. Cross the col and climb 20m under the R flank (E) of the ridge to reach the foot of a 30m chimney-groove which ends on the crest at the top of the initial step.

Climb the chimney-groove, moving L where it steepens (IV: piton), then up a little wall and back R (piton) to arrive on the crest at a small platform. Climb steep rocks above for 15m on the crest (III+ to start with). The ridge levels off; follow it sometimes on the crest, sometimes by ledges and couloirs on the R flank, to a brèche. Rappel 25m into the brèche and then climb a steep slab for 15m (III). Leave the slab by moving R and then regain the crest and follow it to a second brèche. Rappel a further 15m and then climb along the flank to a short chimney formed by large blocks. Climb this and then the final part of the arête, avoiding some gendarmes on the L flank (loose), to reach the easy summit rocks (moves of III/III+). **3hr**

Descend from the summit in the direction of the Brèche Cordier along the NW ridge. Some 20m from this very steep brèche, scramble down L where a rappel is made from a comfortable ledge on the Glacier Blanc flank (lots of old slings usually adorn the anchor flake). Rappel 50m to reach the glacier. With shorter ropes the pitch will have to be broken. There is a second anchor point to facilitate this c15m above the snow.

An alternative descent is by the snowy and often corniced E ridge. The Col du Glacier Blanc (3,276m) is the lowest point on the ridge between the Pic du Glacier Blanc and the Pic du Glacier d'Arsine. The S face track from the col to the Glacier Blanc hut is much frequented and obvious.

Pic du Glacier d'Arsine 3,368m

Another minor summit easily accessible from the Glacier Blanc basin. It is a fine viewpoint.

29a
F
25

NORTH-WEST RIDGE

P Guillemin, Dulbarry, Florentin, Grand, Hayssert and Roche with P Estienne, 8 Sept 1878

This is the most accessible summit from the Glacier Blanc hut and provides the easiest outing in the Glacier Blanc basin. The approach to the ridge is by a permanent névé which recedes in its lower levels as the season advances to expose a boulder field. The route offers a ski outing of modest proportions

From the Glacier Blanc hut follow the track towards the Ecrins hut. Before reaching the S ridge of the Pic du Glacier Blanc, at a height of c3,000m, enter the combe on the R below the Col du Glacier Blanc. Ascend Nwards over snow or boulders and then trend Rwards beneath a buttress to follow an open, snowy gully leading to a less steep slope and the col. From the col follow the ridge, or its R flank, to the summit. There is usually a well used track. 3-3½hr

Montagne des Agneaux 3,664m

W Coolidge with C Almer snr and C Roth, 17 July 1873

A wonderful mountain which makes up by its bulk what it lacks in height. It is situated NE of the Glacier Blanc hut and the Glacier Blanc ice-fall. It has three tops on its summit ridge; the snowy NW summit 3,634m (the Calotte); the rocky Central summit 3,648m and the rocky highest point. Below the summit ridge are four faces; NW, NE, SW and SE, each of which is glaciated to some extent.

30a
PD
27

SOUTH-WEST FACE AND SOUTH RIDGE

F Gardiner and L Pilkington, 30 July 1879

This is the ordinary route and provides an easy, short, mixed route from the Glacier Blanc hut as well as an easy descent route.

Start from the Glacier Blanc hut by a path leading ENE up vegetation and scree slopes to the Jean Gauthier glacier. Ascend the glacier towards the two snow couloirs leading to the Col Jean Gauthier. Do not go up these but turn L up snow and scree slopes to the foot of the rocks of the SE ridge. Turn R and traverse almost horizontally across rocks to the V-notch of the Col du Monêtier. 2-2½hr

On the other side of the col, climb the upper slopes of the Monêtier glacier below the rocks of Pic Tuckett to the foot of the couloir below Col Tuckett, which is a snowy saddle at the foot of the S ridge of the E (main) summit (45min). Climb the couloir to the col and then an easy chimney (III) on the SE face. This avoids delicate slabs on the other flank. Now follow the ridge to the top. A step in the ridge is avoided on the R. 20-30min: **3½-4hr** from the hut

Descend by the same route. It is usual to rappel down the delicate slab into the Col Tuckett (rappel ring in place).

30b   ## SOUTH-WEST SPUR - CENTRAL SUMMIT

D-
27

Mme L Arnoux and L Arnoux, Aug 1948

The pillar, which abuts the central summit, constitutes a good climb from the Glacier Blanc hut. The rock is not always perfect but is good where it matters. The exact start is not easy to find.

Follow the track behind the Glacier Blanc hut towards the Pointe des Cinéastes. Continue on the W side of the ridge into a secondary valley which is followed to a sérac barrier on the Tuckett glacier. This is snow covered in the early season. The base of the spur separates the séracs of the glacier on the L and the tongue of the upper Tuckett glacier on the R at c3,100m (2hr). On the L, gain the foot of the sérac barrier bordering the rocks of the spur. Climb 30m alongside the ice by broken rocks to grey slabs which steepen. Climb these obliquely from L to R for 30m to gain the centre of the spur (III). Bend around R to enter a flared couloir leaning L wards and follow this to the edge of the spur. Climb several slabs to the foot of a steep step of 25m. Overcome this by a large slab, climbing obliquely from R to L to arrive at the top of the step (V: exposed). Continue to the foot of a second step, 35m high; go R to climb an enclosed dièdre, well defined on its R flank (IV).

The spur, from here on, decreases in angle and presents numerous gendarmes. One of these, of a characteristic red colour, is turned on the R (III+), the others are also generally turned by their R flanks. The spur leads directly to the central summit. **6-7hr**

Note: The steep pitch on the first step can be avoided by dodging around the base to find a couloir of loose rocks leading to the top of the step. It misses the difficulties but also the best pitch of the climb.

Descent: Follow Route 30c to the E summit and then reverse Route 30a.

30c   NORTH-WEST FACE - CALOTTE
AD   First ascent party

This is an attractive snow and ice route up a mountain which looks well from the Alpe hut. The standard varies with conditions, being harder late in the season or in a dry year. The angle of the slope is 45° or less. The route described is a variation of the original, the latter has an approach in a glacier couloir with dangerous séracs.

Start from the Alpe hut along the path (GR54) which leads SE to the Col d'Arsine (1hr). Go over the col and continue along the path for c400m to a small lake. Leave the path and head SE, crossing moraines, to reach Pt 2,236m. From here head SW to a position E of the Arsine glacier lakes. Now turn SE again, staying on the L side of a big moraine situated below a very conspicuous, triangular rognon. A tedious ascent leads to the Réou d'Arsine glacier between the rognon and Pt 2,813m. Climb the crevassed glacier SE then SW to a little saddle on the W side near the top. If the séracs of the upper Arsine glacier are stable, a more direct approach to this point can be made via the combe E of Pt 2,875m. Cross the saddle to the upper Arsine glacier and continue up its R bank (crevasses) to the upper snow plateau. Move R and climb a steep snow or ice slope (45°) to the N ridge of the NW summit. This is the summit ridge. Climb along it over the central summit and pass on to the L-hand (N) side of the E summit to climb up rocks (III), which face NE above the Casset glacier, to highest point. 5-7hr: **6-8hr** from the hut

Pointe des Cinéastes 3,203m

This is a feature on the mountainside S of the Montagne des Agneaux, above the Glacier Blanc hut, at the end of a long spur projecting S from the W ridge of the Agneaux between the Pyramide and Tuckett glaciers. The highest point is one of nine along the length of its N-S ridge.

31a
AD
27

SOUTH-NORTH TRAVERSE

A Aulois and J Vernet, 2 or 3 July 1936

The multi-pinnacled ridge provides a pleasant rock climb of character and is low enough to be climbable in periods of bad weather. There is a good deal of equipment in place so it is only necessary to carry a few quick draws and slings. It can quite well be climbed from Cézanne or Ailefroide in the day. The first pinnacle is usually reached by its W flank although a more direct and difficult (max IV+), equipped route is more in keeping with the rest of the climb.

Start from the Glacier Blanc hut, up the grass and scree slopes behind the hut, E and then NE to the W foot of the first pinnacle. Climb easy angled, broken rocks below the third pinnacle to a large ledge. Continue Rwards on this to a couloir descending from the first pinnacle. Climb the couloir to the ridge then follow this to the second pinnacle (III).

The more direct route starts on the E flank of the first pinnacle. Reach the foot of the S ridge which bounds the steep S face on the R. There are two parallel chimneys. Climb the R-hand one, leaving it by moving L on to the crest of the S ridge. Climb the ridge for 30m and then traverse 5m R to a platform at the top of the chimney. Another 30m of climbing leads to the top of the first point.

Descend to the brèche (rappel or down climb: IV), where the route using the ordinary start is joined, and stay on the crest of the ridge over the second point to the next brèche. Go up a few m easily, then traverse to the R-hand (E) face of the third point. Go along a ledge, then up a crack slanting R (IV) to beneath a prominent roof. Turn the roof on its L (unseen hold round the corner: IV) and climb a dièdre for 8m to the top of the third pinnacle and so to the next brèche. Continue over the fourth and fifth pinnacles, without much incident (a 20m rappel is useful for the descent of the fourth point), to the sixth and highest pinnacle. 3½hr

Descend N by a slab with a crack down it (III) and climb the seventh point by its L (W) face. Continue over the eighth point to the ninth and on down the rest of the ridge, which is messy, to a brèche. Descend ledges and scree couloirs on the L (W) side to the moraine on the L bank of the Pyramide glacier or equally well, go off down the R (E) side to the Tuckett glacier. In either case it is a simple matter to regain the route of ascent and the Glacier Blanc hut. 2½hr: **6hr** round trip

31b   **LE VIEUX PITON**

TD

27

D Stumpert and J Flandin, 1992

A pleasant climb on very good rock. Partly equipped. Carry a rack and a couple of long slings. Escape is possible in several places. From the first point the route follows Route 31a but with some variations.

Start L of the lowest tip of the S ridge on a black slab.

P1 4: P2 4+: P3 5+: P4 4+/5: P5 5: P6 5+: P7 5: P8 4 (the top of the first point). To the second and third point is 4 and 3+. Beyond the 3rd point is a pitch of 4+/5 with a move of A0 or 6a. Keep L of Route 31a to the fourth point (5 then 4). The 5th point is IV followed by a 20m rappel. The sixth point is 4 then a rappel. This is the highest point of the ridge but it is possible to continue to the eigth point by one pitch of 4 and two 20m rappels. **5-6hr** climbing

Descend by rappel to the scree/snow.

Col du Casset 3,261m

This is an insignificant col at the head of the Casset glacier on the rocky ridge running E from the Agneaux.

32a   COULOIR DAVIN

AD+
28

Possibly the Abbé J Davin, solo, date unknown
Authenticated by A Cartherade and J Piégay, 28 June 1950

It is often descended on ski and is, not infrequently, the scene of serious accidents. It runs parallel to the Casset glacier, separated from it, on its E side, by a rock spur. It is a straightforward snow climb of 600m, best done and recommended in the early season. The slope is 45° in the upper section.

From the village of le Casset in the Guisane valley take the path which climbs the Petit Tabuc valley (GR54, which continues to the Col d'Arsine). After leaving the wood, leave this path to climb L ward by the moraines of the Casset glacier; climb the lower section of the glacier, move L to pass the foot of the medial spur separating couloir from glacier to reach the couloir proper. 2hr

Climb the couloir, keeping to the centre for the most elegant line. At the top, exit R to the plateau which leads to the Col du Casset or continue direct to the Col des Prés les Fonts. **5hr** from the Casset village

From the col it is possible to climb either of the two adjacent peaks or continue to les Agneaux.

It is quite reasonable to descend the route itself if conditions are good and it is early enough in the day to enjoy sound névé. The normal descent consists of reaching the Col des Prés les Fonts (3,223m) and descending on to and down the glacier of the same name. Continue due E to join, low down, a path alongside the Grand Tabuc torrent to Monêtier-les-Bains.

Dôme du Monetier 3,404m

Lying SW of Monêtier-les-Bains (in the Guisane valley), it is a broad snow (glacier) covered mountain mass with a prominent, yet small peak at its centre. This is the dôme itself although the name is also applied to the whole of the mass. Its SW flank is a complete contrast and is rather hideous in appearance being composed mostly of scree. Along the long crest of the mass are various minor summits the highest of which is the Pointe des Arcas 3,479m.

33a **TRAVERSE OF THE GLACIERS**
PD
P Guillemin, J Gauthier and P-A Reymond, 28 Sept 1876

This is a popular excursion between the Glacier Blanc hut and the Lac de l'Eychauda, from which point it is possible to return to Ailefroide by a motorable route, or continue to Monêtier-les-Bains by way of well used and marked (GR) paths. A popular ski-tour. The views are excellent.

From the Glacier Blanc hut follow Route 30a as far as the Col du Monêtier (3,345m). Once on the Monêtier glacier, descend gently, losing some 200m in height in a SE direction to contour around the E base of the Pic Jean Gauthier. From the base of the spur turn S then SW towards the Col des Brouillards (3,270m) which it is advisable to pass well to its L to climb a fairly steep snow slope of c100m. After having climbed the rimaye (generally easy) not far from the topmost crest (which is better not followed due to bad rock) gain the Pic de Dormillouse (3,409m) without difficulty. The views from here are quite spectacular.

From the summit descend easily to the Col de Séguret Foran (3,333m). From there either make for the Seuil du Rif from where it is easy to attain the Pt 3,406m (Dôme due Monêtier) in a few min or, take in the Pic du Rif by a short detour along with the Pointe des Arcas (3,478m).

The descent of the Séguret Foran glacier is made via the S bank, then go N along the 3,250m contour (crevasses). Dodge the sérac barrier in mid-stream by keeping on the L bank. Gain, as soon as possible by the scree and névés, the moraine beneath the Crête des Grangettes which is followed to the Lac de l'Eychauda which is in turn circled on its N shore. **6hr**

From the lake descend easily to the Cabane du Berger (1,861m) at the foot of the Crête de l'Yret and follow the motorable road to Pelvoux - le Poet. A local bus service to

Vallouise operates in July and Aug, leaving at 3.30pm daily. It is possible to go direct to Ailefroide without going to the village of Pelvoux by taking the path following the water pipe-lines. This expedition is clearly marked on the map.

To return to Monêtier les Bains, cross the Col des Grangettes then follow the path down the Grand Tabuc valley.

Col des Ecrins 3,367m

This long frequented passage between la Bérarde and the Ailefroide valley lies at the head of the Glacier Blanc, between the Roche Faurio and the Ecrins.

34a   **TRAVERSE**
PD
23

F Tuckett, M Croz and P Perren, 12 July 1862

This is a high, much frequented route between la Bérarde and the Glacier Blanc and Ecrins huts. It can be treacherous in icy conditions due to the steep and exposed nature of the upper section on the Bonne Pierre (W) flank (crampons and helmet recommended).

To ascend the W side from la Bérarde, follow the Chatelleret hut path on the L bank of the Etançons stream to the bottom of the Bonne Pierre valley. Cross the two branches of the Bonne Pierre stream and then take the poorly marked path which climbs through scrub on its R bank. It leads up through the Somme stream waterfall and reaches the base of the moraine on the R bank of the Bonne Pierre glacier. Follow the moraine path to where it turns N and then climb steep scree to reach the upper part of the glacier near Pt 2,944m. Cross the glacier E wards to reach a snowy couloir coming down from the Col des Ecrins (3½hr).

This couloir is very broad in its lower part and very narrow in its upper part. Pass the rimaye via a rock rognon or skirt round it on the L. Climb the couloir on the snow as high as possible on the R bank then reach, on the L side, the rocks of th R bank of the couloir. Climb an easy, 12m chimney to reach a ledge and follow this Rwards to reach a steel cable. Climb along the cable on steep slabs for 150m (the cable, which was replaced in 1995, may have gaps in places: gloves recommended). From the top of it, climb easy rocks and reach the R-hand col. 1½hr: **4½-5hr** from la Bérarde

To descend the E side go down from the col on the L edge of the Glacier Blanc to the Ecrins hut. This is very easy and deeply trenched throughout the season.

To descend the W side, stay by the R bank of the couloir and reach the cable (see note above) 20m below the col. Continue on easy rocks to the R bank and go down on to the glacier only when the rocky barriers on the lower half of the couloir have been passed.

Pointe de Bonne Pierre 3,682m

R Toumayeff and J Vernet, 15 July 1926

The Pointe de Bonne Pierre is one of the points capping the impressive wall which rises above the Bonne Pierre glacier and culminates in the Dôme de Neige des Ecrins, a subsidiary summit of the Barre des Ecrins. It is the N most of the two most prominent pinnacles situated just below the point at which the ridge on which they stand turns to snow. The S-most is the Tour de Bonne Pierre.

35a
TD+
29

WEST FACE

P Girod and R Sandoz, 24 Sept 1955

This route is selected as being one of the most interesting and elegant of the half-dozen routes up the wall refered to above. It is unusually steep and of continuous interest on reasonable rock.

Walk from la Bérarde towards the Col des Ecrins as far as Pt 2,944m (Route 34a: excellent bivouac sites at the top of the moraine). Continue up the upper tongue of the glacier keeping R of the spur of broken rock projecting from the Pointe de Bonne

Pierre into the glacier. Get on to this spur at the L extremity of the snow tongue, near a step of copper coloured rock. 4hr: 1hr from the bivouac

Once on the spur, climb a high chimney followed by a couloir. Further up, slant R to the foot of the great, yellowish wall 400m high. The profile of a spur is now seen on the R, with a long narrow crack leading to a little shoulder. Pass beneath black slabs and then climb directly upwards. Move R over an overhang and continue along a steep diagonal line to a point on the spur c10m above the top end of the long, narrow crack (35m: V-, V+ and IV). Now slant L and slightly upwards, pass the foot of a first inviting chimney to a second and steeper one. Climb it (30m: IV- and IV+) and the steep and apparently cracked wall above (V then IV). Move R a bit to within sight of the couloir separating the Pointe from the Tour de Bonne Pierre and climb a step of grey rock leading to the foot of a grey wall 100m high. The line of ascent up this wall is generally towards a rounded brèche between two summits, one grey and the other red. Slant for a rope-length then make a long stride into a poorly defined couloir and climb it direct to a great smooth brown slab at the foot of the second part of the wall (IV: one step of V). Start up this on the R and then traverse L to a vague depression. Now climb up for c40m, partly via a short dièdre (IV+). At this point there are two grey dièdres. Climb the one on the R, the less obvious of the two. It soon bends L and fades into a great, cracked slab, smooth and light coloured. Climb it to the overhang, traverse 2m R (A1) and take the overhang (20m: V/V- then VI, 6a or A1). Move L over steep rocks to reach a wide, easy-angled couloir which leads to the summit ridge. **8hr** climbing

35b **DESCENT BY THE SOUTH RIDGE**
PD
30 In ascent: G Bassac and J Vernet, 26 July 1929
In descent: First ascent party

The route of descent lies over the Tour de Bonne Pierre.

Descend on the E face (a couloir dropping from the N ridge may be used) to the brèche between the Pointe and the Tour de Bonne Pierre. Climb straight up to the Tour and over it down the S ridge. Cross the rimaye and so on to the ordinary route of the Ecrins (Route 37a). Descend this to the Col des Ecrins. The col can then be descended E or W (Route 34a).

It is possible, from the point of arrival on the ridge, to move R and rope down to the Glacier Blanc at the most convenient point. This leads to exposure to the séracs on the E side of the Bonne Pierre.

Dôme de Neige des Ecrins 4,015m

E Boileau de Castelnau with P Gaspard snr and jnr, 21 July 1877

This is little more than a subsidiary summit of the Barre des Ecrins and is climbed by all and sundry wishing to climb an easy 4,000m summit. Its two main faces, the N and NW show two entirely opposite characters. The former, mainly glaciated, merges into the slopes forming the N face of the Barre des Ecrins. By contrast its steep and high NW face consists of steep, rock pillars interspersed with ice couloirs.

36a
F+
30
32

NORTH FLANK

First ascent party

This is the most frequented of the summits of les Ecrins and the route is usually a deeply entrenched track.

From the Ecrins hut follow Route 37a to the rimaye below the Brèche Lory. From the rimaye move Rwards. Cross the crevasse and climb in zigzags towards the ridge which is followed easily to the summit. 3-3½hr

Descend the same route.

North-West face

36b
TD
29

CENTRAL PILLAR (RIGHT-HAND ROUTE)

R Figerou and C Jeanguillaume, 21 and 22 Aug 1973

The pillar presents, in the lower and middle sections, two matching pillars separated by a couloir which, high up, ends below an enormous roof. This climb takes the R-hand branch of the pillar. It is L of Dibona's route of 1913 which climbs the massive ice couloir, the main feature of the face.

Good rock except for the first section. This and the following route conjoin at two-thirds height but separate finishes keep the lines largely independent. 1,000m of climbing.

Reach the foot of the face as for Route 35a and make for the base of the central pillar, trending towards the massive ice couloir. Start close to the lowest point of the rock, a little to the R.

Climb the plinth by easy rock to reach the foot of a Rward slanting dièdre and climb it for 40m (IV with moves of V). Traverse 8m R and climb more easy rock to an inclined chimney. Avoid this by a short crack Lwards (V) then climb a system of cracked blocks (IV) which allow an arête to be joined above the chimney. Follow the arête to end the ascent of the plinth by big slabs on the L flank of the pillar (lll and IV). Start the first step a few m R of the crest by cracks and slabs to a shoulder (lll and IV). Climb a steep,15m wall, make a delicate step L and then climb a flake to reach an easier section (V+). Climb a ramp on the N flank (IV). Reach the crest of the pillar by poor rock and follow it to a big ledge inclined towards the base of the second step. Tackle this by a dièdre just above the R extremity of the ledge (IV, V/A1: 4 pitons: do not go towards a red piton on the L). Traverse L for 8m (V+) to climb large blocks via the N flank to a brèche in the ridge. Follow the arête (IV at first). Here, the Girod - Vivet climb is met.

Turn a gendarme on the L and two others on the R side and follow the base of a large, monolithic step. This is the Grey Tower. By a Rwards traverse reach a characteristic chimney which cleaves the tower. Climb it for c45m (V). Traverse R by a small ledge to reach the W face of the tower. Climb it obliquely on slabs (50m: IV) then take a little couloir to the top of the tower. Follow the ridge to the fourth step. Reach a crack L of a large couloir which splits this step vertically. Climb it to a niche (IV+) and exit R by flakes (V-) to join the couloir where it meets the ridge. Climb the ridge to a brèche beneath the final step. Slant L for 10m and climb a deep crack leading to the crest of the pillar. Follow the crest for 40m (IV+ and IV) then easily to the summit. **14-16hr** climbing

The suggestion is made that the first half of the Girod - Vivet, linked to the upper section of the above climb would provide the best of both...

36c ## CENTRAL PILLAR (LEFT-HAND ROUTE)

TD

29

P Girod and R Vivet, 28 June 1959

This route follows the big pillar in the middle of the face on its L side. It is a big route, the most difficult on this side of the mountain and possibly the best. Climbing is sustained for most of the 1,000m.

Approach as for the previous route. Start at the base of the L-hand part of the pillar and start by a little facet. Climb R, then L (III) to reach a little platform on the crest at the foot of a step characterised by a beak which overhangs on the L. Climb a few m directly and then traverse L below the beak by a smooth slab (V). Climb a corner and force a short overhang directly (V+). Above rises a big wall cut by two ledges. Climb it (III and IV) more or less directly. Next climb a rocky couloir leading L and then follow the crest to a brèche dominating a narrow, verglas-covered couloir.

Climb a sharp spine (IV) and the wall which follows on its L side (IV/IV+) to join the crest once again. Climb it to the foot of a smooth wall which is often verglassed. Take, on the L, an icy couloir which is climbed on the R bank and which gives access to a vast ramp of ice and rock. Climb it directly (very delicate and exposed) to the crest which crowns it and which dominates the big couloir of the NW face. Climb the first gendarme on the L and then a second on the R. Continue almost to the base of a huge, grey, unclimbable step (Grey Tower). On the R flank of its lower section make a long ascending traverse (crossing two ice couloirs) which leads to the junction with the 1913 route at c3,750m. Here, in the L-hand corner of the much steeper summit cliffs, the foot of the NW ridge is reached. The line of ascent varies according to prevailing conditions in this last section. Climb towards this crest either by a short chimney-crack (IV+) and then a couloir 20 m further L (V) or, by a big slab just R of the chimney-crack (V). Follow the airy ridge to the summit **c12hr** from the foot of the climb

36d   **NORTH FLANK DIRECT - LA CALOTTE**

AD   J Giraud and a client, 1944

30

Although not much frequented, this is a fine route in a spectacular setting and much more sporting than the route followed by the masses

Follow Route 37a until level with the summit of the Pt de Bonne Pierre on the R (W). Climb up snow (45°) bearing R to bypass the sérac barrier above. From the R-hand side of these séracs, swing back L to follow the rounded crest of the ridge to the summit. Obviously the climb makes a less crowded alternative from the ordinary route and in good conditions is probably more enjoyable.

Barre des Ecrins 4,101m

A Moore, H Walker and E Whymper with C Almer and M Croz 25 June 1864

The highest peak in the region, this is the only 4,000m peak in France S of the Mont Blanc massif. It is splendidly isolated from its near neighbours and can be seen from many viewpoints, even from many km away. It has a very recognisable, glaciated N face whilst its S flank, mostly rock, presents some fine pillars descending into the couloir below the Col des Avalanches. Its summit is the culminating point of two ridges, the W, at the foot of which is the Brèche Lory separating the peak from the Dôme, and the NE. The former has a subsidiary 'top', the Pic Lory 4,088m. Near the foot of the NE ridge, just beyond the Brèche des Ecrins, is a striking rock pinnacle, the Barre Noire 3,751m

37a
PD
30
32

NORTH FACE AND WEST RIDGE

First ascent party in descent

A *magnificent route without special difficulty and very popular. A fine viewpoint. The state of the glacier varies according to the year. The rimaye at the foot of the Brèche Lory can pose minor difficulties. There is some danger from séracs, especially from those below the Tour de Bonne Pierre as the route crosses the glacier from the region of the Col des Ecrins.*

From the Ecrins hut descend to the Glacier Blanc. Follow the L bank of the glacier almost to the Col des Ecrins (1hr). Cross the glacier towards the N slopes of the Barre, generally crossing an avalanche path in the process. Go by snow slopes in the less-crevassed area of the glacier, passing R of the lowest séracs and L (E) of those next to the Tour de Bonne Pierre (sérac fall danger). Go towards the snow boss which forms the lower extremity of the NE ridge of the Ecrins and, when the slope is less steep, go obliquely R, turning ice cliffs in the process on their E side, to reach the upper plateau of the glacier. (When there is new snow go slightly L, cross a rimaye and the steep slopes above it and then go slightly R on to the upper plateau of the glacier). Make a long, level traverse Rwards under the final slopes of the Barre to reach the foot of the Brèche Lory which marks the extremity of the W ridge of the Barre des Ecrins. Cross the rimaye a little R of the brèche (sometimes difficult) and climb to the brèche (1½-2hr).

The brèche is dominated by a step which cannot be climbed directly. Go around the base of the rocks on the L and climb a short chimney which leads, 10m higher, to a ledge. From there, climb obliquely L by easy rocks below the crest of the step to join the W ridge. (The first ascent party, in descent, climbed down from the ridge a little way before they reached Pic Lory. This route is sometimes followed in ascent today if the rimaye can be crossed.) Follow the ridge directly by its crest or a few m below it by rocks and snow slopes on the N side. Climb up to and past the Pic Lory and finally reach the summit. 1hr: **3½-4h** from the hut

Should circumstances not allow for an ascent of the Barre, the Dôme de Neige des Ecrins provides suitable compensation without much further commitment.

Descend by the same route.

37b ARETE ROUGE

D+

31

33

R Toumayeff and J Vernet, 31 July 1926

Probably as classic a climb as the S Pillar, certainly more elegant but less frequented. It is steep, has few resting places and has sustained difficulties.

There is a risk of stonefall whilst crossing the gorge separating the Arête Rouge from the S Pillar and it is therefore strongly recommended that a very early start is made. The rock i good, the climbing exposed and (amazingly) does not exceed grade IV. 1,100m of climbing.

Approach and start as for the S pillar (Route 37c) as far as the bivouac site on the little, rotten ridge. Get into the bed of the gorge on the R by a system of ascending ledges and scree. Climb the gorge on its R bank and then cross it as high as possible and climb up to a grey spur which is also climbed (stonefall danger a the start). The ridge steepens forming a sugar loaf like pillar, the real climbing starts here.

Climb a slab and a crack/dièdre on the L flank then move to a slab on the R flank where a ledge and a chimney lead to a small ledge on the top of the pillar against the wall. Start up the wall by climbing a step followed by a short overhang. Traverse a few m L to climb a couloir for 20m (all IV from the start). A curving traverse R over a series of slabs leads to the first large, snow terrace. Traverse R, descending slightly across the bottom edge of the snow and the lower part of a couloir. This leads to the foot of a fairly steep wall of light coloured, broken rock which is climbed as far as a second snow terrace. Cross this for 20m to its centre and climb a wall, a small chimney, a crack and a slab (IV), to reach a third snow band which is followed towards the summit. To avoid a ravine, skirt around a spur then climb a 15m crack. Follow a horizontal ledge to beneath an overhang. Arrive, at c4,000m, below a fourth terrace at the foot of a gently rising couloir which is followed to the summit. Alternatively climb a chimney/couloir on the NE arête which leads to the top. **8-12hr** for the pillar

37c
TD
31
33

SOUTH PILLAR

M and Mme J Franco, 15 Aug 1944

This is one of the great, classic rock climbs of the Dauphiné. It is c1,100m from the rimaye to the top and is as demanding as the Couzy-Desmaison route on the Olan, although not as difficult technically. It has a great number of pitches of IV, several of V and one of V+. Unfortunately the quality of the rock is not good, which means that moving together on the grade IV is dangerous, otherwise it is a safe line. It is sheltered from stonefall once the rimaye has been crossed. There are several variants in the upper section of the Bastion, a 300m high step on the ridge, notable above the long chimneys. These end below the two hard pitches immediately below the 'mirror' slab, where the Bastion is completed. These variations are all harder than the route described and most followed. It is better to bivouac below the face where there are excellent sites and water, but take great care that it is not contaminated by other climbers or refuse!

Start from Cézanne up the Col de la Temple path and go along the long moraine on the L bank of the Glacier Noir (bivouacs around the Balmes de François Blanc). Go up the Glacier Noir itself to the complicated system of rimayes at the foot of the

Couloir des Avalanches. 1½hr: excellent bivouac sites and water beneath huge blocks.

Cross the rimaye either at the extreme L end of the initial wall of the SE face of the Ecrins, at the base of this wall, at the base of the couloir itself or, rather lower on the R. Climb the initial wall (II to IV depending on where it is climbed) above the rimaye and slant somewhat L up easy broken rocks to a bivouac site c100m above the rimaye and 50m R of the Couloir des Avalanches. Continue direct to the foot of a large wall. Climb this starting from L to R and then back L up a ledge fading into a chimney. This leads to the upper L extremity of the wall, on a little, rotten ridge (bivouac site).

Climb this ridge and then a little facet for a rope-length moving gently Rwards. Follow ledges ascending L to the crest of the pillar (c3,300m) where there is a bivouac site. Climb the edge easily to the point where it steepens dramatically in a large reddish step (the Tête Rouge). From the foot of the step traverse 5m L and move back by a short slab on the crest (IV) which is climbed for 20m. Take a ledge on the R, go Rwards and climb a dièdre-chimney for 50m (III) which leads to the summit of the Tête Rouge. Above is a short step, the Tête Grise, which is turned by slanting ledges on the R(E) flank (a move of IV); the crest, once gained, is followed without difficulties. Go into the brèche which follows and, by ledges on the L flank, reach another brèche at the foot of the Bastion. 3-5hr

Climb straight up for 15m by a chimney (IV-). Traverse almost horizontally R for 20m (V-: exposed stance). Climb up directly for 5-6m (IV) and then take a chimney-crack on the R (IV) which leans L a little. Climb a second chimney-crack on the R for 20m then straight up a third crack (III) to arrive at the L of the foot of a 'U' shaped trough of rotten rock. Climb this trough and pass the wall which closes it towards the R. Climb R for 15 to take a stance behind an enormous detached flake. From the flake traverse 10m L (IV) and climb up R for 20m followed by another 20m with a little curving move Rwards at the start.

Climb a 10m high, red crack (IV) and, after a few more m, climb steep, loose rocks (IV). 15m higher reach a ledge at the foot of the very steep, 50m high, final step of the Bastion. Follow the ledge R and at the end of it traverse horizontally for a few m to gain the foot of a vague, vertical dièdre. Climb it (V) and then leave it on the R and traverse Rwards to a stance after a few more m. On the R climb a couloir ending in a jamming crack (V) c10m above and R of the stance. Climb obliquely for 3m and go to the base of a depression (V/V+). Climb the scoop (V) and leave L on bad rock to reach an inclined area of slabs (the Mirror). Climb these to the arête at the top of the Bastion (c3,800m). The difficulties are over.

Climb up couloirs of scree and ice or snow on the W side of the crest of the ridge, thus avoiding numerous gendarmes, then back to the ridge and so to the top. **6-10hr** from the foot of the face: 9-13hr from Cézanne

37d SOUTH-NORTH TRAVERSE

AD
32

S face: H Duhamel with P Gaspard snr and jnr, 2 Sept 1880
Traverse: W Coolidge with C Almer snr and jnr, 11 July 1881

The route is less popular today than in earlier times. More popular these days is the route taking the NE ridge to the summit after the ascent of the North couloir of the Barre Noire. The line of the N-S route is not clear in the middle section and is difficult to find in mist (or dark). It makes a natural traverse starting from la Bérarde, returning via the Col des Ecrins. It is a mixed climb at high altitude in magnificent surroundings.

From the Temple-Ecrins hut climb the first zigzag of the Col de la Temple path. Leave it a little before it climbs towards the spur formed by the SW ridge of the Pic Coolidge by a path on the L which rises through the grassy slopes of the L bank of the Vallon de la Pilatte. Reach the SW extremity of the Vallon de la Pilatte glacier and follow its L bank close to the NW flanks of the SW ridge of the Pic Coolidge. If the glacier is badly crevassed, cross it to reach a large rock rognon emerging from the ice. Climb this on the L by easy rock, then scree, and continue up the glacier towards the Fifre. Otherwise continue up the glacier passing W of the Col du Fifre. Climb N past the base of the Fifre and go towards the Col des Avalanches, turning several crevasses on the L. 3-3½hr

Before actually reaching the Col des Avalanches, go towards the S face into a snowy bay (the second one below the col) and a Y-shaped couloir. Climb up via slabs into the R branch of the couloir. Follow this, nearly always wet (III), to where the couloir opens. Reach a terrace of loose, unstable rock. Climb for 20m or so R (E) and then climb a narrow couloir on the L. Don't climb too high in this and do not cross a vein of quartz. Instead climb slabs and cracks on the R to reach the crest of a rib. Follow the crest for c25m and then cross the couloir on the R to reach slabs on the other side (cables). Climb the slabs (III/IV without cables) to reach more slabs (III) leading to the ridge which borders the R bank of a deep, snow couloir (the Couloir Champeaux). This ridge extends from the Col des Avalanches. Get into the Couloir Champeaux and follow it until close to the junction where it splits. Climb the spur between the two branches of the couloir (III). At the top of the spur, climb the couloir on its L side at first on snow/ice icy and then, above, on the R, on easy rock to reach a hanging snow slope (frequently called the Glacier des Ecrins) of the S face (2hr). Climb the snow slope and rock which emerges from it, upwards and R and then climb R and as high as possible by a rib of rock on the R bank of a steep snow couloir. Cross the couloir Rwards to reach the foot of rocks which lead to the summit ridge. Join the W ridge between the Pic Lory and the summit. Climb up R along the crest to the highest point. 1hr: 6-6½hr from the hut

Complete the traverse by descending the ordinary route (Route 37a) to the Col des Ecrins and return to la Bérarde via Route 34a. **12-14hr** for the round trip

37e NORTH FACE DIRECT FINISH

AD

30

W Coolidge, C and U Almer and C Gertsch, 3 July 1870

This is a variation to the N face and W ridge (Route 37a) and should only be attempted if there is a sufficient snow to prevent stonefall. The rimaye may be impossible to cross. The first ascent party took a line further L following a shallow, icy couloir which slants up to the NE ridge close to the summit.

Follow Route 37a to directly beneath the summit on the final traverse towards the Brèche Lory. The route is obvious and takes the shallow grooves above this point, sometimes snow-filled in abundance but often easy mixed ground.

37f BARRE NOIRE NORTH COULOIR

AD

30

F Picard and G Singer, 24 Sept 1954

This route, combined with an ascent of the NE ridge, provides an excellent alternative means of ascent to the summit of the mountain from the Glacier Blanc. It may also be used as a variation start to the N face route (37a). It follows a wide, open couloir and is often frequented nowadays by guided parties. It is safe from objective dangers. The couloir, followed by the ascent of the NE ridge of the Barre des Ecrins, is highly recommended. It is airy and less frequented than the ordinary route.

From the Ecrins hut, follow the L bank of the Glacier Blanc towards the Col des Ecrins. At a point opposite the North Couloir, cross the glacier. Cross the rimaye (normally) on the L, a few m from the boundary rocks of the R bank of the couloir. Climb directly towards the col. At about two-thirds height the angle steepens to c50°; trend Rwards for the final three or four rope-lengths to leave the couloir adjacent to the rocky rib which bounds the L bank. A snowy crest leads to the Brèche des Ecrins. 2-3hr from the rimaye: **4hr** from the hut

Traverse R to join the ordinary route (Route 37a) or follow the NE ridge to the summit (Route 37g).

37g **NORTH-EAST RIDGE**

AD- P Güssfeldt and A Burgener, 18 June 1881

30
31

This is a fine climb of considerable variety which can be combined with the Barre Noire N couloir route or with the N face approach route. The former is preferable. Occasionally the ridge is corniced but this is not usually a problem. Seasonal variations in conditions may increase the difficulties of the ridge by as much as two standards to D.

From the N couloir of the Barre Noire (or from the ordinary route), climb the ridge over a series of snow bosses to reach the rocky part of NE ridge below a steep step at c3,950m. Traverse R on to the N face and climb the second rock chimney which is encountered (III: verglas) back on to the ridge above the step. Now follow the crest of the ridge to the summit. **2hr** from the foot of the ridge (Brèche des Ecrins)

Pic Coolidge 3,774m

W Coolidge and C Almer snr and jnr, 14 July 1877

The mountain lies S of the Barre des Ecrins, filling the angle formed by the two branches of the Glacier Noir. Its N flank provides most interest to climbers whilst its S ridge makes an interesting route for newcomers to the Alps.

38a **SOUTH RIDGE**

F First ascent party

32

The ordinary route, easy and popular leading to a fine viewpoint. It can be started from the Temple-Ecrins hut or from Cézanne.

Reach the Col de la Temple via Route 39a. From the col turn N and get on to the S ridge of the Pic Coolidge at the point where it emerges from the scree. Pass along a ledge on its R (E) side to the second couloir. Cross this (possibility of snow and ice) and climb the easy rocks on its L bank. If the snow conditions are good it is possible to climb the couloir. From the top, slant up R and reach a small brèche on the S ridge. Continue along a good ledge on the E face, descending a little, and then L up steep but easy rock to a small plateau covered with snow and/or scree bordering the E ridge. Cross this plateau Nwards and continue, on easy rocks, up the L (W) edge of the steep snow slope which follows. When this ridge steepens, slant up R across the upper part of this slope to the E ridge. Continue along the ridge over a subsidiary top to the summit. **1½hr** from the col

38b   **NORTH-EAST FACE**

D   Mlle L Bizzari and W Bonatti, 5 July 1955

33   FWA: C Chamel, J-P Chaud, Y Estienne and M Molinatti, March 1974

A fine, open route of some 750m which is relatively straightforward once the hanging glacier has been reached. The upper section receives the sun quite early in the morning and a certain amount of stonefall is possible. The climb is best done from a bivouac on the Glacier Noir where there is a wide choice of sites at the end of the long moraine on the R side of the glacier (Balmes de François Blanc). The best available sites lie beyond a large cairn where the glacier splits and the moraine bends R towards the Col des Avalanches. There is a plentiful supply of water but be careful of human pollution!

Cross the N branch of the Glacier Noir and reach a depression/couloir on the R of the tempting rock buttress and close to the lowest section of the rock barrier at the base of the face. Start up an ill-defined pillar then move L on to a ramp slanting up R. Climb this to the top of the barrier (several pitches of III/IV). Continue up the hanging glacier (45°), passing L of the sérac barrier, to the steep upper wall. Keep L and continue on ice and mixed terrain (poor rock with minimum security) to reach the E ridge. There is no real line here but early in the day this will give easy mixed climbing. Later in the day conditions can become very bad. The summit is reached easily by continuing along the summit ridge. The first ascent party moved R from the top of the ice slope and climbed direct to the summit. This is generally more difficult. **6-8hr**

North and North-East Flank of the East Ridge

On the E ridge of the Pic Coolidge is an obvious boss at
Pt 3,343m. Below this is a series of flying buttresses and couloirs
seaming the whole flank of the ridge. They offer several snow or
ice climbs of which the following three give a representative
sample. The approach from the Pré de Mme Carle takes c2½hr

Descent is by a line on the S flank which is common to all
three climbs described here. Cross the boss and follow snow-
fields and scree to the Glacier Noir midway between the end of
the E ridge and the couloir which climbs to the Col de la
Temple.

38c   **NORTH COULOIR**

D-   J Fédèle, J-M Bourgeois, 19 July 1966

33

39

*This couloir is also known as the Couloir Dérobé or Fédèle. Hidden
from view in the deep couloir L of the Bonatti climb, this 500m route
offers a regular, classic style route finishing at the brèche (Pt 3,301m)
on the E ridge. The only concern, as with the Bonatti, is stonefall late
in the day emanating from the small couloirs of the E ridge. 50° max*

Approach as for Route 39a along the L bank moraine of the
Glacier Noir. From the vicinity of the Balmes de François Blanc
(bivouacs), cross the glacier to the N foot of the E ridge. Climb
the glacier to the entrance to the gully which does not appear in
view until the last moments of the approach.

At the start the couloir is bordered by a strip of snow in the
form of a terrace above the glacier. Take the couloir to reach this
terrace (50°). If necessary traverse a deep gutter then climb in the
couloir, keeping for preference on the L bank where rock gives
some protection from stonefall. Pass a narrowing - sometimes
ice, often rock. Several rope lengths on snow lead to a further
narrowing. Climb in the bottom of this on rock, ice and mixed
ground and surmount the final cornice, which often overhangs,
to arrive at the brèche (Pt 3,301m). **4-5hr**

38d   COULOIR RITCHIE

TD-/TD+ A Martin and B Pleindoux, Dec 1994

39

A surprising, 650m long climb with the difficulty varying according to the quantity of snow/ice in the gully.

Approach as for Route 38c. Start at the top of the avalanche cone L of the spur which itself is L of the previous route.

    Two initial steep pitches (70°: 5+ mixed ground, then 80° for 5m) lead to a snow slope. Climb the snow towards the R then take steep, mixed ground (5+). Climb a suspended snow slope for 150-200m followed by a slanting, narrow couloir on the R (2 rope lengths: 60/70° then 5 mixed ground). This may be avoided by an easier line around the rocks on the L.

    Climb to the summit of the boss via a terminal (easy) snow slope. **6-8hr**

38e   COULOIR DEWEZE

D

S Dewèze solo, winter 1980

33
39

This is the L-most of the climbs and takes the couloir directly to a hidden brèche. 60°-65° max. Dewèze climbed with a single, classic ice-axe and without crampons!

Approach as for Route 38c and start up the L-most avalanche cone.

Climb the couloir without deviation to mid-height and then climb the steeper slope giving access to to the R branch of the couloir. When this steepens and closes, climb L along a ramp for 50m to a second, narrow couloir. Climb this to the hidden brèche. It is possible to descend by the same route but if this is deemed too steep/dangerous, descend as described above.

Col de la Temple 3,322m

The Col lies between Pic Coolidge and the Ailefroide and connects the Gyronde and Vallouise valley (Ailefroide) with the Vénéon valley (la Bérarde). It has probably been known and used for centuries and is easy. For parties wishing to undertake some of the major NW face climbs on the Ailefroide, the significance of the approach route will be obvious.

39a **EAST-WEST TRAVERSE**

F

32

The route is described from Ailefroide to la Bérarde but can equally easily be undertaken in the reverse direction.

Start from Cézanne along the path leading up the valley NWwards and across the stream from the Glacier Noir. Zigzag up to where the path forks and take the L branch (the R goes to the Glacier Blanc hut) along the top of the long moraine on the L bank of the Glacier Noir. Continue to the guide-post at its upper end (1½-2hr). Now traverse across the N branch of the glacier, going S towards a rock island. This island is not far from the foot of the E ridge of the Pic Coolidge and marks the lower end of the moraine on the L bank of the S branch of the glacier. Climb a snow slope, or broken rocks on the R, to a path which leads to the top of this island. Follow the moraine to another guide-post (30min). Get on to the glacier near where it ceases to be covered with scree. Ascend it, keeping near its true L bank and pass L (S) of the spur, which descends from the Col de la Temple, by a prepared track. Climb a loose, sometimes snowy couloir on the S flank of the spur to reach the E edge of the ston plateau below the col. Care needs to be taken in the couloir. Wal W up scree to the col. 1hr: c4½hr from Cézanne

From the col, slant down R over some scree and/or snow (take care if it is icy) on to the Temple glacier. Continue down the glacier, NW then W, to the R bank (sometimes icy) and then turn down scree to the foot of the SW ridge of the Pic Coolidge. Cross over R and join the path from the Col des Avalanches. Turn L down this and zigzag down to the Temple-Ecrins hut (1-1½hr). Follow the path down into the valley and so to la Bérarde. 1½hr: **c7½hr** from Cézanne

In the reverse direction, locate the couloir leading to the Glacier Noir from the ruins of a small hut on the E flank of the Col de l

Temple. The couloir starts just below the ruin. Great care should be exercised in the couloir as there is a lot of loose rock and this is a much used route.

L'Ailefroide 3,953m

W Coolidge with C and U Almer and C Gertsch, 7 July 1870

A large and complex mountain and most impressive, especially when viewed from the N and NW. It has routes of all types to suit almost everyone except those wanting very short climbs. Along its crest, which extends for c2km, are several high points. The true summit is the Ailefroide Occidentale which dominates the mighty NW face, standing above the Coste Rouge glacier, as well as the S and SE faces, which overlooks the Ailefroide glacier. The glacier is split into two parts by a broad spur descending SE from the summit. This spur also forms the boundary between the two facets of this flank.

To the NE of the main summit, beyond the Brèche de Coste Rouge, is the central summit 3,927m. This point is particularly significant in that it is from here that the very fine N (Coste Rouge) ridge descends. Two further, easily identifiable point are located further E. The first is a distinct shoulder, Pointe Fourastier 3,907m, whilst the other is a subsidiary summit, the Ailefroide Orientale 3,847m.

40a
PD
34

SOUTH-EAST SPUR

First ascent party

Athough it is not a popular climb because of the quality of the rock, this is the ordinary route up the W and highest of the Ailefroide's three summits. The route described is a variation of that used by the first ascent party.

Start from the Sélé hut, up the Celse Nière valley to beneath the SE spur of the W summit, which divides the Ailefroide glacier into two branches. Climb up glacier-smoothed slabs and the lower slopes of the glacier towards the cliff terminating the SE spur. Across the face of this will be seen a remarkable rake, slanting up from L to R. Follow it under several waterfalls until the E branch of the Ailefroide glacier comes into sight (at the start of the season it may be better to reach this point up the R bank of the E branch of the Ailefroide glacier). Cross the scree and snow slopes that crown the terminal cliff of the spur going R on to the crest bounding the E side of the spur. Climb this to a snowy shoulder. Now climb the L bank of a couloir whose R bank sports a prominent rock tower. Continue, slanting L up mixed rock and snow slopes to the top. **5-6hr**

40b COL DE L'AILEFROIDE

F

35

34

H Duhamel and P Gaspard snr and jnr, 17 June 1882

This col 3,337m can be used for descent from the Ailefroide W summit and may be reached from the Brèche des Frères Chamois by traversing the Ailefroide glacier below the Cime du Coin. It is closer to reach than the Col du Sélé if pressed for time in descent to the Pilatte hut. It is not recommended as a crossing between the Pilatte and Sélé huts.

From the Col d'Ailefroide, descend a loose, rocky couloir to the Coin glacier and cross it obliquely Lwards to the rocky spur descending from the Pointe du Sélé. Continue down the rocks below the glacier and gain the Pilatte glacier by névés and scree slopes. Cross the glacier to the hut.

40c WEST FACE AND SOUTH FLANK

PD

35

34

In descent: H Baker, T Danby, C Turc and J Rodier, 5 Sept 1893
To the Brèche des Frères Chamois: F Perrin and C Verne with C Clot, P Gaspard snr and J Turc, 3 Aug 1889

This is the ordinary route up the mountain from la Bérarde. The route is rather circuitous: there are no real difficulties above the Brèche des Frères Chamois.

Start from the Pilatte hut by the path which leads S to the Pilatte glacier. Cross it and descend it near its R bank to a point a little below the level of the hut (c2,525m). Leave it here and climb a large, steep scree. Slant up slightly L and up a small, vegetated couloir to reach the L bank of the Gris glacier at its SW edge. Climb the glacier NE to reach the R bank of its N branch and the R branch of a big couloir which is partly snow filled. Cross the rimaye and climb the couloir on névé and rocks on its R bank, then cross it (stonefall) and continue up the rocks on the L bank. Leave it two-thirds of the way up, at a point level with a big slanting ledge covered with scree. Pass along this ledge Rwards, to a narrow, ice couloir. Climb the L bank of this to its easy upper part and on up easy rocks to the Brèche des Frères Chamois. 3½hr.

On the other side of the Brèche, traverse horizontally across the upper part of the S branch of the Ailefroide glacier and make towards a scree slope on the spur dividing it from the small hanging glacier in the middle of the S flank of the Ailefroide. Climb an easy couloir to this slope and continue up indefinite ridges and snow to the SW ridge. Follow this to the summit. 2½hr: **6hr in all**

Descend by the same route. Alternatively, from the Brèche des Frères Chamois descend the Ailefroide glacier to reach the Col de l'Ailefroide and follow Route 40b.

40d   **NORTH-WEST FACE VIA THE GLACIER LONG**
D
36

To the brèche: J de Lepiney and E Stofer, 1982
FWA: G Cavarec and Y Maillard, 26 Jan 1983

A superb glacier climb of 1,000m on this vast face. Remote and rarely frequented. The climbing conditions vary considerably from one season to the next. The climb is best attempted from a bivouac near the foot of the face.

There are two methods of reaching the start from la Bérarde: Follow the path towards the Pilatte hut and the scree slopes below the Coste Rouge glacier. Climb the L side (R bank) of the glacier then traverse across the base of the snow to reach the bottom R-hand corner of the Glacier Long. Alternatively start at the Temple-Ecrins hut and follow the approach described for Route 40e.

From Ailefroide/Cézanne follow Route 40f via the Glacier Noir and Col de Coste Rouge. Descend from the col on to the Coste Rouge glacier and follow it down to the level of the NW face. Continue following the line of the wall and then a partly marked track between rock barriers on a level with the foot of the Glacier Long. There are some good bivouac sites in this vicinity. Both methods are difficult and complicated in the dark.

Start on the L bank of the glacier. Climb the steepening ice to rock and séracs which form an impassable barrier. The best way past this obstacle is to follow a ramp rising from R to L to reach the uniform snow/ice slope above the séracs. Continue up the middle of the glacier, crossing 2 or 3 steep ice walls and rimayes, to reach a snowy saddle on the R near the top of the glacier just S of Pt 3,431m. 4-5hr: 500m

Now cross the upper slope of the glacier (steep and icy) to gain the R side of the face below a large black wall. Climb rocky ribs and icy chimneys to reach the R-hand side of a long snowy ramp above. Follow it back L (ice and loose rock), then climb direct, then L, crossing 2 or 3 rocky ribs, to reach the SW ridge which is followed to the summit. c3hr: **8hr** in all

Descend to the Pilatte hut as for Route 40b. It is also possible, without going to the summit, to descend from the brèche S of Pt 3,431m. Route 40c climbs part way up the couloir below this brèche and so the descent reverses that route from the foot of the couloir. Go down a small couloir on the SW side of the saddle and then descend diagonally L on snow and rock, followed by short chimneys and mixed ground to reach the Gris glacier. Reverse Route 40c from here. The latter section of this presents difficult route finding.

40e **NORTH-WEST WALL**
ED2   L Devies and G Gervasutti, 23-24 July 1936
36 FWA: P Béghin, P Caubet, O Challéat and P Guillet,
34   19-23 Feb 1945

This is a great route up a magnificent 1,050m wall. The rock is sound

*but the technical difficulties are considerable without ever being
excessive. There is usually verglas and some stonefall danger (cross the
big Coste-Rouge couloir as early as possible). Pitches of V+ and with a
short section of 6a (avoidable). There are c40 pitons in place and 1
(old) bolt! The climb has had several British ascents and is rated as
seriously as the Walker Spur of the Grandes Jorasses.*

Start from the Temple-Ecrins hut up the Col de la Temple path
as far as its entry into the Vallon de la Temple. Leave the path
and slant slightly downwards into the bed of the Temple ravine
near the foot of the crags beneath the Temple glacier. Cross the
stream and climb a couloir on the other side to the terraces at the
foot of the W ridge of the Pic de la Temple. Pass SE along debris
covered terraces above the Cloute Favier cliffs and so on to the
Coste-Rouge glacier above the ice-fall (2,800m, 1½-2hr).
Bivouacs at the glacier edge. These can also be reached from the
Vénéon valley - see Route 40d).

Cross the glacier to the foot of the NW wall and climb half-
way up the snow cone at the foot of the big couloir, at this point
taking to the rocks of the R bank of the couloir where there is a
little platform. Climb a chimney, then slant R up an open dièdre
(III). Climb a wall (IV+) and pass along a ledge to the Coste-
Rouge couloir. Cross it (stonefall) at the easiest point to the
rocks of the central pillar (this point can also be reached by
traversing R above the chimney and climbing more or less up the
couloir: stonefall danger, but easier).

The central pillar starts easily for several pitches to the first
step, which is a triangular wall. Traverse L and climb a chimney
(V) on to the crest of the pillar which steepens. Climb an open
chimney (IV) to a letter-box and the vertical crack above to the
crest again (IV). Climb the almost vertical wall which dominates
the crack (25m: V+/VI, 6a). This can be avoided on the R (IV).
Traverse R to the crest of the pillar and climb up it, keeping on
or near the crest (IV) to a deep, narrow brèche. Descend 5m and
make a long stride to the other side of the brèche. Start the next,
big step by a L traverse to a tall, vertical dièdre. Climb straight
up the dièdre (V/V+). Regain the crest of the pillar and follow it

(IV) to its summit (6hr). This point can also be reached more easily from the point where the Coste-Rouge couloir is crossed by the secondary couloir dropping from the top of the central pillar; climb the rocks on its L bank and then up the couloir itsel (P Paquet's variant).

The central pillar is joined to the face by a ridge which is generally snow covered. Above this there is a stretch of steep and smooth, grey slabs, with few resting places for 100m and which are exposed to stonefall. Climb these slabs (V), starting straight up and then slanting R. Climb a little wall (V) and return L to a large semi-circular ledge (1hr: bivouac site above the E end of the ledge). Pass R along the ledge and up a short steep couloir of rotten, icy rocks to a broken, rocky and snowy shoulder (or avoid the couloir on the R up a chimney: III: one step of IV). From the shoulder climb a second couloir by the rocks on the L, thus reaching a scoop slanting up from the R to L. Climb this to the point where it loses itself in the upper cliffs and traverse L under an obvious nose to a sloping terrace at the foot of a deep, 100m chimney. Climb this (V: verglas) until it fades out under an enormous overhang. Take a sloping ledge L (V+) from under the overhang and so to easier rocks which lead to the summit ridge (an alternative exit, from the top of the second couloir above the grey slabs, traverses R and uses the R bank of the ice couloir dropping from the brèche SW of the great square gendarme on the SW ridge). **12hr** from foot of the face

There are now two possibilities: If late it is not necessary to go on to the summit of the mountain. Descend the SE face from a point on the NE ridge close to the point of arrival on the ridge half-way between the Brèche de Coste-Rouge (Pt 3,874m) and the summit. Descend first the R then the L bank of a shallow couloir on the SE face. Continue down L (E) past platforms to the top of the overhanging wall 40m above the Ailefroide glacier Make two overhanging rappels to the glacier and slant down R and join the ordinary route (40a) on the ridge below the shoulder. Reverse this route to the valley to descend to Ailefroide

Cross the Col du Sélé or the Col de l'Ailefroide to reach the Pilatte hut and la Bérarde

To reach the summit, turn R up the NE ridge and go over or round (on the SE side) the square gendarme, then up the last step and along the ridge to the summit. The descent is by reversing the ordinary route (Route 40a) to the Celse Nière valley and past the Sélé hut, to Ailefroide, or via the Col du Sélé (Route 47a), or Col de l'Ailefroide (Route 40b), to the Pilatte hut and la Bérarde.

Central Summit

40f
D
37
36

NORTH (COSTE ROUGE) RIDGE

G Mayer with A Dibona, 1 July 1913

This is a very fine ridge leading to the central summit and marred only by the poor quality of a good deal of the rock; verglas is often encountered. A bivouac at the Col de Coste Rouge is possible.

Start from the Temple-Ecrins hut and follow Route 40e on to the Coste Rouge glacier. Climb the glacier to the R-hand (S) col. 2½-3hr

It is possible to start from Cézanne (this is two hours longer) by following Route 39a until below the Col de la Temple. Continue up the glacier, heading for the couloir leading to the col L (S) of the Aig de Coste Rouge. Climb the snowy couloir by its L bank to reach the col.

From the col climb almost on the crest of the ridge, on its W side, to a deep brèche and descend a little way on the E side. Now continue almost horizontally along a system of ledges, with little ups and downs, to a point a short way beneath the brèche between the Dents de Coste Rouge, the jagged ridge at the top of the first step of the ridge, and the Tour Pointue, the next tower. Cross the E side of the Tour Pointue and descend (step of IV) into the big couloir dropping from the upper part of the Tour du Géant, the next really big step after the Tour Pointue. Now,

either climb the couloir, if it is in good condition, or slant steadily R to the brèche between the Tour Pointue and the Tour du Géant. By a rising traverse, climb the base of the Tour de Géant and pass along a ledge into a couloir on its NE side. Climb the couloir (III: verglas), up its bed and then up the R bank of the brèche at the upper side of the Tour du Géant. An attractive alternative is to climb from the brèche between the Tour Pointue and the Tour du Géant, up the ridge itself or just on its L (a pitch of IV). Continue up the crest of the ridge to the tower at the foot of the final wall. Turn this along an airy ledge on the R (W). The final wall again has two alternatives; either climb chimneys on the W face (IV), or stay on the crest of the ridge for two pitches and then take a ledge for 10m. Now climb steeply at first, keeping L of the walls of crumbling rock; the angle eases to the summit ridge, reached a few m E of the top.
7-8hr for the ridge

40g
PD

DESCENT BY THE SOUTH FACE

X de Grunne and J de Layre with F Engilberge, 3 Aug 1926

In normal snow conditions, this provides the quickest and safest route down.

From the central summit descend the ridge leading W for a little way to where a snow couloir drops to the E branch of the Ailefroide glacier. Turn off down the couloir, on the snow or down the R bank, to the lower part which is narrow and very steep. Here make a wide detour (III) round L (E) and back to the mouth of the couloir. Slant R across the glacier and continue down the ordinary route (Route 40a) to the Sélé hut and Ailefroide.

North Face

The face, below the crest joining the E and central summits, is bordered on its W side by the Coste Rouge ridge. It is c800m high and is characterised by a large hanging glacier. This stands above a steep rock wall and is itself dominated by the steep rocks of the summit ridge.

40h
TD+
37

PILIER DES SÉRACS

B Franco and J-M Cambon, 30 Aug 1981

A good, direct approach to the L edge of the hanging glacier below the sérac barrier. The rock is good; no equipment in place. The route follows the big convex pillar immediately below the E extremity of the hanging glacier. 460m to where it links with the Fourastier climb described below to give a total undertaking of 800m. Rock difficulties of V+ max.

Reach the foot of the face and look for the lowest point of the rock by the side of the couloir descending from the séracs on the R. Start a little to the R up a wall (V+) then follow a ramp climbing R for 10m and return L by a snowy ledge (IV+). Climb to below a big dièdre, reached by steep, rounded rock (V+). Climb by the bed of the dièdre (V: one move of V+) to a pile of loose, unstable blocks. From there either turn L by an unstable ledge (A1/V+), or make a loop R to a block strewn ledge and follow it L wards.

Climb L over smooth slabs to a little dièdre (V/V+) and exit by an overhang on the L (V+: no piton placements!). Get on to a small terrace at the foot of a large, R wards climbing ramp which is followed to its termination (IV+: sustained). Traverse a smooth slab R wards (V) to reach the crest of the pillar and follow it for 20m. Climb a smooth dièdre on the L (IV+/V). Reach a less steep and easier section by climbing a short wall slanting R (V). Continue for 100m on rocks which are often icy (III: one move of IV) and reach the hanging glacier and join the next climb. **6-8hr**

40i
TD-
37

NORTH FACE OF POINTE FOURASTIER - Y COULOIR

M Fourastier, H Le Breton and A Manhès, 1 Sept 1936
FWA: A Giraud and P Pâquet jnr, 5-6 Feb 1964

The climb takes the line of the obvious 'Y' couloir descending from the lowest point on the R bank of the huge hanging glacier. The route is long (800m) and is exposed to stonefall in the couloir.

From a bivouac high on the Glacier Noir, approach the couloir easily and directly from the Col de la Temple track. In a good year the couloir may be climbed from its base, taking the R branch of the 'Y' to join the L edge of the hanging glacier. If there is stonefall or poor conditions, gain rocks on the L of the couloir and climb these for 40m (III) to arrive at a band of ice. Climb this on the L to a chimney and climb this obliquely L passing an overhang in the middle (IV). Traverse obliquely R and reach the foot of a couloir which dominates the rimaye; climb this for 80m to reach a zone of slabs bordering the 'Y' couloir and climb these for about five rope-lengths to arrive beneath a 'head' of brown rock. Traverse the two branches of the 'Y' (rock islands) to gain the L bank of the R-hand branch, which is followed for 40m (stonefall and sérac danger). Move R and climb for 100m on poor rock at the top of which is a dièdre (IV: verglas) which leads to the base of the hanging glacier. 5-7hr

Climb the glacier slope directly (50°), keeping well L of the séracs, then, towards the top of the slope, slant up L to reach a ridge of mixed rock and snow which is followed to the final wall. Climb directly at first and then, by moving L for one long pitch over rock and ice, join and climb a 40m chimney slanting L (IV). By an icy couloir reach the brèche at the foot of the final step of the E ridge of the Pt Fourastier; from there either go R to climb 50m chimney (V) to the summit rocks or pass on to the S flank and, by a big crack and a letter-box, reach the summit. 3-5hr: **8-12hr** from the foot of face

To descend, traverse to the central summit easily and follow the S face descent (Route 40g).

East Summit

40j
PD
34
38

SOUTH RIDGE
L Nérot with E Pic and Giraud-Lézin, 25 Aug 1880

This is the ordinary route to this subsidiary summit. It is long and mainly on snow. The final snow ridge is superb but the descent may be

difficult to find in bad visibility. The route is much frequented, much more so than the ordinary route to the W summit and is preferred to an alternative route (also PD) which climbs a couloir on the L side of the E face, below the summit.

The key to this climb is the straight, shallow couloir leading to the top of a promontory. Each year several parties fail to find this couloir when descending the mountain, especially in misty conditions, so it is important that careful note is made of its location. The guardian of the Sélé hut will advise anyone who asks for details.

From the Sélé hut take the way-marked path towards the Aig de Sialouze and the Coup de Sabre glacier, passing the old Sélé hut (winter hut) which is clearly marked on the map. Follow a track above the old hut towards the rock wall N of it. The path makes a sharp turn L and then climbs towards the Coup de Sabre glacier. Cross a short rock barrier to reach an area of moraine and névé below the glacier. Traverse horizontally W over scree and névés towards the cliff forming the E flank of the S ridge. All of this is well marked when dry (cairns and paint marks).

In the middle of the cliff is a prominent couloir with névé slopes at its base. Just L of this, starting in a small recess, is a straight, shallow couloir (note: the main couloir is hidden from view from below so do not be tempted to take a lower line). Climb the R bank of the narrow couloir by easy rocks (cairns) to the top of a promontory. Narrow ledges and easy rock allow a traverse L, decending slightly below the buttresses of the S ridge to gain the other flank (cairns). Part way along the traverse L an alternative line takes a narrow, snow gully leading to a higher ledge which in turn leads to a snow bowl on the W side of the S ridge. Either way reach a cirque of scree or snow, according to the season, above Pt 3,228m (2hr). Climb the snow, dodging a rock barrier L wards, to continue on more snow to the W side of the upper part of the S ridge. Climb R wards to reach the snowy crest and follow it to the summit. **c5hr** from the hut

In descent follow the same route. In poor visibility the SW flank may be taken with easier route finding, but it is longer.

40k
F
34

SOUTH-WEST FLANK

Useful in descent in poor visibility.

From the Sélé hut follow the route (40a) towards the W summit
via the remarkable rake and continue up the easy ground until it
is possible to get on the Ailefroide glacier. Cross it Rwards (E).
Turn a rock rognon on the L (c3,580m) and join snow slopes on
the W flank of the upper part of the S ridge. Gain the snowy crest
of the ridge and follow it to the summit. **4½-5hr**

40l
ED1
39

NORTH FACE OF BRECHE DU GLACIER NOIRE
L Hardy and N Parks, 17 July 1988

37

*Immediately W of the Ailefroide E summit is the Brèche du Glacier
Noire. A shallow couloir snakes down the N face below this brèche
giving some very steep ice climbing reminiscent of routes on the Minus
face of Ben Nevis. Lew Hardy suggests that the route would be a
superb undertaking in winter or early summer but is unlikely, these
days, to be in condition in mid-season. The difficult middle section
remains in the shade all day and is protected from stonefall by a rock
wall to its L. Belays are not easy to arrange. c700m*

Climb the wide couloir below the col for 150m to where it forks.
Take the L fork (the Marmier-Rabet route, TD-, takes the R
fork: not described) and reach the 250m rock wall in the centre
of the face. Climb a vertical ice smear in two 50m pitches to a
shallow couloir. Four more pitches of gradually easing difficulty
lead to the upper slopes and the brèche. **11hr** from the rimaye

Descend by climbing to the E summit and then reverse Route
40j or 40k.

Pic du Coup de Sabre 3,699m

This fine little peak, sandwiched between the Ailefroide and the Pic Sans Nom, takes its name from the sensational brèche which separates it from the latter peak.

41a   **NORTH-WEST BUTTRESS**
D
39

M Fourastier and H Le Breton, 30 July 1936

This is a serious climb despite having few pitches of high technical difficulty. It is long, over 750m and has quite a long approach.
Bivouac at the Balmes de François Blanc or on the Glacier Noir. Sites are marked by long poles.

Start from Cézanne, up the Col de la Temple path to the upper plateau of the S branch of the Glacier Noir. Cross it to reach the foot of the buttress (Pt 2,902m: 4hr). Start straight up the buttress, via attractive pitches of IV, to where it narrows to a ridge. Move up the ridge to within 10m of the top of a pyramid-shaped gendarme and dodge round L (E) along a good ledge to the next brèche. The ridge now steepens. Climb it, slanting sometimes L, sometimes R, to a point 60m below a three-headed gendarme. Take to the rocks on the R (W) side and pass over the gendarme, avoiding the wide snow slope, to the snowy brèche beyond. Climb a steep snow slope, keeping near the rocks of the L edge, to half-height, then cross it and continue across rocks (piton) to a rib R (W) of the ridge. Climb the rib and up increasingly steeper pitches to an overhanging wall. Turn it on the R and continue up a series of walls to a little scree shoulder. 3½hr

Return somewhat L, up a 20m chimney with an overhang half-way, to the upper part of the ridge and follow it for a little way. Avoid a grey step by a delicate traverse L (E) into and up an icy couloir. Above there is a little brèche which marks the point where the ridge fades out into the upper wall c150m below the summit. Follow an icy ledge L (E) towards an overhang blocking entry to a short, snowy chimney. Climb the overhang by a detached flake on the L and slant R into the chimney. Climb it and then slant up R to make use of a short ledge leading back L. 15m higher follow an indefinite ledge on the R and climb a 20m vertical wall. Continue up steep rock for 30m to a little terrace. Climb a chimney, dodging an overhang in the middle by a slab on the R, then move back L a little along a ledge to another chimney which is short and has a chockstone. This leads to an overhang; climb it (piton). Climb a shallow chimney to the summit ridge and so to the top. This final wall is mostly pitches of IV with one pitch of V. 3hr: **6½hr** from the foot of the buttress: c11hr from Cézanne

41b
PD
34

DESCENT BY THE SOUTH FACE

A Holmes with J and H Rodier, 12 July 1892

The route is included for descent after the ascent of the N buttress. The ascent is hardly worth making except for an attractive view.

From the summit descend the ridge W to a point near a curious rock pinnacle. Turn L (S) and descend the upper wall by a couloir and little chimneys to the snow slope in the middle of this face. Descend the snow and move across R until it is possible to leave the S buttress Rwards on to the Coup de Sabre glacier. Cross the glacier, heading SSE from the lowest rocks of the S buttress, to its lowest point. A little lower is a short rock barrier. Descend this and follow a track down to the old and then new Sélé huts. **1½-2hr**

Le Coup de Sabre 3,448m

This is the central of the three fine cols between the Pelvoux and the Ailefroide. On its N side is an icy couloir, the line of a fine climb.

42a
D
40
38
39

NORTH-SOUTH TRAVERSE

A Reynier and C Verne with C and M Gaspard and J Turc, 17 July 1895

This route is best tackled early in a good snow year. It is steep, the top

reaching nearly 60°. It has been descended on ski and is not infrequently climbed solo.

Start from Cézanne up the Col de la Temple path to the upper plateau of the S branch of the Glacier Noir. There is a bivouac site above the Glacier Noir (marked by long poles). Cross it to the little tributary glacier which drops from the Coup de Sabre and climb this to the rimaye which is often difficult to cross(4hr). Climb the couloir, either near the L bank, or on the rocks of the L bank. In the wider, middle section slant L and then go straight up towards the rocks of the R bank in the upper section. Climb the upper section, either near the R bank, or in the middle of the couloir. The exact line will depend, of course, on the prevailing conditions. 2½-4hr: 6½-8hr from Cézanne

From the col, descend the much easier couloir on the S side using either the bed of the couloir, or its banks, to reach the E branch of the Coup de Sabre glacier. Slant down R, joining the route of descent from the Pic du Coup de Sabre (Route 41b). 1½hr: **c8-10hr** Cézanne to Sélé hut

Pic Sans Nom 3,914m

J-B Colgrove and R Pendlebury with G and S Spechtenhauser, 10 July 1877

Although somewhat dominated by its near neighbours, it is never-the-less a fine peak of some complexity. The W ridge, which rises steeply from the Coup de Sabre, forms a pronounced (W) shoulder, Pt 3,771m, beyond which is a brèche, Pt 3,728m. Further along the ridge is another shoulder (3,805m) and another brèche (3,773m: known as the Fenêtre de Sialouze). This brèche is the origin of the NW couloir. From the shoulder an important ridge runs S, eventually joining that of the Aig de Sialouze. The quality of the rock on the S flank of the mountain leaves much to be desired.

43a WEST RIDGE

TD
38
40

P Allain, J Charignon, J Leininger and J Vernet, 5 Sept 1934

This is one of the most attractive of the pre-war rock climbs in the Dauphiné, with a good many pitches of V and unusually good rock.

From the Sélé hut take the waymarked route past the old hut and then follow the path leading up to the Coup de Sabre Glacier. Reach to the lower edge of the glacier by crossing a short rock barrier and then climb the glacier, at first towards the base of the SSE ridge of the Pic du Coup de Sabre and then up the E branch to the bottom of the couloir originating at the col. Follow the couloir to the Coup de Sabre. 2½hr

From the Coup de Sabre, start up the first few easy rocks of the W ridge and then up a steep wall L (N) of the crest of the ridge. Continue up some interesting pitches, switching from one side of the ridge to the other, the last one being along a ledge on the N side. Next go up a wall and a wide crack to the ridge, cross it to a wide ledge and continue up to another ledge, which is horizontal, at the foot of the superb, 120m tower. The main difficulties of the climb are concentrated in the ascent of this tower to the W shoulder of the mountain.

The general line of ascent is that of the couloir which drops from the final rocks below the W shoulder. Climb 15m up the slabs on the L bank (V: 3 pitons: steep), then traverse L along a ledge and cross a slab (V) into the bed of the couloir above its initial overhang (or, 10m L of the couloir, climb a 12m crack: V: then slant 15m slightly L and traverse horizontally R back into the couloir). Now climb the couloir, moving L on to a platform situated 40m from the start of the couloir. Climb the bed of the couloir for another 40m (IV) past a few overhangs where the side walls are close together and provided with holds; exit on to the ridge at the foot of the last step below the W shoulder and at the top of the couloir. This final step is the top of the continuous wall R of the couloir. Slant slightly up R across this wall, following a ledge which is always narrow and sometimes little more than a few spaced holds (25m:V: piton). The ridge is reached a little W of the top of the W shoulder; turn it across the S face. Continue up the ridge staying a few m R of the crest to a preliminary brèche. Climb a short step by the wall on the L (N), go along a short horizontal section and turn the last gendarme by easy ledges and rotten rocks on the R (S); this leads to the brèche (Fenêtre de Sialouze). Continue easily along the final ridge to the top. **8-12hr** from the Sélé hut

Descend by Route 43h

43b **NORTH-WEST COULOIR**

AD
P Dalloz, J Lagarde, H de Ségogne and G and J Vernet,
11 July 1925
FWA: J-P Fédèle, P Gras and A Ioan, 31 Dec 1968-1 Jan 1969

This is a fine snow or ice couloir which descends from the Fenêtre de Sialouze, the difficulty of which depends a good deal on conditions. There is some stonefall danger, particularly on the L bank of the couloir.

Start from a bivouac or Cézanne up the Col de la Temple path to the upper plateau of the S branch of the Glacier Noir. Cross it to the little tributary glacier E of Pt 2,903m and below the Coup de Sabre (4hr from Cézanne). Climb this for some way to a point c50m below the lower rimaye, which is an extension of the Coup de Sabre rimaye. Go up to the little, well-defined brèche on the NNW ridge of the Pic Sans Nom (the R bank of the little tributary glacier). Climb up the ridge staying more or less on the R, thus dodging the first rimaye. Now climb the snow slope, keeping close to the rocks, to cross the upper rimaye at the extreme L (E). Slant up R across the rocks above the rimaye into the couloir itself. This is c350m high, with an average angle of 54°. Climb its R bank, taking to the rocks where necessary. It ends on the W ridge at the Fenêtre de Sialouze (one pitch of IV: piton). It is not possible to descend from here, the ridge to the summit must be followed. This is easily done. 4-6hr: **8-10hr** from Cezanne

North Face

The face is almost 1,000m high and is mostly rock. The only significant amount of snow is a névé slope situated below the headwall of the E shoulder (Pt 3,829m). The face is split into two parts by a long, central couloir which is always subjected to stonefall. This is bordered on the E side by a steep, slabby pillar (Pilier Chapoutot) which ends at the névé slope. On the W side of the central couloir is a broad dièdre capped by a short, vertical step. Above this is a more gently sloping area of slabs leading to the summit headwall.

43c
ED2

ORIGINAL ROUTE

L George and V Russenberger, 22-23 Aug 1950
FWA: L Audoubert, M Galy, T Leroy and J-J Ricouard, 12-15 Jan 1976

The route follows the rocks forming the L bank of the central couloir, generally following the line of the dièdre mentioned above. It skirts round the vertical step before following the less steeply sloping slabs which slope up from L to R. These are lost higher up the face in scree. In the lower part the route is rock, becoming mixed higher up. It is very serious, very sustained, steep and exposed. In the more difficult lower part, the climbing is very good and never strenuous; protection is difficult to arrange, even pitons, but it is always possible to find decent stances. The rock is excellent (except in a few areas). In the higher part of mixed ground, the rock is good in the difficult sections. Route finding needs care. Rockfalls are a big problem, so the best conditions are when the lower part is very dry and the higher part is verglas or snowy. At the end of a summer's day the sun does not reach the higher sections. Therefore after mid-Aug is considered the 'prime time'.

From Cézanne or a bivouac follow the route to the Col de la Temple as far as the upper plateau of the Glacier Noir. Cross the glacier to reach the base of the face and start 30m R of the big couloir (3-3½hr from Cézanne). Climb up over black, damp slabs cut by ledges covered in gravel, then go obliquely R, towards a block c12m high in the form of a letter box. Avoid it on the R. Enter an area of cracked slabs (IV) that are climbed for three rope-lengths, gradually moving L and crossing an overhang (IV+). A system of poorly defined ledges permits a traverse R (III and IV) in order to reach a secondary ridge that borders the L flank of a large wide dièdre. Now find a very characteristic area of much weathered, black and yellow rock of brittle appearance. Climb up the best line, several m R of the crest of the ridge, for several rope lengths on excellent rock (IV: numerous moves of V). After traversing a wide, snow-covered ledge, go up a couloir of blocks and then come up to a 40m dièdre cut by overhangs. Climb it by the L face, keeping a few m from its bed (V and V+) or, more easily, climb up it for 10m then traverse R for 10m (IV+) and return L to its top. Go up a ramp (V) to reach a scree covered terrace at the foot of a yellow, vertical, c30m high step. 5-7hr

This step is the key to the route. Start it by a dièdre (10m: IV+) on its R (W), then traverse L for c8m (V+/VI, 6a) and climb up several m (V+) to reach a monolithic, sloping, snow-covered ledge. Continue Lwards (IV), then climb a chimney of large blocks. On the L are seen immense, steep, damp, black slabs that make up the higher part of the large couloir. Climb the ridge that borders them on their R (W) side as far as the foot of a small step that overhangs (the bivouac of the first ascent). A horizontal crack of rotten rock (IV: very delicate and exposed) permits a Rwards traverse of 30-40m. Then, on the better rock available, reach slabs on the L which are seamed with cracks (IV and V). Continue for one or two rope lengths directly; this is easy. Traverse easily R along a whole fringe of black, 5m high overhangs to reach a vertical line of snow. Cross it and then go up further on grey, verglas-coated slabs with rounded holds (V: delicate) to reach the first snowy bank of the higher section of the face. 5-7hr

Follow a long ledge obliquely L; it is snowy in parts and easy. Reach the foot of a gorge on the other side from a vague spur that is the highest extension of the large medial step. Go up this gorge and continue over broken rock for several rope lengths (IV: then easier). A steep step is climbed obliquely for one rope length in a Rwards direction (V and V+). Continue moving R on easy ground. A last step, climbed in a L-slanting fashion, leads to the summit rocks. These are climbed without difficulty. 4hr: **14-18hr** from the foot of the face

43d
ED2
40
39

RAIE DES FESSES

J-M Boivin, F Diaferia and G Vionnet-Fuasset, 6-8 May 1976
FWA: B Douillet and P Sombardier, 26-27 Feb 1980

This climb is the bench mark of high altitude winter/ice climbing (V/5). It follows the obvious central couloir, a cleavage between two zones of slabs (the fesses or buttocks). Protection is not always easy to find and a large selection of rock/ice gear is essential. A long period of cold weather (winter and spring) renders the climb safe (in relative terms). Parties usually descend from the top of the N pillar by taking the line of fixed rappels down Aurore Nucléaire (Route 43g). 55m ropes are recommended. There have been several recent ascents (1999/2000) and more equipment is apparent. However, an assortment of pitons should be carried to re-equip belays since stonefall in the summer months can strip existing gear. 550m

Reach the foot of the couloir and either take a hard, direct line to enter the couloir (30m: 85°) or climb 30m R and up two verglassed rock pitches back towards the couloir (IV then IV+).
    Climb for 5 rope lengths (50°) to the foot of a narrowing of the couloir which is the second part of the route. Three sustained rope lengths (70-80°), passing steep walls, lead to the foot of the final wall - the crux. This is complicated by a 'plug' or build up of snow which may need some artificial aid to overcome (one pitch: 85° or more). Continue for 3 pitches (65° then 50°) by a much more friendly angled section which finishes at the top of the N pillar. Allow **10hrs** for the couloir itself

43e   **PILIER CHAPOUTOT**

TD

40

P Chapoutot, J-L Mercadié and J-J Rolland, 12-13 Aug 1970

A great route on excellent rock using traditional equipment and with good belays. Take a standard rack and a few pitons. The climb has lost its popularity to the two more recent climbs on the flank but it would be a crime to omit it. It is not sustained and follows a line L of Raie des Fesses (Route 43d).

Start c30m L of Route 43d. Cross the rimaye and climb a 10m wall (IV) to a large terrace (snow possible). Move L up the terrace to below a small, snow covered terrace c15 higher. On the R, climb a wall of grey slabs to a niche (III) then slant R for 65-70m (III then IV: 1 move V) to the foot of a dièdre. Climb this (IV) and exit L, or pass further L then come back R above the dièdre (III then IV). Reach and climb a balcony (snow/loose rock) bordering the couloir on the R flank.

From here there are three possibilities: Climb a big smooth wall directly by an encased dièdre, a little roof and a crack (V+). This is the original line. An alternative: R of the above, climb a chimney crack (V to VI, 6a), the Agresti variation. Another alternative: 25m R, climb a dièdre/crack then return L (V-/IV+: stonefall possible), the Feulliet variation.

By any of these means attain a second snowy terrace. Climb slabs towards the L, then R to the foot of a smooth step. Climb L up a long, steep ramp for 4 rope lengths (III and IV: airy). Leave this where a small ledge breaks off R and reach an exposed balcony at the foot of a compact wall. Climb this on its R edge (V+), then climb a big slab to an excellent ledge (IV+/V). Follow the ledge Rwards and climb a compact wall of 15m (V) to another good ledge (the dièdre on the L may also be climbed). A little to the R climb a rib (25m: IV) to a narrow ledge leading off R. Traverse R for 70m to turn the edge of the pillar (III then V: exposed). Climb a dièdre against the crest of the pillar on the flank of the couloir and then a line of cracks and slabs for 100m (IV: one move of V: then V+: sustained). Continue by less steep slabs to the foot of a Lward slanting dièdre and reach the top of the pillar with ease in 5 rope lengths (III). 5-7hr

From the top of the pillar, climb along an easy ridge of mixed ground towards the E shoulder as far as the N spur. Reach this L of the triangular tower which dominates the top of the pillar. To gain the spur, climb a couloir with a few delicate moves at the top. From the brèche beneath the final step of the N spur, make 4 slanting rappels to the Couloir du Pelvoux (W branch) and reach the col itself. From there return via the Sialouze glacier and Route 46a to the Pelvoux hut. c5hr: **10-12hr** from the foot of the face

A rapel descent of Route 43g can be made from the top of the pillar.

43f   **MAGIC STONES**

TD+   C Ferrera and J-M Rey, July 1983

40

A modern classic. The climbing is not strenuous, the rock is good and the equipment is traditional but adequate (none the less, a small standard rack is not out of place - winter weather can affect in situ pitons…). 500m to the level of descent by rappel: 6a max.

Start as for Route 43e to the large terrace and then reach a small terrace some 15m higher. Aurore Nucléaire covers the same ground a little further L. This route takes the R-hand line, runs parallel to its neighbour and crosses the original (Chapoutot) climb a couple of times before reaching the top of the N pillar.

P1 4: P2 easy: P3 6a and 5: P4 6a and 5+: P5 5+ and 4: P6 6a: P7 5+: P8 5+: P9 traverses R - meets and crosses the Chapoutot line 5+: P10 5+: P11 5: P12 5+ second crossing of Chapoutot line: P13 5: P14 5+ dièdre: P15 6a: Finish beneath an overhang on the R. Reach the crest of the pillar (easily) by the ridge. **7-8hrs** climbing

Follow Route 43e to the Pelvoux hut, or rappel route 43g.

43g   AURORE NUCLEAIRE

ED2

40

J-M Cambon and G Fiaschi, Aug 1986 in 3 days

Entirely equipped with bolts, including the descent. The rock is good and the climbing sustained. Difficulties up to 6a/b. The first section climbs on slabs, the second follows a pillar. Although it is equipped, take a few nuts. Both climbs here may be continued L wards to the Col du Pelvoux over snow and mixed ground as for Route 43e.

Start just L (E) of the previous climb.

P1 4: P2 6a/b then 5+: P3 5+: P4 V+ then IV: P5 6b then 6a: P6 5 then 6b: P7 6a: P8 5+ then 6a: P9 5+ then 6a: P10 6a: P11 6a/b: P12 5: P13 5 then 5+: P14 3. **5-8hr** climbing

Descend by 15 rappels of 45m back down the climb.

43h   DESCENT BY THE SOUTH-EAST FACE

PD

38

J Colgrove and R Pendlebury with G and J Spechtenhauser, 10 July 1877

This is the ordinary route, but it is so messy and the rocks so unreliable that it is recommended only as a means of descent. The correct route is easy to lose.

From the summit descend c100m down the snowy couloir dropping from the immediate neighbourhood of the summit (or use its L bank). Now slant down L across a succession of couloirs and ribs, in a diagonal line towards the Cols du Pelvoux. Continue in this line until quite close to the cols and 50-60m above the glacier, at which point a buttress provides a line down past the overhangs which cut off most of the face from the glacier. Descend the buttress (unpleasant rock), using its R-hand side in places, to the glacier. Walk down the Sialouze glacier towards Pt 3,229m then follow Route 46a in reverse to the Pelvoux hut. **c3hr**

Aiguille de Sialouze 3,576m

The S ridge of the Pic Sans Nom drops to a brèche at 3,578m (upper Brèche de Sialouze). Its extension S takes the form of a multi-gendarmed ridge. One of the pinnacles, although not the highest, is the Aig de Sialouze. The ridge terminates at its S end at the Brèche du Sialouze. Immediately W of the brèche is the magnificent rock wall forming the SW face. Between the two brèches, on the E flank of the ridge, is another steep rock wall. Both walls present much scope for rock gymnasts.

44a   **SOUTH RIDGE TRAVERSE**

D   To the Aig de Sialouze: J Charignon and P Salmon, 3 Sept 1934

41

42   Complete traverse: M and Mme J Franco, K Gurekian,

38   H Joubard and R Laveyssière with E Frendo, 22 Aug 1942

This excellent route gives delightful climbing on firm, rough rock. It is no longer usual to continue to the Pic Sans Nom due to the scrappy nature of the climbing and the poor descent. However, the continuation is described to provide for the total traverse (AD on the Pic Sans Nom).

Start from the Pelvoux hut by following Route 46a to Pt 3,229m on the edge of the Sialouze glacier. Cross the glacier W wards to the Brèche de Sialouze. 2hr

Climb straight up from the brèche, steeply at first, then up gentle slabs, reaching the S ridge beyond an unstable looking gendarme. Continue up the steep but easy rocks L of the ridge for c40m to the first pinnacle. Dodge round R of this to the next brèche. Climb up steeply to the foot of the second pinnacle and turn it on the R along an exposed ledge (it can be climbed direct). Cross over the third pinnacle by a delightful slab pitch and reach the foot of a big slab. Climb straight up the slab for c15m to just below a piton (IV) and traverse R (IV+) up and across a sloping slab to the top of the step. It is also possible and rather easier but less attractive, to traverse, descending slightly, round L of the slab where a couloir can be climbed to the top of the step. Ahead is a steep wall, c5m high. Climb it by a dièdre (IV), move R along a ledge and climb another steep wall (IV) on to a slanting ledge. Continue along and up this to the foot of the final slabs below the summit. The direct ascent of these provides some more delightful slab pitches (IV), or they can be avoided on the L. 2-3hr

Between the summit and the upper Brèche de Sialouze there are five gendarmes. Descend N to the brèche before the first of these (20m rappel is useful but not essential; if climbing down, start the steep section on the L). Climb the gendarme by the obvious, overhanging chimney which is easier than it looks (IV: the avoiding traverse round R is V+). Either climb the second gendarme direct, or turn it on its R side at half-height (both IV). Climb the third gendarme up a sort of cleft on the L and continue on to the fourth gendarme. Turn this along a scree ledge on the L (W) and do the same with the last, the most distinctive and largest gendarme, to reach the upper brèche. 2hr

There are two possible descents back on to the Sialouze glacier. Early in the season, or when the slabs are snow covered, take the following line from between the fourth and the final gendarme: Descend the couloir (E) for 20m and slant R round to the other side of a buttress where there is a piton. Now make five rappels (the third is obliquely L for c20m, the longest c25m) to the glacier. There is some danger from stonefall from other parties in the couloir.

Later in the season it is usually possible to traverse to the upper brèche as described above. By making a U turn (E), get on to and descend the angled slab beneath the large gendarme. When dry this is relatively safe and easy, a single rappel (40-45m) being sufficient to reach the Sialouze glacier from the lower edge of the slab. It is also possible to make a series of rappel of no more than 30m each from the brèche itself. There is some danger from stonefall from parties above. Return to the hut via the approach route. 1½hr: allow **8-9hr** in all

If continuing from the upper brèche to the Pic Sans Nom; climb up the broken, messy rocks above the brèche to the big overhangs. Just underneath them is a ledge. Follow it R and, where it ceases, climb a little, grey dièdre (IV) which gives access to a big couloir dropping from a brèche on the R (NE) of the SW shoulder. Climb up the R bank of the couloir to the brèche and turn R over easy but rather loose rocks for some way to the summit. 1½hr: **7½-8½hr** from the Pelvoux hut

Descend Route 43h

South-West Face

This is a high (c400m), roughly triangular face which has many steep, smooth and sometimes overlapping granite slabs. It provides scope for both traditional and modern rock climbs in a splendid environment. The top of the face is below the S ridge but this can be easily reached. An ice axe and crampons may be needed for the approach and descent.

44b **VOIE LIVANOS**
TD+ R Lepage, G Livanos and M Vaucher, 13-14 July 1959
42

A very good, sustained climb of c350m, although the first 100m are relatively easy. The rock is excellent. The route lies R of the summit fall-line and then joins the central face and climbs direct to the summit. Stances are sometimes very scarce but the climbing is always safe. Carry a rack of Friends, nuts and pitons as the equipment is traditional - no bolts, although at least one bolt equipped stance is shared! For the cleanest ethic, avoid adjacent climbs and gear.

From the Sélé hut follow Route 43a to the top of the short rock barrier. Now climb the Coup de Sabre glacier NNE in the direction of the Brèche de Sialouze in order to reach the foot of the face (2hr). This is cut on the R by a couloir which descends from the S ridge and is interrupted by a terrace 80m above the glacier. Two parallel couloir-chimneys descend from the terrace.

Start between the two couloir-chimneys and then join the L one that leads to the steeply sloping terrace (IV: one pitch of V). Make a circling move Lwards in order to enter a couloir (V+: exposed), climb it for one pitch and then traverse L across easy slabs, to get into the centre of the face. Above, climb for 2 short rope lengths, up slabs which are obvious, in a gentle L to R angle (V/V+: exposed). Arrive at a second set of slabs dominated by overhangs. Climb up under the overhangs and traverse L (IV and V), slowly descending (delicate) in order to go round an angle. This leads to the foot of a wide wall that overhangs and obstructs the face.

Climb the wall at the place where it overhangs least (A1, 5 pitons and VI, 6a). Climb the crack that follows and exit by moving L (V+: sustained). Climb straight up for 10m (A1 and V) and then go up a crack on the L (V/V+). Continue in the chimney that follows (V/V+). Climb another chimney that leads to a terrace below a slab (IV). Gain the R side of this slab (IV) and climb it (V+: old wood wedges in place on the L should be avoided). A few m R, a short couloir leads to a platform at the top of a gendarme in view of the S ridge. This marks the end of the difficult section.

Climb directly upwards above the platform in order to join a ridge (40m: IV). Next reach an easy section marking the top of the face and which leads to the foot of the last step on the S ridge. By the S-N traverse line described above, reach the summit. **5-7hr** climbing

Descent: All the routes described may follow the same descent, which is by 9 rappels. Ignore any advice that 45m ropes will suffice - they will not! The pitch over the overhangs requires enough spare rope to be able to swing into the wall to reach the chain and security. Thus 50m ropes are strongly urged, as is a back up device.

The first rappel point is to be found by a cairn on a rounded hump of rock at the highest point of the face, some 70m below the actual summit.

The descent described for the traverse (Route 44a) is also possible and may prove preferable if it is unnecessary to return to the base of the climb and there is a lot of traffic causing hold-ups.

44c VENTRE A TERRE

TD+

42

J-J Bonniot and J-M and C Cambon, 1985

Sustained at 5/5+ with some 6a pitches, this climb offers a good insight into the style of climbing on the Sialouze. Equipment is mainly bolts but some old pitons justify attention.

Start in the bay L of the Livanos and climb the slabs some 20m L of a snowy corner towards the first terraces. After crossing the Livanos the route above these terraces bears Rwards, aiming to pass the large barrier of roofs higher up by their R side. This section constitutes the crux. After passing the roofs, the climb returns L towards the summit.

P1 5+: P2 5+: P3 5+: P4 6a: P5 5+: P6 6a: P7 6a: P8 6a: P9 5+: P10 5 (junction with Diagonale du Fou, not described here and crossing of the Livanos): P11 5: P12 5. **5-7hr** climbing

44d ATTAQUE A MAIN ARMEE

ED2

42

S Revel and J-M Cambon, Aug 1985

A good climb, mainly on slabs. It is jusifiably popular. All equipment is in place. 6c max (6a/b obl)

Start just L of the Gurékian route (44f) and take the centre of the first slab before cutting through the overhangs.

P1 short pitch: P2 5+: P3 5 (crosses the Gurékian): P4 6a: P5 5+: P6 6c: P7 6c: P8 5+: P9 6b: P10 5+: P11 5: P12 6a: P13 5+: P14 6a: P15 4. **5-8hr**

44e SUPER PILOU

TD-

42

J-J Bonniot and J-M and C Cambon, Aug 1984

Probably the most climbed route of the crag. There are slabs for the first half and cracks for the upper section. Most of the equipment is in place

but a small selection of wedges and friends may prove useful on the upper pitches. Max 5+

Climb the extreme L side of the wall L of the Gurékian route (Route 44f) to reach the L end of the line of inclined slabs and ramp leading to the WSW ridge. Reach the second ramp and cross the Gurékian route. Continue R of the ridge.

P1 5+: P2 5+: P3 4: P5 5: P6 4 (common with the Gurékian) then 5+: P7 4: P8 terrace: P9 5+: P10 5: P11 4+: P12 4. **4-6hr**

44f
D+
42
38

WEST-SOUTH-WEST SPUR

M and Mme K Gurékian and J Vernet, 7 July 1948

This climb is on the W flank of the SW face. It is not equipped, thereby offering an excellent climb on good granite which contrasts with the modern and harder routes on the SW face. It is less frequented. The hardest moves are V+.

Start from the small inlet of snow L of the direct line from the summit, characterised by a ramp above inclined slabs. Climb up to and follow this ramp, the upper of two such ramps, which traverses under a line of overhangs from R to L, crossing a rib (IV), to reach a zone of inclined slabs. Slant up L to reach the vertical wall on the R-hand side of the ridge (IV: moves of V).

Climb straight up the wall for 10m (V+: piton) then another 12m gradually R (IV+). Above is another set of inclined slabs which are followed Lwards beneath a line of overhangs to reach a platform in a corner of the ridge (III). Leave the SW face and climb the ridge (IV+) and then traverse L towards the couloir which descends from the summit. Climb the couloir (4m: steep and exposed IV, then another 12m: easy) to a shoulder where the climbing eases. Reach a large, gravelly shoulder above the overhanging head of the spur. Turn a step by slabs on the L. Climb stone covered slopes and easy rock then a snowy couloir on the R, below the gendarmes of the N ridge. A chimney on the R (IV+) gives access to the ridge between the first and second gendarmes. Reach the top of the first gendarme by the R flank and make a rappel into the brèche which follows and climb directly to the summit (IV). **4-5hr** climbing: 6-7hr from the Sélé hut

East Face

44g **ORIGINAL ROUTE**
TD+ J-M Guibert and R Prangé, 7 July 1955
41

A good climb, mostly on good rock (see below, Route 44h) with the difficulties arriving in the upper section. Carry a full rack - there is little equipment in place.

Approach as for Route 44a. Start below a block and just R of a chimney which lies directly below the summit of the Sialouze. Slant up diagonally L to the chimney (V) and then climb the overhanging chimney itself (V+), which is best taken on the outside in places, then exit L. Climb slabs alongside a flake for 20m (III/IV) to rejoin the chimney where it emerges on to R ward slanting ledges. Follow these ledges for 30m and then follow a long dièdre which butts up against the summit block. Climb slabs, first L then return R (IV+). Climb a flake on the L (V) then move L to reach the dièdre (V). Climb the entire length of this, passing an overhang (V then V+: poorish rock). It ends on an easy ramp climbing L to a platform below the summit step, formed by steep slabs seamed by cracks.

Layback up a first crack (V), traverse R for 3m (V) and climb a line of cracks for two rope lengths (V+; sustained). After a little loop to climb a short wall, move back L to reach the summit. **c6hr** climbing

There is a choice of descent. See Route 44a.

44h **WAKANTANKA**
ED3/4 B Coignard, J-M Derobert, J Perrier (Pschit) and F Roux, 1990
41

A modern climb with a history of attempts by several well known 'Stars', all of whom failed until Perrier 'carved' the missing links.

Certainly the hardest of the Sialouse climbs (7b: 6a/b obl). Equipment is complete in the upper section. The rock requires some caution, it tends to be friable in places but in general it is good. Carry a range of smaller friends and at least 14 quick draws.

Approach as for Route 44a. The start is by a vague spur just L of the chimney of the original route and directly below the summit.

Start by smooth slabs (5) and then: P2 6b then 5+: P3 6a: P4 6b: P5 7a then 7b (cut holds): P6 6c then 6a: P7 5+ then 6a+. **c6hr** climbing

Descent can be effected via the climb and gear is in place for this. To reach the first anchor point, turn the summit block and find the chain 3m below, close to a little groove.

Col Est du Pelvoux 3,609m

The Col du Pelvoux (Cols du Pelvoux on the IGN map) is situated between the Pic Sans Nom and the Pointe Puiseux of the Mont Pelvoux. There are two brèches (E and W), both easily accessible from the S. On the N side they stand at the top of a most impressive, glaciated couloir which is split in the upper part by the rocks of a gendarme (Aig du Pelvoux).

45a
D

44
39
40

NORTH FLANK

J-P Engilberge, E Estienne and H Mettrier, 23 July 1909
FWA: R Lecerf and M Parmentier, 30-31 Dec 1973

A magnificent route and one of the classic ice climbs of the range with 700m of climbing. The difficulty depends on the state of the sérac barrier in the lower 300m of the couloir and of the rimaye in mid-face which can sometimes be a vertical wall of some 50m. The climb is best done from a bivouac on the Glacier Noir opposite the couloir. There are good sites in the vicinity of a line of long, thin poles 100m above the glacier on the true L bank. The grade applies only in good conditions. The route can be continued to the summit of the Pelvoux via the Mettrier Couloir (Route 46c).

Reach the base of the couloir from the bivouac in c1hr. Thread a way through the sérac area, generally on the L side (R bank) of the couloir for c300m (danger from icefall and more difficult in dry conditions). Above, climb the uniform slope to below the Aig du Pelvoux where there can often be a difficult ice barrier. Now take the L (E) branch of the couloir and climb the ice slopes bordering the rocky rib on the L. Finally traverse R and reach the col in 4 or 5 pitches. This upper section is 50°-55°. **4hr** would be a good time

Descent: Go down the Sialouze glacier and join up with Route 44a near the foot of the Coolidge couloir. Reverse that route to the Pelvoux hut. 1½-2hr

Mont Pelvoux 3,943m

To Pt Durand and, probably, some time later to Pt Puiseux: A-A Durand with J-E Matheoud and A Liotard, 30 July 1828

Bigger and even more complex than the Ailefroide, it has two principal summits; Pt Puiseux which is the true summit and Pt Durand which is 11m lower. These stand just a few m above the head of the Pelvoux glacier which forms a sort of high combe which is bordered on its S side by two further, distinct high points; Trois Dents du Pelvoux 3,683m and Petit Pelvoux 3,753m. Around its flanks the mountain is scored by glaciers and couloirs. The rock forming the intervening ridges is, unfortunately, not very good.

46a
PD

SOUTH FACE
First ascent party

The two variations described are the easiest routes up this important peak; they also offer easy routes of descent. For descent the Coolidge couloir is the best, except in the heat of the afternoon when the Rochers Rouges is safer. Either route can be combined with the descent by the Violettes glacier to make the classic traverse of the mountain. In recent times the Rochers Rouges alternative has become significant once more as a route of ascent due to difficult conditions in the exit funnel of the Coolidge couloir - very loose rock aggravated by diminishing snow cover to bind it all together. In consequence, the line shows signs of traffic.

Start up the path behind the Pelvoux hut, first up some steep rocks and then up a hog's back of scree to reach the L bank of the Clot de l'Homme glacier. Go W across the lower part of the glacier and up scree and snow slopes to alongside Pt 3,229m, which is on the edge of the Sialouze glacier (1½hr). The two routes now diverge:

To climb the Rochers Rouges, return R (NE) along a slanting traverse over scree, easy rock and snow to the foot of the Rochers Rouges. Climb these slanting slightly R to the ridge defining them on the E and continue up to the Pelvoux glacier (2hr). From here it is short and easy to reach either the highest summit (Pointe Puiseux) on the L, or the Pointe Durand on the R. 30min: **c4hr** from the Pelvoux hut

To climb the Coolidge couloir (35°-40°), the normal route in good conditions, go on to the Sialouze glacier and up its L bank to the foot of the large snow couloir which runs the whole height of the SW face. Climb this couloir (possibly using the rocks of the R bank in the upper section) to the Pelvoux glacier where the routes rejoin. Reach either of the two summits easily from here. **c4hr** from the Pelvoux hut: 1½-2hr in descent

46b
PD
43

DESCENT BY THE VIOLETTES GLACIER

C Passavant with A Burgener and P-A Raymond, 25 June 1882

This is the 'other half' of the classic Pelvoux traverse. A relatively quick, knee-wrecking, direct descent, recommended as providing variety after an ascent of the S face. Parties undertaking this descent should be aware that it is quite a serious undertaking, being quite long and complex. It is only suitable for experienced alpinists.

Descend from either of the summits to the Pelvoux glacier and strike off down the middle of the Violettes glacier, turning L under the first séracs. Continue down the L bank of the glacier. If this is very crevassed, try the rocks on the E side of the Violettes ridge. Descend on to the buttress which splits the glacier into two branches and go down its crest to the start of a high, steep couloir on the R where there is a steep little notch (parties tend to collect here: cairns). Descend the couloir (down climb or rappel) on to the S branch of the glacier then cross it horizontally (beware of séracs) to a shoulder at the foot of the NE ridge of the Trois Dents du Pelvoux. On the other side of the ridge, descend a little couloir (III and IV: or make a 30m rappel) to a snow/ice slope. Descend the R branch to rocks and continue down them L wards via a couloir to reach the névé Pélissier, often a dry glacier). Go E down the L (N) part of this glacier and on down moraines etc on the R bank of the Riéou des Planes gorge. This gorge joins another on the L (N); descend to an attractive hanging meadow on the L bank of this, where a path leads off R (SE). This leads across cliffs, following a kind of downward and R ward slanting ramp (Vire d'Ailefroide). Descend the scree (or snow) cone to reach the R bank of the Saint-Pierre stream (look for the well worn path) and so to Ailefroide. 3-5hr: Allow **8-10hr** from the Pelvoux hut

46c
AD
38

METTRIER COULOIR

J-P Engilberge, E Estienne and H Metrier, 13 July 1907

This is a fine, narrow couloir which provides an interesting variation to the normal route of ascent. It sees little sun and has negligible objective danger in snowy conditions, thus making it an excellent choice for a training climb or an introduction to high altitude alpinism. It is in best condition early in the season - by mid-July the middle 'narrows' are often bare rock.

From the Pelvoux hut follow Route 46a to below the Coolidge couloir then continue up L wards on the Sialouze glacier towards the Cols du Pelvoux. 100m before reaching the cols, an obvious, narrow couloir rises diagonally on the R. The main difficulties lie in the middle section of the couloir (1-2 pitches of III if it is rock). At the top, either climb direct over a slab bordered by a steep wall on the L, thus forming a dièdre/chimney, or traverse R and zigzag up loose, rocky steps and ledges (ll and lll) to arrive on the plateau 10-15min from the summit. It is possible to use rock belays all the way. 1½-2hr: **c5hr** in all

Descent: Either by reversing Route 46a, or continue the classic traverse to Ailefroide via the Violettes glacier (Route 46b).

46d   **NORTH RIDGE**

TD

44

39

M Fourastier and A Manhès, 22-23 Aug 1936

This, one of the three great ridge of the Pelvoux, drops from the Pointe Puiseux. It has a total height of almost 1,100m of which the first 350m are easy. It is a classic route despite the imperfect rock.

Start either from Cézanne, or from the bivouac sites of the Glacier Noir. Cross the glacier and move L, below the Cols du Pelvoux couloir, to the N ridge (2½hr from Cézanne). Start by climbing up between the two spurs which form the base of the ridge and then along the hanging snow slopes which border it to the E. When the ridge steepens, slant up L on easy terraces to the foot of a big yellow step. Climb this on the R (W), either direct, or slanting up R (IV) to a collection of couloirs leading back to the ridge. Go up the ridge, then take ledges ascending among detached blocks on the W face. Climb a steep slab (IV) back on to the ridge which is reached at the foot of a little gendarme. Turn this on the E to the next brèche from where a steep, shallow dièdre on the W side leads back on to the ridge (IV). It is also possible to take a ledge across the W face, returning to the ridge up a steep couloir. Now continue up the less steep, but unstable rocks (verglas) mostly keeping on the W side, to a brèche on the W ridge. Follow the easy summit ridge to the top. 6-8hr: **8½-10½hr** from Cézanne

46e NORTH FACE - CENTRAL ICE SLOPE

TD
44
39

P Courtet, H Laurent and P Souriac, 15-16 May 1953
FWA: J Maire, J-C Normand and M Parmentier,
28-29 Dec 1974

*This is a long and serious route with 1,500m of climbing due to the
length of the traverse in the middle section. The rock requires some
caution and the top section is rarely in good condition. The route is
best attempted from a bivouac on the Glacier Noir.*

From the bivouac, go up the glacier to the base of the couloir
issuing from the Cols du Pelvoux and then traverse L to gain the
lower glacier below the N face. Climb the L side to reach an
amphitheatre below a massive rock barrier. Now make the long
rising traverse Lwards to the upper L corner of the amphitheatre
where there is a small chimney. Climb this on loosish rock
(2 pitches of IV), then climb up easy, mixed ground before
making a long Rwards traverse across the many ice runnels and
ribs descending from the Pt Durand. This leads to the base of the
central ice slope (some danger from stones or ice particles in the
runnels). Climb the L side of the ice slope (60° with sections of
65°: rock belays are possible on small islets) to reach the col
between the two summits. **7-9hr** is a fast time

Descent is either by reversing Route 46a or by the Violettes
glacier (Route 46b).

46f VIOLETTES RIDGE

D
43

J Charignon, J-A Morin and G and J Vernet, 10-12 Aug 1935

*This is another of the three great ridges of the Pelvoux. It descends
NNE from Pointe Durand and bifurcates a little N of Pt 3,735m, one
spur descending NW, the other, the Violettes ridge, descending NE.
Both branches provide long, serious routes of considerable character.
The snag is the rock which is decidedly poor. The Violettes ridge is
preferred to the Momie ridge as having rather greater technical
interest.*

Start from Cézanne up the most easterly couloir dropping from
the Momie glacier, situated L of the L-hand (E) outflow of the

glacier. Climb the large scree cone to where the couloir narrows. Slant up L over grey slabs to a vegetated ledge beneath black cliffs; follow this ledge L, down slightly round a corner, on to some grassy slopes. Go up these slopes, still slightly L, as far as a rise from which the lower part of the Violettes glacier can be seen. Now go up R and along a narrow, grassy ledge slanting up R across more cliffs (not the wider slabby ledge below). Climb a scree couloir to a brèche on the R of a prominent shoulder above the small combe N of the Violettes glacier.

Move up R over slabs and grass and up a little chimney to a ridge. Go along over some boulders and up a step in the ridge by means of a 10m crack. Now climb up the N (Cézanne) side of the ridge, keeping on this side past the first series of gendarmes. Continue up easy slabs to the top of another prominent shoulder where the ridge becomes horizontal. Descend the far slope on the L (Violettes) side and cross a deep cleft to the brèche before a second series of gendarmes. Turn the gendarmes on the messy rock of the Cézanne face, return to the ridge and descend to another brèche. Turn another gendarme on the Violettes side and climb up again to another brèche (Pt 2,869m). Continue along the ridge and traverse Pt 3,074m. Dodge round several gendarmes on the R (N) side to an important brèche at the foot of a big step in the ridge (this point can also be reached from Cézanne up the Momie glacier). Climb a first steep slope at the L (SE) corner. Cross the gendarmes which follow by keeping near the crest of the ridge. Climb part of the second steep slope on the R (N) side and then move round completely on to the Momie glacier side (NW), on filthy rock, to another brèche. Continue along the crest of the ridge, or just off it on the L side, to the junction with the Momie ridge.

Continue along the ridge past a number of gendarmes to a big tower. Turn the base of this on the Violettes side to the brèche between it and the next step. Descend 5m on the Glacier Noir side and climb a large snow and rock couloir to the summit ridge above the step. Follow the ridge round several gendarmes to the Pointe Durand. **13-14hr** from Cézanne

Trois Dents du Pelvoux 3,682m

E Boileau de Castelnau with P Gaspard snr and jnr, 31 July 1877

One of the subsidiary summits of the Pelvoux that can be easily climbed from the Pelvoux glacier. Its E face offers some interesting goulottes (steep, narrow ice couloir), mostly climbed in winter conditions. An important feature, on the N flank, rising from the Violettes glacier, is a magnificent ice couloir - the Couloir Chaud.

46g **COULOIR CHAUD**
TD+ V Chaud and E Cortial, 14 July 1950
45 FWA: A Berry and J-M Boivin, 19-20 Jan 1973

This now classic climb was at one time considered the hardest ice climb in the range with an arduous approach and a certain amount of objective danger from the sérac barrier at the top. There are two distinct sections in its 500m. The first averages 50°-55°, but the upper section steepens to 70° and contains at least one almost vertical ice pitch. It does not receive the sun during the day and is almost always totally ice rather than névé. The climb is best attempted from a bivouac on the R-hand extremity of the Névé Pelissier where the route from the Pelvoux crosses. There are some excellent bivouac sites in this area and water is available (5hr from Ailefroide).

In recent summers the lower (easy) section has practically disappeared but the climb remains as a winter or early season challenge.

Get on to the Violettes glacier and reach the foot of the couloir in c30min from the bivouac. Follow the L side (R bank) of the couloir, which is more sheltered, until it steepens. Above is a large cave at about half-height, seen on the L bank below the séracs, which provides suitable respite. Climb to the level of the cave and traverse horizontally R for 2 pitches to reach the sheltered section below the sérac barrier and the cave.

From the cave move steeply L for 2 pitches, then climb a vertical section near to a conspicuous steep and smooth, 20m

high, black rock rognon. After this crux pitch trend L to reach
the rock of the ridge and then zigzag back Rwards through séracs
and narrow couloirs (continuous steep ice work) to reach the
Pelvoux glacier. **5-9hr** for the ascent

Descent is via the Violettes glacier.

Petit Pelvoux 3,753m
E Boileau de Castelnau with P Gaspard snr and jnr, 31 July 1877

A subsidiary summit of the Pelvoux which can be very easily
climbed from the Pelvoux glacier. Its significance is that it is the
culminating point of one of the three great ridges of the Pelvoux,
the SE ridge (Crête du Palavar).

46h
AD
38

SOUTH-EAST RIDGE
J-A and Nea Morin with A Roux, 9 Aug 1932

*This is a rather long route with a circuitous approach. It provides an
entertaining, mixed climb.*

Start from the Pelvoux hut by descending the couloir E of the
hut to the first stream. Cross it and continue E, still descending
obliquely down grassy slabs, to scree below reddish overhangs.
Continue under the cliffs (one short ascent) to near the edge (R
bank) of another ravine. Descend the 100m rocky barrier that
bars access to it, first straight down, then slanting L. Cross the
ravine and slant diagonally up the other side, continuing by
rising ledges to a snowy brèche at the foot of a 350m high step
on the SE ridge. 3hr

     The step can be climbed without difficulty by a long rock
couloir which is rather ill-defined in its lower section. In its upper
section it passes between two conspicuous reddish-brown
bastions. From the top of the step go along the crest of the ridge
to a second snowy brèche under a grey tower (2hr). Traverse R
(N) along a ledge which is 45m long and steeply banked with
snow (exposed). At the far end, climb a very steep, cracked wall

(IV) and a chimney with loose blocks in it to get into a rock couloir dropping from the ridge. The couloir is steep, probably icy and exposed. Climb it (III) to the top of the grey tower c100m above the ledge. Continue to the brèche beyond (W of) the tower and climb the double gendarme which follows. Turn two others and continue over good rock to the last brèche under the terminal wall (4hr). Slant slightly R (N) into the large snow combe between the Petit Pelvoux and the Trois Dents and climb straight up snow or ice slopes mixed with icy rocks to the top of the Petit Pelvoux. 2hr: **11hr** from the Pelvoux hut

From the top, descend an easy snow slope for a few minutes to reach the Pelvoux glacier. Descend Route 46a or 46b.

South and South-West Sector

This section covers the mountains S and E of a line running W from Ailefroide up the Celse Nière valley, over the Col du Sélé and along the Vénéon valley past la Bérarde and finally to Venosc. The S-most peak is the Sirac, somewhat isolated from the rest of the mountains in the region, whilst the W-most is the Roche de la Muzelle. It includes the important summits of Les Bans and L'Olan. See maps 3436 ET, 3437 ET (for the Sirac only) and 3336 ET

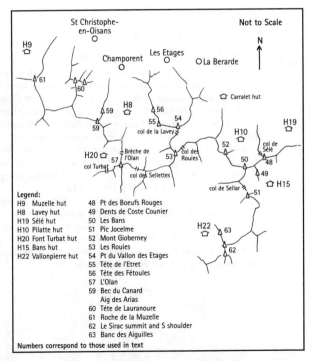

St Christophe-en-Oisans

Not to Scale

N

H9 Muzelle hut

Champorent

Les Etages

La Berarde

Carralet hut

61

60

H8

59

59

56

54

55

col de la Lavey

H10

52

H19

col de Sélé

48

Brèche de l'Olan

col des Rouies

50

H20 Font Turbat hut

57

53

49

col Turbat

col des Sellettes

col de Sellar

51

H15

Legend:
H9   Muzelle hut
H8   Lavey hut
H19 Sélé hut
H10 Pilatte hut
H20 Font Turbat hut
H15 Bans hut
H22 Vallonpierre hut

48   Pt des Boeufs Rouges
49   Dents de Coste Counier
50   Les Bans
51   Pic Jocelme
52   Mont Gioberney
53   Les Rouies
54   Pt du Vallon des Etages
55   Tête de l'Etret
56   Tête des Fétoules
57   L'Olan
59   Bec du Canard
       Aig des Arias
60   Tête de Lauranoure
61   Roche de la Muzelle
62   Le Sirac summit and S shoulder
63   Banc des Aiguilles

H22 Vallonpierre hut

63

62

Numbers correspond to those used in text

Col du Sélé 3,283m

First tourist crossing: F Tuckett with M Croz and P Perren,
14 July 1862

This passage was known centuries ago as it is the easiest link
between the Pilatte and Sélé glaciers and, with the Col de la
Temple, an original crossing between the upper Vénéon valley
and Ailefroide. The upper Sélé glacier is prone to serious
crevassing where care and attention are needed, particularly in
late season.

47a
F
47

WEST-EAST TRAVERSE

The crossing is just as easy in the reverse direction.

From the Pilatte hut descend to the glacier and climb it S wards
to a basin formed by the convergence of the E and W branches of
the glacier below a huge rock rognon. Go L and climb E wards
passing between two zones of séracs and big crevasses. Trend
towards the rock barrier baring access to the col. Pass a small
rognon which is situated below the col and then, above it, climb
up a snow or scree slope as high as possible to reach the rocks
above (2 bolts *in situ*). Move L and climb a chimney to a ledge
slanting up R and follow this to the col. There is some danger
from stonefall caused by other parties. 2½hr

From the col descend a little R to reach the upper Sélé
glacier, traverse the plateau obliquely R to reach the rock wall of
the Pointe Holmes and thread through the crevassed region on
the R. Swing L, still on the R flank of the glacier, and then cross
to the L flank and the moraine which leads towards the Sélé hut.
2hrs: **c4hr** in all: another 2hr to Ailefroide

Pointe des Boeufs Rouges 3,516m

W Coolidge with C Almer snr and jnr, 9 July 1877

A minor peak which is a wonderful viewpoint and has extensive views, particularly of Les Bans and the Ailefroide.

48a   **NORTH-NORTH-WEST RIDGE AND TRAVERSE**
PD   First ascent party

This is a relatively easy scramble in a fine situation. The rock is poor on the W side at first but then improves.

From the Col du Sélé (Route 47a) follow the horizontal section of the ridge keeping on the W flank and then the crest to a point where some gendarmes are encountered. Dodge these by a long ledge on the W flank and regain the crest after the last of them. From this point, the ridge steepens to the summit and the crest is followed to it. **1½hr** from the col

Descent is by the same route. Take great care with the loose rock that abounds, especially if you have not ascended the route and are unfamiliar with it. An alternative means of descent to the Col du Sélé is: from the summit, descend a little couloir on the S side to reach the SW ridge. Follow this, more or less on the crest, to the Col de la Condamine (3,422m). From here get on to the Pilatte glacier and descend it towards the W side of the Col du Sélé. Reach the col as for Route 47a.

It is also possible to descend from the Col de la Condamine to the Bans hut, creating a link between La Bérarde and the Pilatte hut and the Entre les Aiges valley and Vallouise. From the col descend L wards to reach the top of a rock spur (cairns). Go down a short chimney then trend R along ledges to a rappel point (metal stake). A single, 50m rappel (can be split) leads to the Fournet glacier. The rimaye might be quite open in some seasons. Move S below the spur and continue down the glacier between rock outcrops to reach a long moraine. This leads S wards to the cairned path leading to the Bans hut. The track follows first the R and then the L bank of the Ravin du Fournet. **2-2½hr**

Dents de Coste Counier 3,025m

These are the rock teeth which form the lower extension of the S ridge of the Pointe de la Pilatte. The two highest points (3,025m and 2,829m) of this section of the ridge are marked but not named on the IGN map.

49a
AD+
46

SOUTH RIDGE

E Bordeaux, solo, 15 Aug 1948

This is a good climb on sound rock and is a classic. It is longer and more sustained than both the S ridge of the Pic du Glacier Blanc and the Cinéastes traverse. There is no difficulty of glacier or snow and as such it makes an early valley start possible.

From the Bans hut follow a track into the Vallon du Sellar to reach the mouth of the Ravin de Coste Counier. Emerging from the ravine is a cascade and L of this is a large rocky barrier forming the end of the long rib which delineates the W side of the ravine. Climb this barrier by an indefinite line and then the rib to where the angle eases and where the torrent from the Bans glacier can be crossed. Once across the torrent, gain the broad, slabby terraces on the W side of the ridge below the first point. 1½hr

Traverse slightly downwards along easy terraces to reach the R-hand most chimney, which is long and bends L wards, leading to the first brèche of the ridge. The chimney carries a fair amount of loose rock, so it is a good idea to avoid it if there is another party ahead. Climb the whole of the chimney, avoiding a first overhang by a rake and another chimney on the L (III). Follow easy slabs back to the main chimney (III) and continue up to the brèche. From here climb the ridge by a narrow slab (III) and then the crest to the next point (Pt 2,829m). Descend the W flank at first then the E flank to a point below the second brèche. Climb to the brèche by a wall and a few short steps. Climb a big slab inclined at 45° and, after a short, steep section, keep on the W flank and climb a vertical wall (III+). Follow a ledge, then broken rocks leading back to the ridge. Follow this on its crest to the final, steep step. Climb this (IV) then continue along the crest with several delicate sections to the summit. 4hr: 5½hr from the hut

Descend by retracing the route for 15m to a cairn marking a vague rake which descends the E face (overlooking the Fournet combe). Go down this rake and then get back on to the ridge by a knife-edged flake and then a short chimney leading to the next brèche (Brèche de Coste Counier: usually a rappel is made into the gap).

Descend the couloir on the E (Fournet) flank of the brèche to a cairn and, after c30m, follow a faint but distinct path which traverses the flank of the ridge Lwards on the Fournet side. Reach the track leading up from the Bans hut (cairns). 1½-2hr: **7-8hr** total

It is possible to rappel and scramble on the Fournet flank from the first tower. Follow a ledge to below the second brèche and descend directly below this (2x45m rappels). Continue down the line of the obvious couloir (much equipment in place). From the foot of the couloir it is necessary to climb up scree and/ or snow to reach the normal descent path to the hut.

49b
TD-
46
48

DIABLE PAR LE QUEUE

C, J-M and S Cambon and H Jaillet, 1990

This popular climb is on the SE face of the first point (tooth) on the ridge and takes the lower buttress of the tooth. It is very close to the Bans hut.

The first section is sustained at 5/5+ but some may find it harder than expected for the grade. The mid-section follows grassy ledges and short rock steps. A pleasant corner pitch leads to the pillar proper. This has pitches of 4 and 5. Descent is possible, as described above, or the full traverse may be enjoyed. All equipment is in place up to the point where the S Ridge route is joined.

Start at the foot of the wall on the E of the Coste Counier ravine, a little way R of a couloir leading to an overhang.

P1 5: P2 5 and 5+: P3 5: P4 5: P5 4: Easy ground (2 and 3) to the corner (5-)

The detached tower gives two pitches of 5-/5 then 4 to the top. Join Route 49a at the brèche beyond this point. **5-6hr** to this point

An easier start may be made R of the original (4 with one section of 5+). This line joins the route described at the end of the difficulties (P5) by grassy ledges.

Les Bans 3,670m

W Coolidge with C Almer snr and jnr, 14 July 1878

A complex mountain whose summit is at the culminating point of three ridges; the ENE ridge provides the line for the normal route of ascent, the NW ridge, which has three subsidiary summits and the S ridge which forms a prominent shoulder. A feature of the S ridge is the conspicuous oval shaped patch of névé (*névé ovale*) which sits below the ridge on its E side. E of this névé is a steep buttress known as the Contrefort Médian.

50a
PD
47

EAST-NORTH-EAST RIDGE
First ascent party

This is the ordinary and easiest route to a popular summit situated between three major valleys. The views are magnificent.

From the Pilatte hut gain the middle of the glacier and climb it up to the central basin, avoiding an important crevassed zone caused by the curving in the glacier and without going too near the séracs which dominate on the R above a rock rognon. By a steep slope and a zigzag route to avoid crevasses and séracs, arrive directly below the Col E des Bans. After climbing the rimaye, take a short, steep slope to the col (3,351m). Reach the Col W (3,404m) by a snow slope and the crest of the ridge, which is sometimes rock and sometimes snow (watch out for cornices). There is a short step to descend Rwards just before the col. 3hr

From the Col W des Bans follow the crest of the ridge by easy rocks to the foot of the step that forms a big gendarme. Go round it on the L (S) flank, climbing by a small chimney and then traverse the flank horizontally to join the brèche which follows. Follow easy ledges L and rejoin the crest of the ridge by climbing obliquely on its S flank. Continue by the crest to a small platform situated at the bottom of a small couloir bordered on the R by another step of the ridge. Climb the couloir for nearly 30m and leave it, moving R, by a small rock wall (III+: very steep) leading to a shoulder on the ridge. Follow the crest and break into the couloir that borders it on the L. Climb it in the middle on a large slab with good holds. From the top L-hand corner of this and a small step, gain a small brèche on a secondary rib leading to another couloir. Climb it on easy rocks to the summit. 1-1½hr: **c5hr** total

The route can be reversed to the Pilatte hut and this is described below in descent. It is also possible to descend to the Bans hut and that option is also described below.

To the Pilatte hut: leave the summit in an ENE direction down an easy couloir as far as a small brèche on the L (do not continue further down this couloir). Pass through the brèche (rappel slings usually found here identify the point) to another couloir and descend by its bed which is a large slab well-supplied with holds. Get on to the ridge on its L and go down it to a shoulder. Below is a step into a couloir on its R; descend R down a steep little wall into the couloir and go down it for 30m to a small platform. Go on down the crest of the ridge leaving it for a bit where easy ledges lead to a brèche. Now dodge the step in the ridge by moving across the S face and down a little chimney. Carry on down the ridge to the Col W des Bans. Continue along the crest to the Col E des Bans. Turn L (N) at this point on to the Pilatte glacier and descend it by the route of ascent. c4hr from the top to the Pilatte hut

To the Bans hut (Entre les Aygues valley): there are three options, the most reliable is via the S ridge and SE flank and is described in ascent: Route 50b

Early in the season, descend via the ENE ridge to the Col E des Bans from where it is possible to descend S. At the level of the Brèche de Coste Counier (Pt 2,998m), N of the Coste Counier summit, a series of ledges lead Lwards (E) linking the glacier with the brèche. From the brèche, the Coste Counier descent is gained which leads over easy, non-glaciated ground to the hut (cairns).

The third alternative is to follow the S ridge to a position above the *névé ovale*. Descend a rib separating two couloirs to the Nmost edge of the névé. Immediately on setting foot on the snow, turn L and find two rappel placements *in situ*. Two 50m rappels lead to the upper part of the Bans glacier. (The glacier can be heavily crevassed and impassable from mid-season onwards). Follow it down and Rwards to where the valley beneath the Contrefort Médian can be reached by a short wall. Follow the valley (scree or snow) to the slabs beneath the E face route and Soleil du Satan. Finally get on to the névé leading to the foot of the Coste Counier ravine.

50b **SOUTH-EAST FLANK AND SOUTH RIDGE**
PD In descent: J Chenais, R Picard, P Schermann and J Vernet,
46 July 1938
48

This is the ordinary route from the Bans hut. It is an interesting line as well as being a good line of descent throughout the season.

From the Bans hut climb the L bank of the Sellar stream into the gorge issuing from the Brèche des Bans. Pass the Coste Counier ravine and continue up the gorge to a height of c2,700m. Continue heading W, keeping S of the spur projecting E from Pt 2,858m. At a height of c2,800m, turn R and climb a couloir, situated between two rock bosses, to the point where it narrows and steepens. Continue climbing, on the L bank at first and then the R bank, until it is possible to move along a short ledge on the right bank. Climb to the top of the boss on that side. Climb to the base of a large, inclined, snow and scree covered ledge, easily seen from the approach route. From the R-hand (N side) of the ledge, climb a steep, narrow ridge for 40m (III). Next climb the couloir on the R of the ridge and then bear a little R by rock which deteriorates as height is gained. Reach the S ridge 150m N of the big cornices of the S shoulder (3,496m). From there follow the ridge, keeping slightly on the W side at first and then on the E side, to the summit. **6½hr**

50c **NORTH-EAST COULOIR**
D
47

M Bourde, L Dubost and R Duplat, 25 June 1950

This is a fine and by now classic ice route with slopes up to 60°. The amount of snow and ice in the lower section of the climb varies with the season. Sometimes the rimaye and sérac barrier are impassable by the route described but it has been possible to enter the couloir proper by the R side (L bank), reaching the couloir by a traverse, which is sometimes mixed ground.

From the Pilatte hut, follow Route 50a towards the Col E des Bans and swing back R to below the outflow of the NE couloir (2½hr). Move L to the first rimaye, which is at the foot of the spur forming the R bank of the couloir and below the séracs which support the lower part of the couloir. Deal with the séracs by climbing a steep, narrow couloir (possible stonefall) on the true R bank. Continue up to the second rimaye. Cross this rather on the R side and climb a direct line of 50m up ice to the foot of a rock rib forming the L bank of the couloir. Move to the centre of the couloir and climb it towards the NW ridge. If conditions are poor, climb the rock of the rib for 100m (poor rock) and then traverse some little, secondary ice couloirs using either the rib or the couloir. Continue up the steep snow of the upper funnel of the couloir to the brèche on the L of a gendarme. 7hr

From the brèche, climb R up a little chimney which is slightly overhung at the top. Now cross the reddish wall on the SW side of the ridge, take a chimney back to the crest and follow it to the N summit (3,662m). The ridge is now very jagged, forming six teeth; stay on the crest of the ridge over all the teeth, the fourth is the highest (Central summit 3,667m). Beyond the teeth, turn a brèche on the N face, returning to its bottom by traversing R for a few m. Avoid the step beyond the brèche by the R (Valgaudemar) face and continue up easy rocks to the S and highest summit. 2hr: **11-12hr** from the Pilatte hut

Descent is by Route 50a

50d NORTH-EAST PILLAR

D
47

B Goodfellow and T Graham-Brown with A Graven and C Rodier, 1 Sept 1933

A classic route on good rock. A more direct finish can be made from the point at which the pillar steepens abruptly (mostly IV and IV+).

Follow Route 50a from the Pilatte hut to the upper slopes of the Pilatte glacier and traverse R when level with the foot of the pillar (2hr). Start at the lowest rocks and climb the cracks and slabs up the E side of the pillar. Eventually the pillar steepens and forms a little gendarme in its upper part with a small brèche behind. Traverse some m L into the bed of a steep, narrow chimney cutting the E side of the gendarme. Climb it to the brèche. The pillar now steepens abruptly. Traverse L to a large, gently-sloping and stony couloir. Climb its easy rocks to the foot of an overhanging chimney which continues above as a couloir cutting the E side of the crest of the pillar. From the foot of the chimney traverse horizontally L along a ledge for c15m and then climb back up to the couloir above the chimney. Continue up the couloir keeping R until it becomes slabby and then get into the bed of the couloir. Climb out L by a rock wall then a ledge slanting up the large easy slabs which form a parallel couloir. Climb this couloir up broken rocks to the N summit (3,662m: 4hr). Continue as for Route 50c to the highest point. 1½hr: **7½hr** in all

50e SOUTH-EAST FACE DIRECT - VOIE GIRAUD

TD+
46

48

Guides J-P Fédèle, A Giraud, T Langevin and J Lepeut, 8 Aug 1963

A magnificent, sustained climb of 450m which is on excellent rock for the most part. Piton placement is not always easy due to the

compactness of the rock, but protection is always good on the hard sections (up to 6a). The route has several variants and is now a classic.

From the Bans hut follow Route 50b towards the Brèche des Bans to c2,700m. On the R is a rock barrier which is climbed into a valley below the Contrefort Médian. Climb the valley which may be snow filled, or the stony ground on its E side to the rock crest at its head, which separates it from the upper basin of the Bans glacier, above the séracs. Climb to the base of the face a little L of the foot of the couloir descending from the Col W des Bans. 3½hr

    The face is cut by an immense dièdre which appears to descend from the summit (in reality, it descends from a small brèche 100m below the summit). The route climbs the face L of the dièdre. Climb it from its base, or slightly to the R by a large flake which permits a return to the line after 10m, for 35-40m (chimney-crack: V: sustained) and exit L below a vague bulge. Climb this (V+) to reach a relatively easy ledge. Follow this ledge L for c15m and then climb an easy section for c40m trending back towards and finally attaining the dièdre. Above, climb the length of a vague spur a few m L of the dièdre for two rope lengths (V+ then IV) to reach a large, damp cave in the dièdre.

    From the cave traverse L across slabs for 15m, descending slightly (a few moves of V), to the foot of a small couloir. Climb this (in the back), then by the pillar bordering its R bank (IV), to a niche forming an overhang at the top of the couloir (35m of climbing). Climb up to a barrier of overhangs and pass below them, moving R for a rope-length (V) before climbing the extremity of the barrier by a cleft. Again slant obliquely R to the vicinity of the dièdre. (From the the cave, the first ascent party moved L by an ascending traverse of 6-8m to a chimney-crack (VI), which they followed for another 10m (V/V+) before reaching the same point at the side of the dièdre by two easier rope lengths). Climb steeply for another pitch (V). A series of easy ledges then leads L, c50m from the depths of the dièdre. An obvious line leads back R; follow this for 40m to a characteristic flake forming an excellent belay. Climb straight up 10m (V: delicate) to a small platform (stance) and then up a 5m high, shattered wall directly above (VI, 6a). (From the stance the first ascent party did a descending traverse of 3-4m (V), climbed an overhang (IV) and traversed R (V+) to finish above the shattered wall). Continue by a dièdre-crack which is less steep (IV) and marks the end of the difficulties. Reach a relatively easy couloir which leads in one rope length to the summit ridge some 20m to the W of the top. 7-8hr: **c12hr** total

Contrefort Médian

A considerable number of climbs have been developed on the E face of this readily accessible buttress. Some are equipped with bolts whilst others require more traditional means of protection. A distinctive feature of the buttress is the square brèche on its crest, some 400m above the base.

50f   **ORIGINAL ROUTE**

D

48

J Chenais, R Picard, P Schermann and J Vernet, 28 July 1938

A very good climb on rock which is generally excellent and compact. Exposed and sustained. Traditional protection: 400m to the square brèche. The climb can be continued to the summit of Les Bans.

From the Bans hut follow Route 50e into the valley below the contrefort. Climb névé and/or scree to reach the base of the cliff. 1½-2hr

The start is found on the L of the face directly below the L (S) edge of the big, square brèche situated on the ridge above. Two rope lengths lead to a large, grey ledge which is followed Rwards. Turning a small spur, gain the foot of a large dièdre-chimney which is climbed (III/IV). When the chimney becomes too steep, a short pitch Rwards (III+) gives access to another big couloir-chimney, c15m away from and parallel with the original, which is climbed to beneath a black slab. Continue up, moving

R to a spur which is climbed before moving slightly R again to some cracked slabs. Climb these (IV), moving back L on to the dark rock of the spur (IV+). Climb the spur to a level area. Traverse 15m L (III) to where the whole of the square brèche is seen and climb below the R corner of the brèche in order to reach it (c3,150m: 3hr). The hardest climbing is now over.

Climb up to find a ledge crossing the back of the buttress above a couloir. Follow the ledge, which is snow and ice covered early in the season, until it fades near the couloir. Climb higher until a traverse into and across the couloir is possible. Easier rocks now lead on to the *névé ovale*. Follow the ridge on the R side of the *névé*, to reach easy rocks which lead to the S ridge. Follow the S ridge to the summit. 5hr: **7-8hr** from the hut

50g
ED1
48

PAS D'ASILE POUR PAZAZU

C and J-M Cambon and P Chapoutot, 1993

A more sustained and steeper climb than the next route. Difficulties up to 6a+. The whole climb and the descent are bolt equipped.

Start in the snowy bay E of Pt 2,858m at foot of the SE ridge of the contrefort. It shares the first pitch with Route 50h, leaving Rwards after one and a half pitches, passing just above the start of the Route 50f and then climbing straight up to the summit crest of the contrefort.

P1 5+: P2 4: P3 5+: P4 5+: P5 5+: P6 5+: P7 5+ then 6a+: P8 5-: P9 6a: P10 5+ then 6a: P11 5-: P12 3. The route finishes at a small brèche. **5-6hr** climbing

Descend from the brèche by rappel.

50h
TD+
48

SOUS LE SOLEIL DU SATAN

C and J-M Cambon, 1989

A good climb, mainly on slabs and fully equipped. The rock is good. 500m of climbing up to 6b (5+ obl).

Start as described for Route 50g with which it shares the first 1½ pitches. The climb takes a line just on the R flank of the SE ridge of the contrefort. After the communal section the line is direct, climbing to the upper part of the ridge.

P1 5+: P2 5+: P3 5/5+: P4 5/5+: P5 5+: P6 6b/A0: P7 5: P8 5-: P9 4: P10 4: P11 3, on the summit ridge. **4-5hr** climbing

Descent: Move towards a little notch in the ridge where Route 50g finishes. The rappel descent by that line is considered the preferred choice.

Pic Jocelme 3,458m

F Gardiner and C and L Pilkington, 12 July 1879

A modest peak but a fine viewpoint, which is situated due S of Les Bans.

51a **NORTH-EAST COULOIR**
D
49
46

A good climb. This route is recommended early in the season. Stonefall and open crevasses make the descent very dangerous in dry conditions.

From the Bans hut follow the L bank of the Sellar torrent by scree and grass slopes. Cross the torrent and follow a large couloir of mixed snow and rock debris R of the NE ridge of the Pic Jocelme. The couloir steepens and continues for 700m. Climb it (35°-45° for 400m, the rest is 50° and sometimes 55°) to reach a small col on the NE ridge. Traverse 30m L on slabs. A 5m chimney (III) and then slabs (IV+: good rock) lead to an easy section before the rotten summit rocks. **5-6hr**

51b **DESCENT BY THE BONVOISIN GLACIER**
PD
49

Follow the SE ridge easily to the Brèche de Bonvoisin (3,298m). Traverse Lwards from here to reach the Bonvoisin glacier (rappel) which is followed, trending back R at first and then keeping on the L side of the lower glacier to reach the line of ascent from the Bans hut. **c2½hr**

Mont Gioberney 3,352m

W Coolidge, C Almer and P Bleuer, 21 July 1873

This is a much frequented mountain near the head of the Vénéon valley. The Pilatte hut stands at its NE foot.

52a
F
50
47

NORTH-EAST FLANK

M Paillon, P and E Estienne, 12 Aug 1898

The normal route to a magnificent belvedere which is easy and frequently climbed.

From the Pilatte hut go up to the highest point on the small basin of scree situated behind the hut. Go up R on the rocky barrier above by a short slope of steep grass, then on a traverse ascending L on a rocky staircase, to reach easy slopes. Go up them towards the R in order to reach a couloir of broken rocks that lead to the foot of a large area of slabs. Cross these from R to L and go up the couloir that follows to gain a higher terrace of scree. Most of this is by a cairned track. Traverse for a long way S (several cairns) in order to reach the slabs forming the base of the central spur of the NE ridge at c2,900m.

From this point, either veer L across the slabs by a traverse around the flank of the spur and then go up a large scree cone, or go up R on easy rock and follow a ledge that leads to the top of the scree cone. Continue traversing towards the S in order to go around the base of the S spur of the NE ridge (Pt 3,064m) and so reach a pile of scree at the foot of the Gioberney glacier. Go up it over the névés on the L side (R bank), then go round on the L-hand side of a large rocky rognon that emerges from the glacier and climb steep slopes as far as the higher névés. Traverse towards the SW in order to reach the Col du Gioberney (3,238m).

From the col, follow the ridge skirting several small projections by means of easy ledges on the W side. Gain the ridge at the end of the crest and follow it as far as the summit. **2½hr**

Descend by the same route or by Route 52b.

52b **NORTH-EAST RIDGE**

PD   First ascent party

50
47   *A pleasant and somewhat varied climb.*

From the Pilatte hut follow the previous route to the base of the central spur of the NE ridge. Climb up over slopes of easy scree in order to reach the R bank of the small glacier situated between the central spur and the N spur of the NE ridge. Climb up the névés of the R bank and reach the crest of the central spur by a fairly steep, rocky chimney. Alternatively scramble directly up the buttress of the central spur. Reach the snowy crest of the NE ridge and follow it without problems (small cornices on the N side) to a rock step which is climbed slightly R by a steep crack. Easy climbing leads to the summit. **2-2½hr**

Les Rouies 3,589m

T Cox, F Gardiner, W Pendlebury and C Taylor with H and P Baumann, P Knubel and J Lochmatter, 19 June 1873

Les Rouies lies NW of the roadhead (Chalet du Gioberney) in the Valgaudemar valley and is one of the easiest summits of the massif to reach. It commands superb views and is often climbed on skis in springtime. Its mainly rocky SE flank is quite massive, some 2,000m high, whilst its W and NE flanks are mostly glaciated.

53a **NORTH-EAST FLANK**

F   First ascent party

50
      A fine outing in spring (ski) and in summer.

From la Bérarde walk towards the Refuge du Carrelet as far as Pt 1,883m. Cross the Vénéon river by the bridge and then follow the path across the Chardon stream to the junction with the path above the R bank of the stream. Follow this path to its junction with the path on the NW side of the valley. This same point can be reached from la Bérarde by crossing the river by the bridge below the village and following the path on the L bank. Climb the moraine and then the L bank of the Chardon glacier by névés and snow slopes. Leave the glacier near Pt 2,568m by scree and earth slopes and climb easily up little rock barriers and grassy chimneys. Eventually, go slightly L (W) to the lowest part of the Ane glacier. 3hr

Cross the glacier, still heading W, to its R bank. Below Pt 3,015m, descend (via the Passage de l'Ane) on to the Rouies glacier above the sérac fall. Climb the L bank, contouring around a rocky spur, to reach the upper plateau of the glacier. To reach the Col des Rouies, go L (SE) towards a rocky outcrop (marked 3,388m) and pass R of this to the col. This col can be reached easily from the Pigeonnier hut by climbing the L bank of the Rouies glacier in c3hr. To continue the climb, go to a little dip marking the foot of the NW arête (SE of the Pt 3,527m). Follow the snow crest and then rock to the summit. c2½hr: **c6hr** from La Bérarde

Descend by the same route.

53b **SOUTH-EAST RIDGE - VOIE REBUFFAT**
AD+ A Duchaussoy and E Frendo, 29 July 1935
51 Route described: J Bouisson and G Rébuffat, 24 June 1941

The ridge is 800m high and projects deeply into the combe on the SE flank of the mountain. The rock is good and the climbing offers some fine situations. The first ascent party avoided the more difficult central section.

From the Pigeonnier hut follow a good path NW until below the S ridge of the W peak of the Pics du Vaccivier. Turn SW and get on to the névé below the Col des Rouies and traverse horizontally below the E face to the foot of the ridge (1hr).

Start in a little snowy bay on the E side of the ridge. Climb grassy slopes to get on to the ridge and then follow this, mainly on its E side, for 100-150m to a small brèche. Most of this is easy. From the brèche follow the crest easily to the first step and the start of the difficulties. Traverse L along a ledge to its highest point. Continue the traverse, descending slightly, to below a massive block. Climb it by its face and a dièdre to reach the top of the step (40m: IV). 200m of easy ground leads to the second step. Traverse horizontally L for 5m round a faint rib to enter a dièdre. Climb it (30m: IV/IV+) before moving R by an exposed traverse (V-) on to the ridge. Alternatively traverse further L and get into and climb a couloir parallel with the dièdre. An exposed traverse leads to the ridge.

The ridge becomes much narrower as the angle eases and then turns slightly L before merging with the final slopes somewhat R (NE) of the summit. The last step can be avoided by the couloir on its R (E). The summit is now easily reached up the NE ridge. 6-7hr: **7-8hr** total

Descend Route 53a to la Bérarde, or follow that route to the Col des Rouies then descend E and get on to the ridge (cornices) near Pt 3,228m. Descend a snow couloir running S (keep L to avoid possible ice fall) to rejoin the ascent route from the Pigeonnier hut.

53c   **SOUTH-EAST FACE - ORIGINAL ROUTE**

AD   A Manhès, H Tête and M Vincent, 12 Sept 1945

51

Approach as for the previous climb. Skirt around the base of the SE ridge and enter the central cirque of the Grande Roche glacier. Climb to the rimaye and cross it on the R to reach the slopes forming the base of the SE face. Start directly below the couloir flanked on its L bank by the SE ridge. Climb the steepening part of the base then climb the couloir. In mid-face, slant L gradually above the high, vertical SE wall. Continue directly to reach the SW ridge (IV: delicate move) 50m L of the summit. **5hr** from the hut

53d   **VOIE DE LA RAMPE**

D+   B Botta, B Olphand and G Vincent, 5 Sept 1970

51

A good climb on compact rock apart from one section at the end of the approach traverse. It is sustained and exposed. Some equipment is in

place but wedges and pitons (some short and some very thin) should be carried.

Reach the start by following the SE ridge (Route 53b) to the top of the dièdre on the first step. Now descend slightly and make a long traverse across the W flank of the ridge to a brèche (moves of IV at the end of the traverse) giving access to ledges and terraces at the foot of the SE face. Traverse L and start by some black streaks (bolt *in situ*). 3-3½hr

Slant up and R for a rope length (lll then IV+ with a move of V) to bypass a wet terrace. Keep moving R for another pitch (IV) and reach a big ramp slanting R and passing between two zones of yellow overhangs. Climb along the ramp for two rope lengths or so (IV/IV+: 1 move of V) and leave Rwards (lll) to traverse along some vague ledges for two more rope lengths (lll and IV: short section of V). Reach the top of a shoulder above (IV+). Climb a rope length slightly R, then slant gently L via slopes and little steps (lll). This is the link with the 'Mafia' variant described below. Climb a steep wall (IV) then slant R to come on to the summit ridge (IV+). Follow the crest to the summit, avoiding a steep step by the N flank. 6hr: **c10hr** in all

53e **LA MAFIA**
ED2
51 J-L and B Botta, F Grand and J Vincent, Aug 1983

The hardest route in the area, it has 400m of climbing on the wall. Partly equipped but a rack is still required.

Climb the previous route to the top of the first two pitches on the wall itself (c3½hr). Traverse L, reaching a flake above the starting terrace (V: 1 rope length). Climb straight up then slant R for two pitches (IV+/V) to reach some ledges. Follow these R to tackle a series of overhangs slanting Lwards for two short rope lengths (6b and 6c). Continue straight up a yellow wall directly below a cave for 2 pitches, with a little loop L at the end of the first pitch (6a/b). Reach a Rwards slanting ramp on the R and follow it for 4 rope lengths (6a then IV+ and lll). Here the route rejoins the previous climb. 8-10hr climbing: **c13hr** in all

Pointe du Vallon des Etages 3,564m

A Salvador de Quatrefages and F Perrin with P Gaspard snr and jnr and C Roderon, 27 June 1878

The peak is situated at the head of the Etages valley immediately S of the Etages hamlet in the Vénéon valley. Although less popular than it once was, it remains an excellent viewpoint. Its rocky N face, which rises above the broad sweep of the Vallon de Etages glacier, is the feature of most interest to the alpinist.

54a   **NORTH-EAST RIDGE**

PD   G Mieg with J-B and H Rodier, 22 July 1890

52

This attractive route, of a fairly low technical standard, is included as giving an expedition practicable from la Bérarde in the day.

Follow Route 53a to the Ane glacier (3hr). Climb the L bank of the glacier and then move R towards a stretch of smooth slabs running with streams. Climb these slabs, dodging the upper cliff on the R, to the little upper glacier situated S of the NE ridge of the Pointe du Vallon des Etages. Climb straight up the glacier to the foot of the ridge and then up a rotten chimney to its crest. 1½hr

Climb SE up the ridge using the easy rocks just under the crest on the S side. The step which is encountered can be turned either by a chimney on the S face, or by slabs and a little chimney on the N face. Continue up to the E (highest) summit. 1-1½hr: **6-6½hr** from la Bérarde

Descend by the same route.

54b   **VOIE DU GRAND DIEDRE**

TD   P Livet and L Rama, 13 Aug 1975

52

This route, which climbs the N pillar of the W summit, is comparable with the original (Route 54c) with which it shares the first 4 pitches. The difficulties are concentrated in the bottom and topmost sections of the face. The rock is good to excellent. In the top section, th

pillar divides into two to provide a superb dièdre. There is no equipment in place.

From les Etages cross the Vénéon river and get on to either of the paths leading up the Vallon des Etage. Climb the valley continuing past Pts 2,040m and 2,065m (1½hr). There are beautiful bivouac sites in this area below the moraine of the Vallon des Etages glacier giving the option of leaving the bivouac equipment, since a return to the same spot is quickly achieved on the descent.

Follow the moraine on the L bank of the glacier to its highest point to bypass the big crevassed zone. Go down slightly L to get on to the glacier. Climb it and turn a little rocky rognon below the central pillar on the R, then go back L to reach the W flank of the central spur. 2½hr

Reach a little platform by climbing a vertical slab with several narrow cracks (IV). Climb 10m, vertically, then a steep section by cracks and continue towards a little niche (IV+). Join the crest of the spur to reach a little balcony and continue on the E flank of the crest to beneath smooth slabs. Follow a ledge on the W flank of the spur to a corner in the wall below an overhang. From this point, either traverse into the corner, below the overhang, by a broken ledge (IV+) and reach the R of the break to climb steep rock and a rib to little terraces, or leave the ledge before the break to climb a vertical slab to its upper edge; bear R and go up an overhanging chimney (V) to reach the little terraces. Climb a wide, easy chimney R of the rib to a little brèche.

From the brèche climb the arête on the R, directly beneath the big pillar of the W summit. Start it by slightly delicate rock slabs (III) which improve as they progress. Leave the slabs well before they butt up against a wall barred by a rotten overhang. Traverse and climb Rwards (III) and then, by cracks (IV), reach another arête of brown rock. Climb by its crest or the R flank (III and IV) to the top of the brown rocks. From here it is possible to escape towards the W ridge at the level of its double pointed gendarme. Descend a little and traverse L (IV: 15m). Traverse then slant up over yellow, cracked rock (IV and IV+). Climb an ascending traverse L for two pitches (III and IV) to within sight of the superb dièdre which splits the pillar. This is soon a deep gorge which forces and twists itself into the wall. Reach its bed by a ramp (V) then climb it (ice and snow). The first pitch is IV/V followed by 20m of V/V+ and then 10m of IV+. Exit L on to a slab (V) and, after c20m, reach the N ridge of W summit. Follow it to the W summit over poor rock. The traverse to the main summit, via the S flank of the interconnecting ridge, is PD. **9hr** from the foot of the face

54c **NORTH FACE**

TD M Fourastier, M Laloue and H Le Breton, 26 July 1935

52 FWA: M Mariet and Y Seigneur, 2-4 Feb 1964

The N face of the Vallon des Etages dominates all the views S from the Dibona region. It is 600m high and split down its entirety by an immense couloir-chimney descending from a brèche between its two summits. The chimney is interrupted at mid-height by a steep, stony ledge. The couloir in the lower part ends in an overhang some 80m above the rimaye. A rib bordering the lower part of the couloir falls vertically to the glacier to form the central pillar. The climb is serious, best attempted in good conditions (no ice) though there is always the possibility of some stonefall high up the climb.

Approach and start as for Route 54b by the same four pitches just to the little brèche. Leave Route 54b here.

Move on to the E side, then climb an easy chimney and leave it the moment it steepens, bear L and traverse verglas-coated slabs, covered in grit, situated below the mouth of a big couloir (stonefall). A last slab leads L to a vertical escarpment which is climbed by a short chimney ending in the big couloir. Climb its bed, then rocks on the R bank which lead to the foot of a high, narrow and icy chimney (IV) of 40m. From there move out of the bed of the couloir and climb some little walls and rubbish covered ledges. The slanting line being followed splits;

on the L an ascending ledge does not lead to the summit, on the R is a very steep chimney-crack. Escape up this for two rope lengths. Dodge a long ice slope by using rock on the R bank of a chimney-crack. Climb 25m vertically and leave the chimney L wards (black, detached block) and climb a cracked slab. Turn an overhang on the L side (IV) and reach a large ledge formed by big blocks. Traverse R to reach a brèche on the summit ridge. The summit is a few m away. **6-10hr** from the bivouac

Descent: Go down the NE ridge to the Col de Clot Chatel then, by the N facing snow-slope, descend to Vallon des Etages. It may be easier to descend N from Pt 3,282m a little further along the ridge. Alternatively it is possible to descend the S slopes towards the Vallon du Chardon and the Refuge du Carrelet. PD

Tête de l'Etret 3,559m

E Boileau de Castelnau with P Gaspard snr and jnr, 4 Sept 1876

Circling round the head of the Vallon des Etages glacier on its S and W side are three high summits. The Tête de l'Etret is the central one. It is the culminating point of three ridges, the NW ridge carrying a subsidiary peak, the Clocher de l'Etret.

55a
TD
53

NORTH-EAST FACE DIRECT

M Fourastier, H Le Breton and A Manhes, 31 July-1 Aug 1935
FWA: J-P Bougerol and Y Morin, 15-16 Mar 1973

The NE flank is split for the whole of its height by a steep, ice couloir (60° for 250m) which forms the line of ascent. It is sustained and there may be some stonefall. Ice conditions vary considerably from season to season. The climb is now a classic. A bivouac in the Vallon des Etage is advisable.

Approach the bivouac as for Route 53a. Continue by the same route to the top of the moraine and get on to the Vallon des Etages glacier. Climb the glacier to a height of c2,700m before turning NW towards the rock spur which descends E from the

Pointe d'Entre les Cols and which carries the Aiguillette de l'Etret. Pass below the spur and then turn L in a wide arc, eventually moving horizonally below some séracs, to reach the N side of the spur. Cross the rimaye and climb on to the crest of the spur. Climb to its highest point then move L across the flank of the spur to gain the foot of the couloir. At mid-height the couloir becomes narrower, steepens and then forms a very narrow couloir of ice. 3hr from the bivouac

Climb the L bank to where the couloir steepens and narrows dramatically at mid-height. Climb two very steep pitches up this bottleneck. Continue to a second narrowing and climb two more very steep and difficult pitches. Above this more mixed terrain is encountered. Climb this, not without difficulty. Exit from the couloir at the brèche between the N (Clocher de l'Etret) and main summits. **5-10hr** from the bivouac

Descent is normally to the Lavey hut via the S flank. Go down a small crest in the middle of a snow couloir leading to the Etret glacier. Traverse this L wards, thread through the rocks to take the Rmost couloir and reach the foot of the Lavey glacier (Lac des Rouies). Continue to the hut.

55b
D-
53

NORTH FACE DIRECT

F Mantel, P Deboeuf, B Macho and P Vuillard, 28 Aug 1975

The 500m face, L of the ice couloir, rises in three steps and is directly below the summit. The rock is fairly good and there is no equipment in place.

Approach as for Route 55a. Before reaching the spur descending from the Pointe d'Entre les Cols, turn SW to reach the lowest rocks at the foot of the face. Start the first step on the L side (easy). Reach the foot of a ramp directly below a big crack formed by a flake (IV). Climb this crack (V) and continue to a bank of snow at the top of the first step. Climb directly to the foot of the third step (III). Follow an obvious line Rwards to the summit for five rope lengths (III and IV). **4-5hr** from the foot of the face: c10hr from les Etages

Tête des Fétoules 3,459m

E Boileau de Castelnau with P Gaspard snr and jnr, 29 Aug 1876

This is the N-most of the peaks above the head of the Vallon des Etages glacier. It has little of interest apart from the fine pillar on its S side.

56a **SOUTH PILLAR**
TD A Charbonnier and J-J Lainex, 29 June 1973

This is a fine climb of c500m on good rock. It is not well equipped so carry a few pitons and a rack. Start from the hut or from a bivouac below the route.

From the Lavey hut cross the river in the valley bottom (bridge) and then walk up the R bank a short way to a bifurcation. Take the L fork and follow the track as far as Pt 2,323m. Leave the path here and head E into the Creux des Fétoules valley. Continue by heading Rwards below the Aiguillette des Fétoules to reach the combe below the vast S side of the mountain.

From the bed of the combe scramble up stony slopes to the base of the pillar which is L of a well defined, snowy couloir. Start slightly R of the pillar at the foot of a narrow chimney-couloir. By slabs, gain the crest of the pillar (IV: one move of V) and follow it to the top of the first step (III). Climb easily to the foot of the second step. Climb this in two pitches by a chimney-couloir (III: a bit of IV). Reach the base of the third step (100m high). This is the hardest part of the route. Climb the Rmost of two cracks situated well R of the crest (this overhanging crack is V+/A0). Climb delicately and obliquely R to a stance (IV). Climb a steep wall by slanting slightly L (V: sustained), then climb back R (IV: exposed) and finally climb a corner to get to a belay. Climb obliquely R for some m (IV) then climb back L, by a ramp (IV: exposed), to reach the obvious corner which splits the whole of the step. Climb it until it is possible to traverse R (V) then traverse obliquely R to a belay some m from the top of the step. Reach the crest and make a descending traverse on its R

(E) flank to the brèche which follows (III).

Climb another step by an obvious chimney R of the crest (III-IV: 2 pitches: a step of IV+) then by the crest itself (IV then III). Follow the arête (exposed) for a rope-length to the foot of the last, overhanging step. Traverse horizontally on its L (W) flank for several m (IV: exposed) and then climb, by a line of cracks, to the top of the step (IV+/V). Follow the easy, horizonta arête and turn the last gendarme on the L (III). Reach a brèche where the S pillar changes its orientation. Gain the summit in three pitches by the last step (III-IV). **9-11hr** from the Lavey hu

56b **DESCENT BY THE SOUTH-EAST RIDGE**
F
Mlle E Capdepon, J Boissière, J Capdepon and E Piaget,
30 May 1909

Go down the easy SE arête to the Col N de l'Etret. Then, by a system of ledges, reach the combe at the bottom of the S face of the Fétoules. At the beginning of the season there may be steep snow so it would be wise to take an ice-axe and crampons.

L'Olan 3,564m

W Coolidge with C Almer snr and jnr, 29 June 1877: the centra summit had been climbed in 1875

L'Olan lies N of la Chapelle-en-Valgaudemar although access from this side is of little value. More importantly, it lies at the to end of the Valjouffrey which provides the approach to the magnificent NW face. L'Olan is one of the finest mountains in the region, quite simple in form with four ridges and four faces. It has two summits, the Nmost being 6m higher than the centra summit. A prominent shoulder a little further S at 3,514m is sometimes refered to as the S summit. It is well seen from the summit of Les Bans from where it dominates the view W.

57a
PD
54

NORTH RIDGE

A Cust, P Gaspard and C Roderon, 5 Aug 1880

A thoroughly worthwhile climb in its own right and a normal route of descent. Described in descent below.

From the Fond Turbat hut reach the Brèche d'Olan by Route 58a. The same point can be reached from the E side starting from the Lavey hut by Route 58b although from this side it is not necessary to climb to the col. By either approach, get on to the upper plateau of the W branch of the Sellettes glacier and climb a couloir leading on to the N ridge between Pt 3,115m and Pt 3,228m. Pass round the latter point on its NW side and reach a snowy col. The ridge becomes steeper now and is climbed by a series of chimneys leading gradually L on the NE side of the ridge. Get back on to the ridge and again move L into a couloir slanting back to the ridge. Climb the couloir and then the ridge direct to the top. 2½hr: **5hr** and **6½hr** respectively from the two huts

In descent: Cross the N summit (30min) and from there descend the N ridge a little way to where a slanting couloir drops down R (NE). Descend this to its lower end and then traverse L back on to the ridge. Now take a series of little chimneys, also down the NE face, staying quite near the ridge and return L to a snowy brèche at the foot of the steep part of the ridge. Ahead is a hump at 3,228m. Before the hump a couloir, the L-hand of three couloirs, drops down to the Sellettes glacier. Descend it (pitch of III: or rappel) and cross the rimaye. Slant L (N) down the glacier to meet the route over the Brèche de l'Olan and return over the brèche to the Fond Turbat hut, or continue on down to the Lavey hut. **c3½hr** from the top

North-West Face

This immense face is the most imposing feature of the mountain. From the gap between the two principal summits, a great couloir descends the full height of the face (c1,100m). In its upper reaches it has two branches separated by a buttress below the central summit. The most obvious line, climbed by Devies and Gervasutti, follows the line of the pillar forming the L bank of the couloir and finishes close to the S shoulder. The more serious and more direct routes to the highest point climb the steep wall L of the couloir. Whilst these routes are harder than the Gervasutti, their difficulties are concentrated into the upper part of the face.

57b   ORIGINAL ROUTE

TD   L Devies and G Gervasutti, 23-24 Aug 1934

54   FWA: F Audibert, R Desmaison, G Payot and J Puiseux, 18-22 Mar 1960

This is a great rock climb, with quite considerable difficulties and the typical atmosphere of the Dauphiné N faces. There are pitches of V and one of 6a. Some of the rock is poor but the route is out of range of the stonefall down the great, central couloir.

Start from the Fond Turbat hut by following the path to the Brèche de l'Olan for 15-20mins, then cross the Bonne stream and walk up a moraine/névé to the little Maye glacier. Climb this to the foot of the wall (2,530m:1hr). Start 20m R of the waterfalls issuing from the central couloir up slabs and then a line of rather indefinite cracks (IV). Continue up on good holds to the first of the three caves which are visible from below and R of the central couloir. Exit R from this and climb chimneys and cracks to the rib separating the central couloir from a smaller, rock couloir on the R. Climb the steep and airy rib on good holds for more than 100m, keeping a little L of its crest, to a shoulder (cairn) near the central couloir. 2-3hr

Slant R up easy rocks to the foot of a yellow tower-like step. Traverse R along ledges and up little walls towards a deep, grey chimney which is cut by several overhangs. Start up the yellow wall 30m L of the chimney. Climb a vertical pitch and continue straight on to a loose, detached block below a yellow wall.

Instead of climbing the wall (it can be climbed: V+) traverse 20m R and then up and slightly L for three rope-lengths to a block-covered terrace (to this point the yellow wall is all IV/V: c120m gained). There follows 30m of easier rock leading to an over-hanging dièdre. Traverse further L (IV) to a couloir parallel to the dièdre and climb this (IV+). An oblique overhanging crack behind a partly detached flake leads to a minute platform below a great, bulging slab. Climb this L wards (VI, 5+/6a) to the first of two niches beneath some overhangs and then move R along overhanging flakes (IV+) to the second niche. Climb an overhanging crack into the conspicuous depression above and then more cracks up broken rocks to the shoulder at the top of the step, near the little ice slope in the central section of the big couloir. 2-4hr.

Climb a few pleasant pitches (III and IV) up grey rock L of a tower to the upper gorge of the big couloir enclosed between the rocks of the central summit and a secondary rib further R. Its bed is usually ice-filled. Climb the couloir for 30m (IV/V: exposed) and then, if the couloir is ice free, climb straight up it on to the summit (S) ridge. Otherwise, climb on rounded holds on to the bounding rib on the R (IV: not far away, under an overhang, is a sheltered bivouac site reached by descending a 3m slab). Go up the rib to the foot of a step. Traverse L and climb the rocks of the L bank of the big couloir, not far from its bed (hard with verglas around), to reach the summit ridge near the brèche which is the origin of the big couloir. Alternatively, cross the couloir c45m below the brèche and continue the top of the central summit (3,514m). 2-3hr;

7-11hr from the Fond Turbat hut

57c
ED1
54

COUZY-DESMAISON ROUTE

J Couzy and R Desmaison, 3-5 Aug 1956
FWA: M Grohens, J-C Marmier and D Segier, 9-13 Jan 1977

This route reaches the L-hand and highest of the summits and runs parallel to the Gervasutti route from which it is separated by the couloir. The lower part of the L-hand face is easy angled but the 450m diamond-shaped, upper section is extremely steep and provides the difficulty of this route. It is still one of the more serious climbs included in this guide and, with the N faces of the Pic Sans Nom and the Meije, probably amongst the best of the classics in the Dauphiné at present. At the time of its first ascent, comparison was drawn with the original route on the W face of the Petit Dru. The second ascent was not made until July 1966. Much equipment is now in situ. Pitches of A1, A2 and VI (7a free). The rock needs care and there are clear signs of damage caused by a plane crash. The route sees c20 ascents per season and modern protection enables its completion in a day.

Approach as for Route 57b, but some way below the foot of the central couloir move to the L edge of the snow slope. Cross the rimaye and climb up Lwards via a system of ledges to a couloir. Climb this and then head back along more ledges on to the crest of the spur forming R bank of the big couloir. Climb the crest (delicate in places) and then follow a series of ledges slanting up towards the central couloir. Continue by climbing several pitches (IV/IV+ at the top), L of the couloir, to reach the upper part of the face close to the R bank of the central couloir and adjacent to the highest snow patch in the centre of the face.

A couloir/dièdre slants up R towards the central couloir. Climb this for c75m (III and IV: verglas). Leave it by climbing an overhang on the L (IV+) up to the ledges, visible from lower down, which lead back L on to the wall below the lower of two big dièdres dominating the R-hand side of the face. Traverse L to the end of the ledge on easy but rotten rock and then climb up to a small perch on the open wall (IV). Continue to the foot of a reddish overhang. Climb L of the overhang (A1/A2: 5 or 6 pitons: 6a free) to the R-hand crack in the lower of the two great dièdres. Climb the crack for c35m (V: a move of V+: 2 or 3 pitons). Continue up R for a rope-length (IV) to some good terraces. 2hr: Couzy's first bivouac

Climb the R-hand crack in the next dièdre for 80m with stances at mid-height and at the top (V+: pitons: exposed finish)

A rope length on the L (IV) now leads to the overhanging area; the route lies between the enormous overhanging wall, seen from a distance, on the L and a region of little white overhangs. Climb a L-slanting dièdre (A1/A2: 10-12 pitons) to a stance in etriers under the little white overhangs. Climb over a considerable overhang at its L extremity (A2: 8 or 9 pitons or wedges) to a stance in étriers on the R. Traverse 5m L via a flake then climb an overhanging dièdre (A1/A2: 11 pitons). Two pitches across ledges of rotten rock, exposed but relatively easy, lead to a wide area of terraces in the centre of the wall. This marks the end of the main difficulties (Couzy's second bivouac).

Climb the slopes above, first L then R and then slant R for two rope lengths (moves of IV+/V: pitons) to the hollow at the foot of the upper of the two big dièdres. Climb a vertical crack, on brown rock up the L side of this hollow (IV: good holds) and then traverse to the R-hand side of the dièdre and climb up a slab (V). Continue easily for 20m and then for 40m up cracks in grey rock in the bed of the dièdre on the L (6a and A1: pitons: 7a free) and exit R. The dièdre deepens into a couloir-chimney. Climb the first 20m easily and then the 40m overhanging chimney up the R-hand side of its bed (V: pitons: sustained). Continue straight up for 20m and up a last little wall on the R (V: piton). Follow ledges leading L to where c50m of easy slopes lead to the summit ridge. **10-12hr**: 1hr approach

57d | **DIRECT ROUTE**
ED3
54

P Bouilloux and P Wilmart, 15 and 16 Aug 1977
Direct finish: J-M Cambon and B Francou, 1981

There is little equipment in place. A large, varied rack including a large friend or two for the diagonal traverse below the summit, plus some thin pitons is recommended. The rock is excellent and very compact although the lower section is difficult to follow and it is suggested that a dawn arrival at this point renders the route finding easier. There is still some pretty unstable rock in this zone which has already seen the brutal demise of one party.

With a total height of 1,100m it is strongly urged that would be climbers treat this route more seriously than sport climbs, it is cold and a bivouac cannot be ruled out, if only on the descent. Difficulties up to 6c and A3.

Approach as for the Couzy route which is followed towards the central couloir. As the Couzy breaks Rwards a section of IV leads to the foot of the wall proper. Start L of a large black stain and 50m R of a big chimney-crack which splits the L side of the face. After a little plinth (IV), climb a dièdre bordering a not too obvious spur on its L side (6a).

Follow terraces R then take a slanting line L for 2 rope lengths (V/V+: unstable blocks). Follow a line of superficial cracks (VI, 6a/b and moves of 6c) to reach the L side of a big black stain in the centre of the face. Follow this edge of the stain to a small terrace (several pitches of V and VI, 6a/b). From there climb up, trending slightly R (VI: section of A3) or, move R along diagonal ramps for two pitches (V/V+). Either way, the middle terraces are reached at the foot of the final section (link with the Couzy route, which climbs off Rwards).

Climb one rope length L of rust coloured rock (IV+/V) to a terrace. Climb the cracks under the grey summit wall just to the height of a spur (V+). Follow a diagonal crack L (V then 6c or A2). From the rib which borders the crack, climb a less steep slab (IV then easy) before traversing R on to the steep rib (V+/VI, 6a) and rocks close to the summit. **14-18hr** climbing

Note the possibility of avoiding the top wall by taking the Couzy route Rwards.

Brèche de l'Olan 2,970m

First tourist crossing: A Cust and R Pendlebury with G and J Spechtenhauser, 6 July 1875

This, probably long used, col forms a passage between the Vénéon valley and Valjouffrey. It is situated between L'Olan and

the Aiguille de l'Olan and provides, for the alpinist, an approach
to the Font Turbat hut and the NW face of l'Olan from the N.

58a   **WEST SIDE**

F   First tourists

From the Fond Turbat hut take a path leading NE up scree
slopes. Follow the R bank of the W-most stream and then cross
the stream and slant R up a grassy bank and then straight up to
reach the cirque containing the Pissoux lake (2,632m). Cross the
cirque of scree/névé to the lake. Slant R and climb a couloir,
which is generally snow filled, direct to the brèche. **2½hr**

58b   **EAST SIDE**

F

From the Lavey hut follow the track on the L bank of the stream
until it forks at Pt 1,926m (easy to miss in the dark). Take the R
branch which slants gradually up the hillside, cross a couloir and
continue by rock steps to a stony hollow. Zigzag up this and head
R to a spur (cairn). Climb this for a little way before traversing L
via occasional rock steps to the moraine overlooking the Sellettes
glacier. Follow the moraine to the top and then continue, by the
L bank of the glacier, to the couloir below the brèche. Climb it
easily. **4hr**

In descent to the Lavey hut it is important not to descend too
low on the moraine. Look carefully for the traverse track (easily
missed).

Bec du Canard 3,269m and Aiguille des Arias 3,402m

E Rochat with P Gaspard snr and jnr, 11 July 1878 and
W Coolidge with C Almer snr and jnr, 4 July 1876 respectively

These relatively minor peaks are roughly W of the Lavey hut.
They present a rocky, interconnecting ridge of some interest.

59a   **NORTH-SOUTH TRAVERSE**

AD   Réthoré and Fortuné, 14 Aug 1933

An interesting, airy traverse which is quite long. The rock is reason-able. The S-N traverse is possible but more difficult and not often followed.

From the Lavey hut take the path S on the L bank of the torrent and leave it fairly soon to take a small path R towards the Col des Aiguilles. Branch R a second time to reach the Lac des Bêches (2,401m). Climb on to the E ridge of the Bec du Canard either taking a high or low line. After having turned a step on the N flank, follow the E ridge then the last steps of the NE ridge to the summit. 4-5hr

From the Bec du Canard descend the SW ridge crossing or skirting round several gendarmes. Pass through a narrow fault between two grey gendarmes and then avoid another gendarme by the SE flank to reach the first brèche. Climb a red gendarme and descend it by means of a dièdre that scores its face to reach the next brèche (Pt 3,155m). From the gap follow the crest of the ridge and then, on the Lavey side, gain the top of a gen-darme. Descend easily down to a platform above a deep brèche by a 20m rappel. Climb up via a chimney and some slabs on the Lavey flank to rejoin the crest of the ridge formed by rather unstable flakes of red rock. Continue over these as far as the summit of the Pointe O'Gorman (3,248m). From the top rappel 25m to reach a narrow gap. Continue on the Mariande (W) side following a ledge which ends at a bulging wall (exposed). Climb a short chimney on this flank and then reach the top of a grey gendarme. From this point rappel 30m to reach a 'V' shaped brèche at the foot of another grey gendarme. The ridge then offers a horizontal line broken by three pinnacles. Pass the first on a steep slab on the Lavey side and the following two along the crest. A brèche (not too deep) is reached. Traverse a 20m gendarme by a gently sloping slab in order to reach the brèche situated at the foot of the NE ridge of the Aiguille des Arias.

From this brèche climb the ridge, on snow at first and then slabs, up to the brèche close to the summit. By means of a steep wall, 10m high, attain the final ridge and the E summit. 5-6hr (The W summit, 3,400m may be reached by an almost level ridge in c1hr)

Descend by following the length of the SE ridge, leaving the crest from time to time. Arrive at the Col d'Entre Pierroux (3,169m) and slant L to reach an enclosed couloir which leads out on to the Lac glacier. Return to the Lac des Bêches, passing several rognons *en route*. 3-4hr: **12-15hr** total

Tête de Lauranoure 3,325m

A grand looking mountain rising to the S above St Christophe-en-Oisans in the Vénéon valley. Despite its appearance the N flank has little to offer. Of more interest is the remote W flank, at the top of which is the highest point, the central summit.

60a
TD

55

SOUTH-WEST FACE

E Brun, P Faure and G Turc, 22 July 1945

The W face of the Tête de Lauranoure is a 450m high wall, split down the middle by a deep couloir issuing from the cleft between the S and central summits. It is bounded on the R by the W spur descending from the S ridge of the S summit; on the L the wall curves and faces SW. This SW face of the central summit, bounded on the R by the deep couloir has, in a direct line below the summit, a spur which soon disappears. The face is cut obliquely by a couloir (not visible from the valley) coming from the NW ridge of the central summit which projects into the main couloir at the lower end.

Approach the face from Lanchâtra in the lower Vénéon valley by the path to la Selle. Just beyond la Selle the track bifurcates at Pt 1,935m. Take the L fork and climb the slopes on the lower, W flank of the mountain. Where the path starts to descend to the valley, leave it by traversing S across stony slopes, climbing steadily, to reach the scree combe on the W flank of the mountain. Climb scree to the barrier at the L of the mouth of the big couloir. 4hr

Climb the big, easy-angled slabs which lead to a ledge (of which the L end is dominated by a chimney). Follow the ledge R to the edge of the big couloir and climb a chimney to a platform. Climb steep slabs, well furnished with good holds, which lead to the diagonal couloir issuing from the NW ridge. Climb a big slab on good holds (do not attempt to go L up the vertical grooves). Gain a little ledge and follow it Rwards to a couloir. Descend a few m into the couloir and then climb a long chimney which ends under an overhang. Exit R on to steep slabs which lead to a ledge below an overhang. Cross the overhang on the R and take a small crack which leads back L above it. Go directly up a vertical dièdre (30m: fairly closed) which finishes on a small platform. From the start this is all IV/V.

Climb L of big, loose blocks to reach a hollow. Continue by slanting L to R up a slab which ends under an overhanging wall. Climb this on the R where it is less steep and, by a succession of delicate little walls, reach the foot of a long couloir ascending Lwards (IV+/V to here). Climb this easily to reach a big ledge slanting up R to L which is followed to the foot of some big, steep grooves. Don't look for an alternative but climb these directly (delicate) on to a big ledge cut off by a vertical wall on the L. Follow the ledge R and descend a delicate, airy chimney. Traverse a few m R to the base of a big wall which is climbed (exposed: good holds). Reach a ridge on the R, which forms the R bank of a diagonal couloir, having its origin L of the summit and falling to the big couloir of the SW face. Cross this couloir and reach the summit by some big slabs. **6-8hr** from the foot of the face

To descend: There is a choice of going to the Alpe du Pin hut or to the start of the climbs described.

To reach the Alpe du Pin hut follow the NW ridge and get on to the W branch of the Pierroux glacier. Descend its L bank to pick up the path passing through grassy pasture and scree in a

NE direction to the hut. F: c2½hr

To reach the foot of the SW face follow the NW ridge. Shortly before a snowy saddle is a little gendarme with a small brèche beyond it. From the brèche, reach a couloir-chimney which descends obliquely R to L across the SW face and leads almost to the bottom of the snowy couloir which separates the S and central summits. Follow it to that point but do not descend the couloir itself (stonefall). Make a rappel of 30m and then go down slightly (easy) before making a traverse R and descending a tight, 10m chimney. By a 30m rappel gain a large platform and then follow this obliquely R for 100m. Return L to reach the base of the face and join the route of ascent. PD: c1hr

60b
AD
55

WEST SPUR

G Dalou, G Turc and UNCM course members, 20 Aug 1956

The spur is well marked on the map. It is a fine climb on good rock and is highly recommended.

From Lanchâtra follow Route 60a into the combe on the W flank. Cross the lower part of the combe to the bottom of the spur (bivouacs). 4hr

Climb it easily to the foot of a step. Slant L to reach a little brèche on the N flank. Climb the arête and arrive at a notch (III). Move R (a step of IV) to continue by the crest, which becomes easy, and reach a terrace. Climb the gendarme which follows by keeping R (III). From its top either rappel or climb (III) to the brèche behind. Climb the second gendarme (III and IV) and descend easily from it to the third gendarme. Climb this (III and IV). From the top, descend slightly and then continue easily along the crest. Reach a facet which forms the W side of the S ridge. Either reach the ridge directly and follow it to the summit or, more interestingly, climb slanting R to L and arrive close to the summit (III and IV). Follow the ridge Nwards to the central summit. **4hr** from the foot of the spur

Roche de la Muzelle 3,465m

W Coolidge with C Almer snr and U Almer, 2 July 1875

This is the W most of the main peaks in the region and is located more or less S of Venosc in the lower Vénéon valley. It is a fine viewpoint on account of its detachment from surrounding peaks. It has a long summit ridge which has three distinct tops; SW 3,465m, central 3,450m and NE 3,418m although only the former is indicated on the map. Probably because of its relative remoteness, it is fairly unfrequented.

The Muzelle hut not only offers the base for the present day ordinary route, the W flank and NE ridge, but it also serves rock climbs on the Tête de la Muraillette, 3,019m. These have barely been visited by British parties and are recommended when the higher climbs are out of condition.

61a WEST FLANK AND NORTH-EAST RIDGE

PD   M Bouvier and Clerc, 22 June 1928

A pleasant climb and the only one on the Muzelle which sees much traffic. The entire NE ridge was climbed by the first ascent party

From the Muzelle hut climb the steep, grassy slope past the Roche Percée on the SW side of Pt 2,328m, then continue SE and S to climb a series of humps and rock outcrops on the crest of the ridge to the Muzelle glacier. It is possible to turn Pt 2,328m on its N side at the beginning of the season to reach the glacier direct. Climb the L bank of the glacier, in the direction of the Col Jean Martin, then get over the rimaye to climb the steep, wide snow slope to the col. 2-3hr

From the col traverse R (W flank of the ridge) to a couloir. Climb this (sometimes icy) to the foot of a spur and then continue up this to the crest of the NE ridge. Follow the ridge, on its W flank at first and then on the crest, to the NE summit. The highest point is reached easily from here. c3hr: **5-6hr** from the hut

Descent is by the same route. From the Col Jean Martin it is possible to descend to Lanchâtra by reversing Route 61b.

61b   **EAST FLANK AND NORTH-EAST RIDGE**
PD   First ascent party

The route is not much frequented today but is useful for descent.

From Lanchâtra head S towards the Col des Berches up to the large higher shelf of the valley called Le Plan (2,154m; 2½hr). Cross the Pisse river and climb W up scree slopes passing between two small rocky barriers S of the Rif du Trou. Reach a rocky spur (2,818m), separating the Grande Montagne glacier into two, that goes towards the rocky E spur of la Muzelle. Climb it or go N round it to get on to the glacier. Head NW across it to reach the foot of the Col Jean Martin which is reached via a short rocky slope (3hr). From the Col Jean Martin follow Route 61a to the summit. **c7hr** from Lanchâtra

Descent by the same route.

Le Sirac 3,441m

W Coolidge with C Almer snr and jnr, 2 July 1877

The S-most of the big peaks in the region, it is the prominent peak looking SSW from the summit of les Bans. The main routes of access to the mountain are from the W and in particular, for the routes described, via the Valgaudemar.

62a   **NORTH-WEST FACE - VOIE HERAUD**
AD   P Héraud and a companion, 1945
57
56

The climb is on the R-hand side of the face and is similar in form to the next climb; a steep first plinth, a mid-section of light coloured slabs and a steep final section. It is separated from the Biju-Duval route by a secondary spur. The rock isn't wonderful but what it lacks in this respect the climb makes up in ambience.

From the Vallonpierre hut head E to the foot of the face. Climb the avalanche cone on the R (S) side of the rounded secondary spur almost to its highest point, below a short, debris covered slab. Start up the slab and then climb the chimney bordering the spur, situated on the R bank of a big couloir (lll and IV). Reach the top of the spur at a shoulder.

Continue easily for several rope lengths to reach slabs of poor rock supporting the central névé. Climb these slabs (lll and IV) on the L side, follow a couloir (with a cave on the L) and then several terraces. Cross the big névé of the lower third of the slope on the R side. Tackle steep, light coloured slabs in the centre of the face, moving L a little to join a system of ledges. Follow these and, by a chimney with a chock stone, reach the foot of a secondary rib on the R. Here you reach the upper part of the face. Climb to the top of a névé slope and continue by a snowy couloir and easy blocks to reach the ridge where it merges into the summit block. Continue to the top by a chimney of very good rock (lll). **9hr** from the hut

62b
TD

56

NORTH-WEST FACE DIRECT

P Biju-Duval and H Foucher: 13 Aug 1989

A long climb (900m) on good rock. There is some gear in place. Carry a rack.

Start as for Route 62a, keeping L of the avalanche cone, to reach the rounded spur on the R side of the lowest point of rock. Climb a rounded crack (60m: lll and IV) which leads to the foot of an obelisk, seen from the start. Pass to its L by slabs and steps for over 100m (IV+: the last wall is V-). Now climb easier angled slopes by a long ramp slanting R (lll), back L then straight up to the foot of the summit triangle. The starting point for this is not easy to find. Look for a round cave c100m higher (seen from the hut) and start c25m L of a vertical line from the cave.

Climb on a Rwards sloping ramp then go up an 8m crack (V+) to meet some overhangs. Pass a corner, descending gently R, to a stance on a smooth slab. Climb the easy depression on

the R and a cracked wall leading to a niche (IV+). One rope
length straight up (V/V+: exposed: poor rock) leads just L of a
cave where a shattered ledge carries a perched block. Traverse L
along the ledge to a fine crack. Climb this and the slab above,
with a small loop L (IV+: sustained) and then four rope lengths
up a line of obvious cracks on the R (fine pitches, slabs, dièdres
and good rock). 15m below its top, leave the dièdre where it
overhangs and exit L by a steep slab (V). Here the N ridge route
is joined and followed to the summit. **9hr** from the hut

62c
AD
56

NORTH RIDGE

P Lloyd and J Longland, 17 July 1932

*The classic route on the Sirac. Interesting and direct. The ridge
descends quite steeply from the summit to a prominent brèche at the
S end of the Banc des Aiguilles. The brèche is immediately N of
Pt 2,597.9m*

Climb E from the Vallonpierre hut to the névé (in the early
season) below the W face of the Banc des Aiguilles, generally in
the direction of the brèche mentioned above. Below the brèche
and c50m R of the couloir descending from it, climb névé slopes
to reach a big, horizontal ledge which leads across the W flank in
the direction of the Banc des Aiguilles. Leave the ledge directly
below the brèche, just before it runs out, by a short chimney
pitch of IV (piton). Four rope lengths lead to the brèche and into
the sun! 1½hr

In the mid/late season (or in a dry year) the névé melts to
expose scree and boulders. Take the L edge of the scree cone
below some obvious large ledges and rock barriers. The line
taken is open to choice but breaks into the barriers and needs to
be studied in advance in order not to lose time reaching the
brèche.

From the brèche, climb easy slabs on rounded holds with
superb friction and then move L wards towards the foot of a big
step. Climb the step more or less directly (bits of IV/IV+).
Continue above the step on or close to the crest (III and IV). On

the upper part of the ridge it is necessary to make a few moves L before returning R (III/III+) on to the summit ridge. Climb this by the snow slopes on the W side. 4hr from the brèche: **c6hr** in all

62d DESCENT BY THE WEST FLANK
PD
56

Go down easy couloirs on the SE flank. A good ledge leads to a brèche on the S ridge which is crossed. The rest of the descent is made on the W flank. Don't be tempted by the couloir descending from the brèche but instead climb the ridge for 5m then follow a horizontal ledge R (facing out) before descending a short wall. Now take a descending line Lwards in a dièdre towards the couloir for c100m. Go straight down for 20m and then easily reach the foot of the couloir. Go down the L bank of the Vallonpierre glacier and to the hut by scree slopes.

Banc des Aiguilles 2,750m

This is a long ridge prolonging the N ridge of the Sirac beyond the brèche at its foot. There are now at least four climbs on the Banc des Aiguilles itself and these are to be found on its S side. Details are contained in the guide book *Escalades en Valgaudemar* by Rémy Karle. Two of these are described.

63a STEAK A L'ANCHOIS
TD+
58

R Karle and P Biju-Duval, in 3 attempts, Aug-Sept 1987

Totally equipped by bolts and on excellent rock. Rappels require 50m ropes.

Approach easily from the hut and start directly below the summit, L of a small detached gendarme in a small dièdre (bolt) The route passes L of a lozenge shaped overhang, then turns R above the roof to climb more or less directly towards a black wall. The climb finishes L of 'Oscar'.

P1 5+: P2 6a+: P3 6a: P4 6a: P5 6b: P6 5+: P7 5+: P8 4:
P9 4: P10 3: P11: 5+: P12 5+

Rappel back down the climb.

63b **BRAVO OSCAR**

AD+ P Biju-Duval and J-C Bonsignore, July 1987

58

IV+: with one pitch of V: 350m: Good rock. 50m of ropes and a standard rack will be required.

Reach the obvious couloir/chimney on the L flank of the buttress by a slab (IV). Climb the break for some 175m (III/IV-) to below a jammed block (do not climb above the block). Climb the slab Rwards to an open corner groove (V: bolts). Follow the slabs by their natural weaknesses, up and Rwards, to below the final wall. Piton belays are all in place. Beyond the jammed block are several variations, mostly between IV+ and V, some old pitons are in place and nut/friend placements may be found. All these lines lead to the base of the final crack. The crack line up the final section is obvious (IV) and leads directly to the summit. 3-5hr from the hut

Descent: Whilst it is possible to traverse the summit ridge Rwards to the brèche leading to the NE ridge and then reversing the Longland route (62c), it is both difficult to find and tortuous. Better to take the fixed rappels of Route 63a.

Rock Climbing

Climbs are graded in two ways. They are given an adjectival grading, as used for the mountain routes, which is quoted in the margin. It indicates the overall seriousness of the climb. Climbs are also graded for their technical difficulty. The technical grade utilises the French grading system for sports climbing. In the introduction to each climb, the highest degree of technical difficulty encountered on the climb is given and subsequently the grade of each pitch is given.

Visitors who are unfamiliar with the French grading system should study the International Comparison of Grades table (page 41) provided in the General Information and should also be cautious on their first climbs. They are well advised to start on climbs one grade lower than they would normally expect to lead with comfort. In this way they can assess the style of climbing and the grading system used in this guide and in 'topo' diagrams in locally produced guide books. Slab climbing in particular is of a high order and, despite *in situ* bolts, many will find that if they cannot climb the grade the bolts (spits) will not help...Most bolts are very well spaced.

It should be noted that in this guide we use French grades as set out in the table (numbers in arabic). All the locally available guide books use French grades but with roman numerals.

Sports climbs are usually, but not always, fully equipped with both bolts and rappel points. The local French guide books use a star rating to indicate the extent of this bolting. We have used a rating system for the same purpose and this appears in the margin of the text below the route number and grade (a # is used to avoid confusion with the star quality rating familiar to British climbers). Note that it differs from the French system:

- indicates a fully equipped climb.
- indicates a climb with ageing gear or a mix of modern bolts and traditional pitons.
- means that a normal rack of friends, nuts and slings etc should be carried.

A most important feature of modern sport climbing is the need to descend via multiple rappels from *in situ* bolts. These anchors are mostly made up of two bolts linked by either chain or full-weight rope. In addition to the technical issues involved it is not always easy, or possible, to see the next rappel point. It is therefore recommended that climbers take great care to place a protection device on their harness - rope linkage and tie the two ends of the rappel ropes before leaving the stance. It is often necessary to make a diagonal swing (or 'pendule') in order to reach the stance and bolts below.

Since many of the newer climbs are over 400m long, it will be appreciated that practise in multi-rappel situations will make the difference between a return to base or a night out on the crag! It is now essential to use 50m ropes.

The General Information section carries an up to date list of guide books to the region. Whilst they are written in French, they contain 'Topo diagrams' which should need little or no translation. For this reason the author does not see fit to give an exhaustive list of valley based sport climbs around the massif. Most of the guide books may be purchased locally at little cost but for the serious sport climber it is essential to buy the latest guide book by Jean-Michel Cambon, *Oisans Moderne - Oisans Sauvage* which is published privately.

The climbs recommended are chosen from personal experience as being among the best and most typical of the particular site. Most have already become 'Classics' of their genre. In this matter of selection the author is indebted to Murray Hamilton and Carol Nash for their help. Not only are they active at the highest levels, it is true to say that as full time residents in the region they are already set to replace the current author as the 'local experts'.

As a final note, there has been no attempt to consider the scores of crags within easy reach of the main massif. This is in part because they are so numerous but it is also because they are dealt with more effectively in regional publications relying almost exclusively upon topo diagrams, which require no translations.

The only feature of development which is unusual is the creation, to date, of seven *via ferrata*. Other projects are already in the course of construction and local Tourist Offices will provide the relevant information.

Ailefroide area

In this section the climbs described are ascribed an equivalent British grade for the benefit of the user who is unfamiliar with either the standard of climbing in the area and/or the French grading system.

Fissure Buttress

Situated behind the village campsite. From the site office follow the roadway to a footbridge over the Celse-Nière river. There are two routes, each is highly recommended. Further R on the crag there is a bouldering area.

r1
D
59

Fissure
L Terray and party, 1955

British VS: 250m. This is the original route of the crag. It is not bolted so a normal rack should be taken. The line is obvious and well marked through use. Belays are always comfortable. Harder when wet - there are several waterfalls.

The descent follows the well marked track which climbs at first and then trends L to cross the deep gorge (care needed) before descending through trees to the meadow.

r2
TD-
59

Snoopy
M André, B Gorgeon and Snoopy, 1973.

###

British HVS: 6b+ (5+ obl): 250m. This climb, L of the Fissure, has now been bolted to give an excellent route, varied in character and of sustained difficulty. On pitch 3 follow the dièdre above the ledge, the variation on the R is sustained 6a.

Palavar Sector

r3
D-
60
###

Palavar les Flots

J-M and S Cambon, 1990

British VS: 2 pitches of 5 (4 obl): 400m. This is a classic of the easier grade routes in the modern idiom. It is justly popular and repays an early start to avoid the crowds in high season.

The approach track starts c100m up the main path (to the Pelvoux and Sélé huts) from the large information notice at the edge of the woods. Turn R and upwards by a huge boulder with a bivouac site below it. After c30min reach the tree line at the base of the Palavar ridge. The start is c50m up and L of the base of the ridge. There is no route finding problem.

Descent is best done by rappelling back down the last two pitches of the climb, then take a direct line down the slab via two prominent trees and then a final pitch to a brèche (*in situ* bolts and chain). From here the track descends easily to a notch above a chimney on the R. A fixed rope (*in situ*) enables the easy path below to be reached. Follow this to regain the start of the climb.

Etoiles sector

Take the path on the R which starts from the small parking area behind the Engilberge Hotel.

r4
D+/TD-
61
###

Orage d'Etoiles

P Paillasson, F Augé and G Fiaschi

British HVS: sustained 5/5+: 450m

The approach path leads to the Etoiles slabs, an equipped training crag. Pass R of the slabs and scramble up the gully below the steep upper wall to just below a large jammed block which is the start of the route. There is a direct variant (6a) on the R and below the block. The climb offers superb and often delicate slab climbing. Descent: rappel the line of ascent.

Pear Buttress

The Pear is reached in c30min from the Engilberge Hotel. Between hotel and the river a path leads up the valley towards Cézanne. Follow it, first through woods and then across a tributary stream coming from the L. Move diagonally L over broken but easy ground to the foot of the climbs. There are routes of all grades, the harder ones to the L of the gully, which gives the line of descent, and more amenable climbs on the Pear itself. Of these the following is probably the best.

r5
###
Cocarde
J-P Flandin and D Stumpert, 1987

British HVS: 5 and 5+ with a move of 6a: 200m. This is a good, varied climb on excellent rock.

Start below the small overhang at the foot of the slab which is bounded on the L by the obvious deep gully.

Descent: the 1st rappel point is hidden behind the top stance. Care needs to be taken with shrubs on the first two rappels and with stonefall once the gully is reached.

Tête de la Draye sector

From the village of Ailefroide follow the road towards Cézanne (Pré de Mme Carle). c500m beyond the bridge are two waterfalls on the R-hand side of the valley, beyond the 'Ecole d'escalade'.

r6
###
Cascade Blues
J-M and S Cambon, 1992

British HVS/VS+: 5+ and 6a: 200m. The climb is quite varied.

The climb starts R of the waterfalls at the slightly overhanging base of a narrow slab. Depending upon the state of the waterfalls, wet feet from traversing both obstacles (which are unavoidable) are likely! Descent is by three rappels (*in situ*) then by a footpath which returns to the valley.

Massif des Cerces

This chain of limestone peaks lies NE of the Guisane valley. E of the chain runs the Clarée (or Névache) river.

Briançon represents the S boundary, whilst to the N lies the Galibier to Valloire road (D902), the Maurienne valley and the Mont Tabor group. The chain is not broken transversally by a motorable route, although the mountain bike enthusiast will find old mining tracks linking the obvious valleys which penetrate the group. Anthracite was mined in the Vallon de la Moulette, which may be entered either from the old track (known as the 'Chemin du Roy') running N from the Col du Granon or Monêtier les Bains.

Climbing here is relatively recent with most of the developments taking place after the 1970s. The first French guide book appeared in 1983, written by Suzy Péguy in collaboration with Jean-Jacques Rolland, which covered the Hautes Durance and Montbrison. This is no longer available. The guide by J-M Cambon *Oisans Moderne - Oisans Sauvage* is the current reference. He tends to concentrate on climbs in the top grades and ignore many of the earlier classics of the J-J Rolland and S Péguy 1960/70s era. However, a new book: *Les Plus Belles Escalade Calcaires des Hautes Alpes* J-P Bizet, P Giraud and J-J Rolland (2000) Private publication is now available and gives some good coverage.

The most useful maps are the IGN TOP 25, 1:25000 series: Névache and Mont Tabor - Ref: 3535OT and Briançon. Serre-Chevalier. Montgenèvre - Ref: 3536OT.

Access to the climbs described is either from the Guisane or Clarée valleys.

Climbs on the Crête du Diable, Crête du Raisin and Crête du Queyrellin are easily accessible from the Chalets de Fontcouvert in the upper Clarée valley. The Chardonnet hut, at 2,219m, is a good base. There is a shorter, direct path, avoiding the hut, to the Queyrellin climbs leading from the N end of the camp site close to the Refuge la Fruitière (parking) via the

Couzy-Desmaison Route on l'Olan (Route 57c) Dore Green climbing
Simon Richardson

Chalets de Queyrellin and the true L bank of the stream. 1hr

Access to the Tête Noire is either from Monêtier les Bains or by a footpath which leads from the Col de Buffère. This col is reached by an unmade but motorable road from a distinctive, sharp hairpin bend (snack bar in summer) c3km below the summit of the Col du Granon on the Guisane flank. Climbers are strongly requested to leave vehicles at the Col de Buffère. There is no official permission to use this access or parking but the practice is tolerated. Local shepherds follow the lower level (wide) continuation track for higher pasture access, using four wheel drive vehicles. The temptation to do the same is to be repressed in the interests of the environment. It is now common to follow the upper (narrow) track which leads from the col and descends gently to contour the first spur. This section of track is clearly marked but at mid-distance it becomes indistinct and at one point an obvious, steeply rising line must be avoided in favour of a grassy line (cairn) to reach the obvious continuation c150m further on. The path now leads directly to below the crags of the 1st Tower and the Pear buttress. The line is difficult to follow in mist.

In winter most of the torrents feeding into both rivers freeze to give easily accessible ice routes of modest standard which are great fun.

Ski touring potential is good. The circuit of the Cerces is possible using huts or, by shifting from valley to valley, for day excursions. Skiers are advised to check locally with the Tourist Offices regarding winter availability of facilities. Since several huts and gîtes are privately owned, they cannot be guaranteed to be open.

The Cerces contains a section of the GR5 long distance route which may be completed either on foot or ski. (See: *Grande Traverse* by Malcolm and Nicole Parker: ISBN 0-906371-81-3: Published by Diadem).

Finally, the Cerces is a nature reserve into which bouquetins (ibex) have recently been reintroduced with success. Please respect the wild life and the environment in general.

Tim Noble climbing on the Tête de la Maye Ian Smith

Note: The sketch map (page 38) and much other material in Rébuffat's *100 Plus Belles Courses* is incorrect - do not use this as a reference.

The climbs: A good, modest level of introduction to the style of climbing might be on the Aiguillette de Lauzet, 2,611m, which has quick (45min to the start of the *via ferrata*) and easy access from Pont des Alpes, between the Col du Lautaret and Monêtier les Bains. The *via ferrata* (vf1) and the Voie Davin (r15) are described. Peaks are listed anti-clockwise starting from the Grand Galibier above the Col du Lautaret.

Grand Galibier - Tour Termier 3,070m

This is the first distinctive peak seen NE of the Col du Lautaret *en route* for Briançon. Below the *paravalanche*, the old route to the Col du Galibier can be seen on the L (in descent). This is motorable with care. This road swings R, then takes a sharp hairpin L wards. Park here (Pt 2,084m). From the parking spot a faint path leads to the face in c1½hr. The climbs described are on the W face.

r7
ED
64
###

Le Feu Sacré
J-M Cambon and G Fiaschi, 1987

7a max (6a obl): 300m: 5-7hr

P1 6a: P2 6a/b: P3 6a/b: P4 ledges then 6b+: P5 6a ramp: P6 6b: P7 7a: P8 6b: P9 6c: P10 5+

Descent: this is equipped with double bolts and chain. At the mid-point (5 rappels) is an obvious ramp. Climb R (facing out) down ledges to reach the last rappel point, which leads to the gully. It is possible and easy to descend the ridge to the Col Termier but this has the disadvantage that it arrives c200m below the start of the route!

r8
ED+
64
###

Ici mieux qu'en face

J-M Rey, L Lesueur and P Giraud, in 4 days, 1991

7b/c max: 250m: 5-7hr. The climb takes the big white wall R of the big dièdre and follows a line L of the dark, wet streaks in the middle of the wall. It is considered to be one of the hardest climbs in the Cerces. It is sustained (6b-7b) and escape is not easy from beyond the eight pitch.

P1 6b: P2 7a+: P3 6b+: P4 7a: P5 5+ - short pitch: P6 6c+: P7 6b: P8 7b: P9 7a: P10 7a: P11 6c+

Descent: follow ledges Rwards (S) to reach the line of 6 *in situ* rappels of which the fourth is diagonally L (N).

Note: A third climb is possible R of 'Ici mieux...' This is 'Allo la Terre' (TD: totally equipped) which takes a line well to the L on the more amenable section of the slabs.

Tête de Colombe 3,023m

Parking is by the second tunnel (Tunnel des Vallois) below the col, after passing the avalanche protected section of road. From there a track leads directly to the crags.

Roche Colombe must not be confused with the Tête de Colombe which lies behind and to the SE.
    The sector is composed of two distinct zones: The 'Ecaille' (literally, the Flake) and the SE facette. The Ecaille is the impressive, detached pillar/flake which dominates the view of the peak from the main road. To reach this section, walk through the wood and, on leaving it, turn L. 1½hr

r9
TD
65
###

Ecaille de Roche Colombe

Rapin, Raymond and Renaud, 1962

5+ max: 200m: 5-6hr. The classic route of the sector. It can be cold before the sun reaches the rock at c11am and any seepage makes the climb more difficult and less pleasant than it can be.

P1 5+: P2 4: P3 5: P4 5+: P5 5: P6 5: P7 5: P8 4: P9 4

Descent: from the top of the flake rappel Lwards (N) to the brèche between it and the wall. From there climb L for 150m (2 and 3), then traverse gently downwards on steep scree to reach the foot of the face. Not nice in rock slippers! 1-1½hr

A rappel descent is possible and probably preferable. Each rappel point has double bolt and chain, the first two of which are well L (N) of the route itself. Because of high winds which regularly rake the face is it recommended that on the free sections the rope is clipped to bolts two or three times to avoid difficulties. This descent is preferable in rock slippers!

r10
D/TD-

66
###

Voie de la Scuola Gervassuti

U Manera, C Unione and four students, 1977

5/5+ max: 350m: 5-6hr. This route is a classic. It is used regularly by local guides.

P1 5+: P2 5+: P3 4: P4 4+: P5 5+: P6 5+: P7 5: P8 5: P9 5: P10 4+

Descent: from the top of the face a rappel leads to a huge ledge which is followed L. A line of rappels leads to the Ecaille.

r11
TD

66
###

Les Gradins Dauphinois

J-M and S Cambon, 1992

6a max: 350m: 5hr. A climb which is broken by ledges and grassy sections. Despite its lack of continuity it gives some fine climbing and uses the best of the rock.

P1 5: P2 5+: P3 6a - 1st brèche: P4 5: P5 5+ - 2nd brèche: P6 2: P7 5+ - short traverse R: P8 5+: P9 6a: P10 6a: P11 5: P12 2 then 6a: P13 4

Descent: either by the previously described route, or by rappels down the face, initially by the route itself then trending R (E) of the climb. Care is demanded in locating these rappel points, which are equipped.

r12
TD
66
###

La Valse des Boucs

J-M Cambon and D Levaillant, 1991

6a max: 250m: 5-6hr. The climb exploits a zone of slabs R of 'Bal des Boucas'. Above the shoulder it is possible to avoid the pitch of 6b (P6) by taking the line on the R (6a/5+).

P1 6a: P2 6a: P3 6a: P4 6a: P5 6a. The climb now follows a horizontal ledge system (the shoulder) to the foot of an arête. P6 6b or 6a: P7 5+: P8 6a: P9 5+: P10 4

Descent: either rappel for five pitches down the climb (difficult and awkward as the line trends Rwards for much of the way), or from the start of the upper, difficult section, rappel Lwards to reach an obviously well equipped line, which is quick, if airy. The alternative is the take the previous (tedious) descent route from the top of the Tête Colombe.

r13
TD+
66
###

Le Bal des Boucas

D Maure and P Pellet, 1985

6b/c max: 250m: 5-6hr. This is one of the best routes of its standard in the Cerces. It is not sustained but finishes up a steep and difficult final pillar which gives the hardest climbing. The lower slab pitches are much used.

The name of the climb derives from the day of the 1st ascent when a bouquetin ferociously attacked Daniel Maure's dog at the foot of the climb!

P1 5: P2 6a: P3 6a: P4 5+: P5 4: P6 5+: P7 5+ - cross the shoulder: P8 6b: P9 5+ - common r12: P10 6b/c - Rwards

Descent: by rappels described for r12 but easier to pick out whilst on the climb.

Arêtes de Bruyères 2,619m

r14

AD

67

\#\#

Ridge Traverse

3 and 4 (not sustained: pitons): 3-4hr. The Arêtes du Bruyères (2,619m) is probably the best known feature and classic climb (together with the Aiguillette de Lauzet) accessible from the Pont de l'Alpe and the chalets of the Alpes de Lauzet (Gîte d'étape).

There is a well worn, broad and much frequented path connecting with the GR57. Park at the bend in the road at Pont de l'Alpe or on the unmade road alongside the stream which descends to the bridge above the main road and restaurant.

Follow the track via the chalets to reach the GR57 at Pt 2,209m. Turn due N and continue along the base of the arêtes. Climb up Lwards to the start of the ridge. The route follows a line NW-SE. and overlooks the lake between itself and the Roche Colombe. 1½hr from Pont de l'Alpe

Start directly below the last little gendarme on the ridge, a small cave marks the beginning of the climb. Ledges on the Guisane flank offer alternative lines to the crest itself.

Descent: this is easy to find with an obvious trail continuing in a SE direction. After 10min scrambling (one 25m rappel useful - slings in place) a good grassy path is reached which joins the GR57 at Pt 2,209 about half-way between the start of the arête and the Alpe de Lauzet chalets. Don't leave gear at the start of the climb!

Aiguillette de Lauzet 2,726m

The routes described are on the SW face. Approach from Pont de l'Alpe as for the *via ferrata* and turn R before the chalets of Alpes de Lauzet. Pass through a wood before skirting the base of the mountain along a well worn, wide track to the extreme (S) end of the cliff. c2hr

r15 Voie Davin

D

68

#/##

Abbés Davin and Blanc, 1940s

4 and 5 max (4+ obl): 250m: 4hr

The climb follows the obvious chimney/couloir L of the main summit. To reach the start is not obvious but small tracks zigzag through rocky barriers and grass ledges to the foot of the couloir. Alternatively, climb the first pitches of 'Voie de l'Etoile' (r16) to reach the large terrace and then traverse L to the couloir.

Escape may be made Lwards at the obvious shoulder (Vire Davin - a big ledge) below the last few pitches to join the *via ferrata*. It is important to traverse L at this ledge to reach a chimney on the ridge (4) made up of big blocks. Other direct lines on the face itself have sustained pitches of 6a.

Descent: very easy from the summit: at first via a good track (NE then E) leads to a steep scree couloir and then grassy slopes leading S, then SW. Regain the original approach below the crag.

r16 Voie de l'Etoile

D+

68

###

S Péguy, J-M Cambon and B Francou, 1980
Direct start described here: G Fiaschi, 1993

6b/A0/A1 max (5+ obl): 300m: The artificial section, level with the 'Vire Davin' has been climbed free and directly at 6c and is reputedly hard.

P1 5: P2 5: P3 cross ledges then 5+: P4 5+ - cross ledges: P5 5: P6 2 - trend up Lwards along a curving ledge: P7 6a: P8 6a: P9 either: R 6c or L 6b/A0: P10 traverse R, 5+: P11 A1: P12 6a: P13 5+: P14 6a: P15 5

Descent: as for r15

r17 Beaux Quartiers

)+/ED

68

###

G Fiaschi, 1986

6b max (6a/5+ obl): 300m: 5-6hr. A fine climb which is not sustained but with magnificent upper pitches. Escape can be made on to Voie

Davin (Route r15) to avoid the hardest pitch. By this means and by using aid the climb can be accomplished at a British 5c grade.

P1 6b: P2 the overhang - traverse L beneath it: P3 6a: these three pitches may be avoided by taking the Voie Davin approach P4 6a: P5 short, 5+ - cross ledges: P6 5+: P7 6a: P8 5+: P9 6b -Vire Davin: P10 6a+: P11 6a: P12 6a: P13 5

Descent: as for r15. The rappel descent is not recommended!

Vallon de la Moulette

From the Col de Buffère (parking) do not drop down to the the wide track but follow a higher, smaller path, always follow the horizontal line as described in detail in the introduction to the massif. 1hr either way

Tête Noire 2,917m

First Tower - SW face

r18
AD+
69
##

Voie de la Poire

M Vaillot and E Martin, 1956

3 and 4+: 4-5hr. This is the original route on the Poire and one of the rare, easy climbs.

Descent: from the top of the last slab pitch, traverse L for 150m to descend by an easy path.

Note: This climb is often used by parties of young people from centres.

r19
TD+
69
###

Voie de la Grande Mère

S Péguy, Capt Marmier, Adj Peeters and M Pichot, 1968

6a max/A0 (5+ obl): 350m: 5-6hr. This is a classic climb opened by the doyenne of climbing in the Cerces.

P1 5: P2 5/A0: P3 5+: P4 5+: P5 5: P6 L of the big roof, 6a/A0 then 5: P7 5+: P8 5/4: P9 5: P10 4

Descent: as for r18

r20
ED
69
###

Ayla

P Mach, P Pellet and L Pilar, 1987

7b+ max (6a/b obl): 370m: 6hr. A remarkable and varied climb which takes a direct line up the wall R of the rib. The route regenerated interest in this hanging valley.

P1 6b then 5: P2 6a: P3 6b: P4 6a: P5 6b then 7b: P6 6b - R of the big roof, then 5+: P7 6b: P8 5+: P9 5+

Descent is by rappel.

Second Tower - SW face

r21
TD+
69
###

Premières Mesures

J-M Cambon and J Saez, 1990

6a with 1 move of 6c (6a/5+ obl): 300m: 5-7hr. A climb which makes use of the lower grey slabs of the tower, then follows the edge of the S pillar to finish.

P1 5+: P2 5+: P3 5 then traverse R, 4: P4 6a+: P5 6a+: P6 6a+: P7 7b (6a/5+ obl): P8 6a: P9 6a: P10 6a

Descent: by rappel. Two 50m ropes essential as the first pitch is 44m long!

r22
TD
69
###

Vaille que Vaille

C and J-M Cambon and Y Ghesquiers, 1991

6a max: 300m: 5hr. A fine route, easier than 'Premières Mesures', with which it shares the first pitches. It strikes L independently (avoiding the old line of 'Voie Vaillot' which is L of the equipped route) to follow a superb line of sustained grade 5 climbing which Cambon (and others) describe as 'A big step towards paradise!'

P1 and P2 as above P3 5 then move R: P4 5+: P5 5+: P6 6a: P7 6a: P8 5+: P9 5+: P10 5+

Descent: by rappel between the two climbs described..

Climbs from the Chardonnet Hut (Clarée valley)

The final section of this collection is concerned with climbs from the Clarée valley, the NE flank of the Cerces. The hut is at the hub of the three main crags of interest and is therefore a logical base. Bivouacs?...Take your pick.

Crête de Queyrellin 2,936m

The towers of the Queyrellin offer the highest walls in the massif attaining 400m. However, the closest climbing to the hut (20min walk) is an outlier, the Pavé du Chardonnet at the SE end of the ridge and close to the Chardonnet torrent. The climb described is on the E face.

Pavé du Chardonnet

r23
TD
###

Retour en Névachie

G Fiaschi and N Izquierdo, 1994

5+ max: 200m: 3-4hr. Due to its popularity and the stone covered ledges, a helmet is recommended.

From the L edge of the buttress (cairns), follow ledges Rwards to a perched block and continue a little further to reach the start.

P1 5: P2 4+ traverse R: P3 4: P4 cross the grassy ledge, 3: P5 5+: P6 5: P7 cross the ledge then 4+/5: P8 5+: P9 5

Descent: either rappel back down the climb, or take a 15m rappel behind the summit to reach a grassy gully facing S.

A second climb, by the same authors a year later, climbs the L edge of the buttress. (Grade 4/5, one move of 6a or A0)

Aiguillette du Queyrellin

This summit lies L of the Pavé and c10min walk from it. It offers other relatively short climbs of quality.

r24
TD+

70
###

Nulle part ailleurs
G Fiaschi and L Gally, 1994

6a: 150m: 3hr. The climb is particularly recommended: excellent rock. Other climbs are recorded in the Hut Book but the routes on this section are all of similar standard and fully equipped.

The start is just beyond the low point of the buttress.

P1 5+: P2 5+ one move of 6b+ or A0: P3 6a: P4 6a

Descent: for all climbs here is by 3 *in situ* rappels of 40m

Second tower - West face

r25
ED
71
###

Les Dents de Cyrielle
G Chantriaux and A Paret, 1992

6c/7a max: 350m: 6-7hr. An exceptional climb by virtue of its and scale. It is one of the best routes in the group.

The climb is reached by taking the path towards the Col du Chardonnet (GR57). The stream swings NW below the 1st tower of the Aiguillette. Follow this track facing the main summit, so as to avoid crossing the boulder field until the last moment. 1hr from the hut

P1 3: P2 6c: P3 6c: P4 6a: P5 6c: P6 6c: P7 6b: P8 6c: P9 6c+: P10 6a: P11 6c: P12 6c

Descent: rappels *in situ* alongside the climb.

Crête du Raisin 2,818m - West face

From the hut take the footpath to where it joins the GR57 and follow this Swards towards the Col de Roche Noire. 45min-1hr

r26
D-/TD
72
###

Le Raisin Giclera 3 Fois
G Fiaschi and N Izquierdo, July/Aug 1997

6a max: The climb is not sustained.

Start beneath a brèche below the third steep step in the ridge, L of a zone of black slabs. Follow the pillar, then, at mid-height, move Rwards to the summit.

P1 5+: P2 6a: P3 5+: P4 5: P5 4+: P6 traverse Rwards, 2: P7 6a: P8 6a: P9 5: P10 6a: P11 traverse R across the ramp, easy: P12 5: P13 5+

Descent: from the summit follow the ridge Swards then a couloir on the R towards the Col de Roche Noire and the GR57. 1 rappe of 40m

r27 **Les Mystères de l'Ouest**
TD-
72
###

G Fiaschi and N Izquierdo, 15/16 Aug 1996

5/5+ with one short section 6a: The climb is mainly on slabs which border a couloir, which in turn separates this climb from the previous route further L. The rock is good.

Take the GR57 as for *Le Raisin Giclera ..* (r26) and leave it just before the final zigzags. 45min-1hr

P1 5: P2 5: P3 5+: P4 5: P5 4 - ledge: P6 5+ - passing a blac overhang which is on the R: P7 5+: P8 5 - cross grassy ledge then 3: P9 5+ - trend R: P10 diagonally L easily then 5+: P11 6a, 2 then 5 to belay on a ledge which is L of a black niche: P12 5

Descent: as for r26

Crête du Diable 2,869m - West face

r28 **L'Enfer du Décor**
TD+
73
###

G Fiaschi and C Malthieux, July 1996

6a with 1 pitch 6c/A0: 250m+: The 6c/A0 direct variation of P3 ma be avoided on the L and this is clearly marked on the photograph. Th upper section is sustained.

From the hut, climb up the Grande Manche valley (45min). There is a huge cross on the summit and the climb follows a lin from directly below this.

P1 6a: P2 5+: P3 6c/A0 direct, or 5 then 3 on the L:

P4 descend easily L: P5 5+: P6 6a: P7 6a: P8 6c/A0: P9 6a:
P10 6a to the cross

Descent: by 6 rappels down the climb to the 4th belay then take
a direct line down the slab for 2 pitches.

Montbrison

The group extends from Prelles, minutes down river from
Briançon, to Vallouise and lies roughly W to E. The main
summits are the Pic de Montbrison 2,818m and Tête d'Amont
2,815m. Slightly lower is the Tête d'Aval 2,698m.

Approaching from Briançon the most obvious features that
come into view above the village of Prelles, where the D4 turns
Rwards to les Vigneaux and Vallouise, are the distinctive, two
pronged form of the Tenailles (tongs) de Montbrisson. The
sinuous D4 road traverses the steep hillside perched high above
the Durance. It becomes extremely difficult in winter and is
rarely cleared of snow and ice. Reliable winter access is via
l'Argentière la Bessée, c8km downstream, from where the D994E
leads more reasonably to Vallouise and the upper valleys.

Montbrison is a limestone massif, dolomitic in stature and
form, with steep, wooded slopes forming the plinth above which
spring the cliffs which attain c500m in height. The general aspect
is S facing, posing problems in summer with fluid intake. There
are numerous springs along the base of the cliffs but it is wise to
take bottled water, just to be sure....

The climbs are varied and steepness is broken by broad
terraces which soften the continuity of the Tête d'Aval buttresses.
The climbs described here are but a small sample and the
Cambon books are essential for a wider and more complete
coverage. In the authors view, early or late visits are well worth
considering. Access is open from early May and extends to late
October. Out of season the crowds may be avoided on the best
(most popular) climbs, it is cooler and climbing is generally more
pleasant.

Access to Tête d'Aval is from the village of les Vigneaux. Just beyond the church a forestry track climbs to a parking site by a large block, marked 'Ecole d'escalade' on the map. From there a track zigzags through the trees N and NW and leads to the cliffs via a spring (Font Marcellin) at Pt 1,714m. Look for a large, obvious block on the path which is directly below the main tower and red wall above. 1½-2hr

The names and start points of most climbs are either scratched or marked. The climbs criss-cross which makes route finding difficult. This is exacerbated by lines of bolts. Some top British climbers have simply climbed the line they most fancied on the day. However, the descent lines are well equipped and common to climbs sharing close finishing pitches.

To reach the Tenailles, follow the narrow, unsurfaced road leading to Bouchier (sign) which is c800m on the Prelles side (N) of the hamlet of Villard Meyer. It is clearly marked on the sheet 3536 OT (Briançon). Beyond this point the road is only suitable for high clearance, 4wd vehicles. Turn sharp R before the hamlet and continue up this road with caution (mountain bikers in summer!) passing la Blétonnéc, which consists of two or three ruins and habitable chalets on either side of the road. Some 750m higher at a R-hand bend in the road is a stream and small bridge. Park either above or below the stream. Space is limited. A track on the true L bank leads W through woods and meadows, swinging almost due S to below the Tenailles. A narrow path climbs steeply over scree to the climbs. Allow 1¼hr from the road and at least 2hr on foot from Bouchier.

Opportunities for a comfortable bivouac abound in the upper meadows. There is running water and wood in abundance - no need for a stove! The saving of wear and tear to the vehicle justifies a two day, two climb trip at least.

Tenailles de Montbrison

r29
TD

Eperon Renaud

M Gérard, R Renaud and E Rozan, 1964

6a+ (5+ obl): 300m: 6hr. The climb has been a classic almost since it was discovered. The crux pitch was originally climbed with pitons. It is now entirely bolted. Care must be taken to avoid equipment on the L of the route in it's lower section. Expect the climb to be crowded in holiday periods

P1 5+: P2 4+: P3 4 and 5 or 5+: P4 4+: P5 5: P6 4: P7 3: P8 20m rappel: P9 3 then 5+: P10 6a+: P11 5+: P12 5+: P13 5 or 5+

Descent: either, make a rappel of 30m W of the summit of the 2nd tower. Scramble down for c20m then climb back through a brèche which leads to a track. Scramble down to join the well trodden path in the screes S of the Tenailles. This is more comfortable in trainers! 45min

Or, it is possible to rappel in 6 pitches: the first section takes the arête of the 2nd tower, then one rope length above the brèche, use the *in situ* rappel points on the S face.

Doigt Central

r30
ED
L'Ecume des Jours

J-M Cambon and G Fiaschi, 1987

6c max (6a obl): 400m: 6-7hr. A fairly sustained climb which follows the best of the lower slabs and the upper, grey tower which face SE.

Access is obvious from the path.

P1 4: P2 3: P3 4+: P4 6b: P5 6a: P6 6b+ and 6a: P7 6b and 6a: P8 6a+: P9 2 (ledge/terrace): P10: 5+ and 4: P11 rappel 45m: P12 6a+: P13 6a and 6b: P14 6b and 3

Descent: look for the obvious cairn at the highest point of the W facette. Rappel down this facette to reach the descent from the Tenailles.

Tête d'Aval

The climbing here is extraordinary but the criss-crossing of routes make the purchase of *Oisans Moderne: Oisans Sauvage* by J-M Cambon essential. Of the possible climbs here, the following routes have been done by English speaking parties and are recommended.

r31 **Ranxerox**

ED

75

###

J-M Cambon and C Ferrera, 1983

7a max (6a/b obl): 500m: 8-10hr: A few small nuts may be useful. A classic route on extremely good rock. The start is clearly marked, and lies just R of the large block. Thereafter the true line is devious and difficult to follow due to the excess of equipment in situ, on adjacent climbs.

P1 6b and 5+: P2 6b and 6a: P3 6a: P4 6a - ledge: P5 6a and 5+ to a broad grassy terrace: P6 5+ and 5 - communal pitch (Pilier Rouge Hebdo - r32) to stance then straight up: P7 7a and 6a: P8 move up avoiding line on the R 6b+: P9 6b and 6a: P10 6c and 6b: P11 traverse R, 5: P12 straight up to a broad terrace and a well marked path leading to the red wall. The climb continues for seven more pitches as: P13 6a and 6b: P14 6b - taking the L option: P15 6a: P16 6a: P17 6a and 6b: P18 6b and 6a: P19 5+ to the crest of the spur.

Descent: either, continue easily up the ridge then turn L (W) to follow a faint track then a broad rake (beneath a steep wall) leading down the face to a good track at the base of the crag.

Alternatively, by rappel, the normal means of descent. Scramble from the last anchor, marking the end of the difficulties, down the E flank into the gully. 15m below the crest is an obvious (equipped) rappel point. Follow the line of 2 to 3 rappels into the gully which leads to the large ledges in the middle of the face. Four more rappels, the first over a large roof, leads to scrambling and fixed ropes to the base. 50m ropes are essential.

r32 **Pilier Rouge Hebdo**
TD+
J-M Cambon and G Merlin, 1981
75

6b max (6a/5+ obl): 300m: 5-7hr. This climb is considered to offer a good introduction to the crag. It is relatively short, ending at the top of the lower wall. Climbing is well sustained, mainly cracks.

Start by the first pitch of the the route 'Pilier Kelle' (not described here), a prominent pillar with the route marked.

P1 4: P2 climb the L option then break out R, 6a: P3 traverse R, 5+: P4 straight up above the stance, 5: P5 5+ and 5: P6 5+ and 5: P7 5+ and 5 - to arrive at the L-hand edge of the terrace. Scramble to the mid-point of the ledge and climb: P8 first L, then R, to the stance: P9 6b and 6a+: P10 6a and 5+: P11 traverse R then climb directly, 5: P12 5+ and 6a: P13 5+ then 4 to the ledge and the finish of the route

Descent: traverse L with care over the broad terrace and rappel over the large roof on the L as described for r31 above, or use the descent on foot described for that route.

r33 **Le Père Ubu**
ED
J-M Cambon and C Ferrera, 1988
75

7a max (6b obl): 500m: 8-10hr. Reputably one of the best. The climbing is sustained at a high level and varies between superb grey slabs in the first section and steep walls in the 'Red Wall', upper half. Exposed!

Start from the R-hand end of the fixed rope section of the descent. The start 'proper' is reached by climbing a diagonal line shared by at least four routes.

P1 3: P2 5 and 5+: P3 6a+: Le Père Abu lies between 'Les Elfes' and 'L'Epinaustère': P4 5+ and 6b: P5 6c: P6 6b and 6c: P7 6b and 5+: P8 6b: P9 6a and 6b. This point is level with a broad ledge on the R: P10 climb slightly Rwards, then straight up, finally continue Rwards to the stance, 6b+ and 6a: P11 6c and 6a: P12 7a: P13 7a: P14 6c: P15 5+: P16 6b and 6a. From this point, climb slightly up and over the rib to find the descent equipment.

Descent: three rappels of 45m lead to the large ledge and the rappels via the roof as described for r31.

r34 Cristal Majeur

ED+

75

C Ferrera, F Roux and R Mohamed, over four Aug days in 1994

7b: 400m: 6-8hr. A very hard, steep and technically sustained climb away from the main cliff and as such, offers a more serious atmosphere. Fixed equipment is incomplete and a rack must be carried. The climb has two sections reached via an easy ramp. The first section, of four pitches, gives a firm indication of what is to follow. An easy descent (II) down the gully on the R leads to the section known as 'the Lozenge', which provides eight committing pitches.

From the easy ramp: P1 6a: P2 6b: P3 6c: P4 5. Descend R into the gully: P5 4: P6 7b: P7 6c: P8 A0, 1 peg and 6b: P9 4: P10 6b/c: P11 7b: P12 6a

Descent: by 7 rappels R of the climb. It is possible to descend the lower section by rappelling back down the route. Equally, the gully may be followed with one further rope manoeuvre..

r35 Voie des Dijonais

TD+

75

J Boivin, J-M Cambon, P Jeannot and G Pétrignet, 1973

5+ and A1: 600m: 8-10hr. This climb is in its original form, a few old pegs, perhaps the odd fixture. It is occasionally climbed these days by the connoisseur seeking a traditional route. A rack, pitons and an étrier should be carried. The climb takes the start and finish of a still earlier climb by René Demaison. The line is not too difficult to follow and the top section, R of the obvious heart shaped slab, is characterise by a ramp (which Demaison followed in its entirety). The Dijon line direct from below and R of the start of the ramp itself.

Start by the gorge above the fixed descent ropes, L of a shattered area with a roof at its L-hand side.

P1 5: P2 3: P3 4: P4 3: L5 5+: P7 5+: P8 5+: P9 5+ and A1 P10 5: P11 3 and A1: P12 4 and 3: P13 5: P14 climb up a few m then descend, traversing L: P15 5+: P16 4: P17 on... via the ramp in five pitches at grade 4 with a final, short section of 5+

Descent: traverse L and pick up the descent on foot described for r31. It is also possible to go R, descending the ridge above the red wall, to the rappel descent used by r31 and r32.

La Bérarde

The village is the centre of activity for the N sector of the Massif des Ecrins. From here many of the best known summits may be climbed. It has the advantage of being close to the main routes of access from Grenoble and is served by bus in summer. It has two (dis)advantages; it becomes inaccessible in winter to motor traffic and the weather is less reliable than in the southern portion of the massif.

As elsewhere in the Alps climbers have, over recent years, developed alternatives for when the high peaks are out of condition. The alternative is sport climbing and, as at Ailefroide for example, this branch of our activity has become, for some, an end in itself.

Directly adjacent to the village is the Tête de la Maye, 2,518m and higher up the Vénéon valley are superb slabs lying on the true R bank of the Encoula glacier from which their name derives. They are easily accessible in 20-30min by a good footpath of long standing which rises gently alongside the L bank of the river. Both crags are equipped and have climbs of 400m in length. Visitors expecting to find accurate overall grades (eg AD: TD: ED: etc) will find scant recognition of UIAA standards. Sport climbers tend to ignore the notion that the existence of one pitch of a high grade, automatically changes the overall standard. It is wise to study the pitch grades and assess the ability of the party to get up the climb. The presence of bolts (spits) doesn't always mean that you can 'frig' your way up!

The existence of both UCPA and CAF training courses, based in the large centre at the top of the village, means that student groups will be encountered on middle grade routes. Spring and particularly autumn see la Bérarde virtually deserted.

Please do not tamper with equipment *in situ*. Remember also that this centre is well within the National Park boundary so please respect the environment. Out of season visitors will be astonished at the amount of wild life which roams around and in the village itself. The photographer is amply rewarded. Other, less important crags have been developed both around the village and down valley.

Encoula

The crag divides naturally into two parts ie L and R of the imposing waterfall, easily identified from the valley. The R flank (N) is known as the Encoula slabs, the L flank (S) as Barfly.

Access: cross the bridge in la Bérarde to reach the true L bank of the torrent, then follow the well used path up the valley. Below the Encoula buttress is a zigzag track which leads to a fixed rope giving access to the path below the climbs. The whole sector is covered with shrubs and is generally much greener than la Maye. Being NE facing it holds the wet (snow in early spring) and is in the shade more progressively as the year ages.

Barfly Sector

Access to the climbs from above the fixed rope is by a track which traverses the whole section.

r36
TD
76
###

Pourquoi Pas?

C Buffière and C Riquet, Aug 1990

6a max:: 200m: 3-5hr

Start L of an overhang just beyond the gorge.

P1 to P4 all 5+: P5 5: P6 4: P7 6a: P8 4

Descent: by rappel R (S) of the climb in the first part, then direct.

r37   **Rikikitavi**

TD+

76

\#\#\#

6b max (6a obl): 200m: 4-5hr

J-M Cambon and P Chapoutot, 1993

Start immediately L of the gorge, the first pitches are the hardest.

P1 to P3 all 6b: P4 6a: P5 5+: P6 6a: P7 much easier!

Descent: by the rappels of r36.

r38   **Barfly**

TD

76

\#\#\#

F Birachi and S Rosso, 1987

5+ but 6b if the 1st pitch is climbed: 250m: 4-5hr

Start in the middle of the huge slab directly beneath a large overhang above the second tier. The climb stops short below the final upper slab.

P1 6b - can be dodged by taking the ledge on the L and traversing back R: P2 to P7 all 5+: P8 4+: P9 4

Descent: rappel down the climb.

r39   **La Bataille des Aigles**

TD

76

\#\#\#

J-M Cambon and J Saez, 1992

6a: 300m: 5-6hr

Start L of the overhanging wall and R of Barfly. As with the previous route, the first pitch is the hardest (less so than its neighbour) and may be similarly avoided.

P1 6a: P2 3 - the ledge: P3 5+: P4 5+: P5 5+: P6 5+ - with a variant on the R at 5: P7 to P9 all 5

Descent: rappel down the climb.

Encoula Sector

r40   **Voyage dans l'Eau de Là**

D+

77

\#\#\#

C Buffière, C Riquet and D Lainé, Aug 1989

5+, the most generous of the climbs here abouts: 350m: 5-6hr. Sited close to the waterfall, this is the one climb best avoided if the snow above is melting fast! The name is a delightful word play (au dela - space, extra terrestrial)

Start at the L side of the large approach ledge, before a large overhang and below a smaller roof 100m. higher up the cliff. Climb the easy first pitch Lwards towards the water...

P1 3: P2 5+: P3 3: P4 4+: P5 5: P6 and P7 4: P8 5: P9 and P10 5+: P11 4+: P12 5

Descent: rappel L of the route.

r41   **Un Grand Pas vers le Bon Dieu**
ED-
77
###

6c max (6a obl): 400m: 5-7hr

Start R of 'Eau de Là' beneath the R-hand end of the roof. The climb passes R of this. The first section is mainly cracks and the upper is via slabs which are not so sustained. The upper roof is also climbed on it's R side.

P1 5+: P2 6c: P3 6a: P4 6b+: P5 5: P6 5: P7 6c: P8 5 - the traverse below the roof: P9 5+: P10 5: P11 6a: P12 5+: P13 5: P14 6b: P15 3

Descent: by rappel down r43 to the R (N).

r42   **Disneyland**
TD
77
###

5+/6a with one move 6b (5+ obl): 400m: 4-6hr. There is a direct start (6c) up the initial slab which is harder than any other pitch on the route. Several sections are polished and require confidence in footwear. Above the triangular pillar the route first veers L, then returns R, to the roof.

Start at the L-hand edge of the obvious triangular shaped slab, clearly seen from the approach path.

P1 and P2 4: P3 6a: P4 5: P5 6a: P6 5: P7 4+: P8 3: P9 easy - traverse R (N): P10 6a: P11 5+: P12 4: P13 5+: P14 6b - one move: P15 4. Descent: via rappels on r43 on the R.

r43

ED-

77

###

Zycco Folies

C Buffière and D Lainé, 1988

6c, for 1 move, and A1 (6a obl): 400m: 5-7hr. An interesting and sustained climb. The lower section is often damp, the upper slabs are very fine, threading between the wet streaks!

P1 5+: P2 6b: P3 5+: P4 3: P5 6c/A1: P6 4: P7 4+: P8 5: P9 ledges: P10 5+: P11 5+: P12 6b: P13 5+: P14 5+: P15 5: P16 5

Descent: is by 12 rappels the first 4 of which are down the route then the line becomes direct and lies L (in descent) of the climb.

Tête de la Maye

The S facing cliff is split by the impressive ravine from which an obvious broad ledge climbs Rwards to link easily with the normal footpath used by walkers to reach the superb summit with its orientation plaque. The summit is justifiably much visited. The views are stunning. The names of climbs are amusing, the word play reminiscent of student humour with 'Li Maye Laya' translating most readily! It makes a change from 'La Voie du pilier'.

Crag access: the only path which does not cross private property starts from below the village almost opposite the sign 'La Bérarde'. This path is strongly recommended, so avoiding would be clashes with land owners. Allow ½-1hr to reach the crag.

Starting from the L flank is one of the easier climbs which suffers from the presence of several ledges breaking continuity. This is:

r44

TD-

78

###

Pain Grillé

C Buffière, D Lainé and C Honneger, 1987

5+ max:: 250m: 4-5hr

Start L of the niche, beyond the block at the L edge of the face.

P1 5+: P2 2: P3 4: P4 4: P5 5+: P6 4+: P7 4: P8 5

Descent: continue to walk/scramble to the summit of la Maye then take the tourist path.

r45 · Li Maye Dulfer
TD+
78
###

J-M Cambon and P Corréar, winter 1992

6b max: 300m: 5-6hr. The name gives the clue to the nature of the route - layback cracks! These make a change from the generally slabby nature of climbing. Gritstone climbers will be at home.

Start from below the block R of a small overhang.

P1 5+/6b: P2 5+: P3 5/6b: P4 5+: P5 ledges: P6 4+: P7 5+: P8 3 - ledge: P9 6a: P10 5/4

Descent: as for r44

r46 · Pêcher Mignon
ED-
78
###

C Buffière, C Riquet, D Lainé and F Chevaillot, 1989

6c max (6a obl): 300m: 5-6hr. A good mixed style of climbing, trending L of the large roof in the upper section.

P1 2: P2 6b: P3 6a - climb the overhang Rwards: P4 5+: P5 6c/6a+: P6 ledge: P7 6a+: P8 5+/6a - the L edge of the big roof: P9 6b

Descent: either walk off, or take rappels on the L (in descent) of the route, taking the first roof direct. From the ledge below this, follow the next 2 pitches of the climb then keep once more on the L.

r47 · La Marre Maye
TD+
78
###

J-M and S Cambon and Y Ghesquiers, 1989

6b max (6a obl): 350m: 5-6hr. An airy climb, the crux (and best) pitch is the light coloured slab above the first ledge.

Start L of the cave below the white slab.

P1 6a: P2 traverse the ledge: P3 4/5/6a: P4 6b/5+: P5 5:
P6 5+: P7 5+/3 - cross the ledge: P8 5+: P9 6a: P10 5 with
one move of 6b: P11 5

Descend: as for r46

r48
TD-
78
###

Abbé Hard

C Buffière, B Guerillot, D Lainé and C Honneger, 1986

*5+ max: 400m: 4-6hr. This was the second 'big route' of the cliff. The
second half crosses several ledges which spoils the continuity but the
lower section is good.*

Start L of the cave and then follow the line R of the white slab.

P1 5+: P2 5+: P3 easy - cross the ledge and move L to the slab:
P4 5+: P5 2 and a move of 5: P6 4: P7 cross the ledge: P8 4:
P9 traverse the ledge Rwards: P10 5+: P11 4: P12 5: P13 3 -
then cross the ledge: P14 5+: P15 2: P16 3 to the ledge and
way off.

Descent: continue to the top of la Maye then take the footpath.

r49
ED-
78
###

Tu Ris Maye

J-M and S Cambon and P Corréard, 1990

6c max (6a obl): 400m: 5-7hr

Start by climbing out of the cave on its R and traverse immediately L over the hole to its centre, then directly to cross 'Abbé
Hard' at the top end of the ledge. Trend Rwards on to the big
slab.

P1 5/6a: P2 6a: P3 6a+: P4 6b: P5 4 - cross the ledge: P6 6a:
P7 6a: P8 5+: L9 6a: P10 5+ - traverse R: P11 5+/6c: P12 3

Descend: as for r48

r50
ED-
78
###

Maye oh naise

J-M Cambon, 1992

*6b/c max: 400m: 5-7hr. A hard, sustained first section, the upper half
is more characteristic of the crag.*

ROCK CLIMBING

Start at the R-hand edge of the ledge which rises above the caves close to the ravine.

P1 6a: P2 5+/6b: P3 6a/6b: P4 5+/6a - the black streak:
P5 6b/6c: P6 2 - cross the ledge Rwards (escape possible):
P7 5+/6a: P8 6b/6a - black water streak: P9 4: P10 5/3:
P11 6a: P12 cross the ledge, then 3 to the top

Descent: as for r48

r51   Pujolidal.
D
78
###

5 max: 350 m: 3-5hr. This is the most frequented climb of the sector. Make an early start to avoid the crowds! It finishes at the broad grassy ramp which leads easily to the descent path.

P1 3: P2 3+: P3 3: P4 2 - move L across the ledge: P5 4+/5:
P6 4+: P7 cross the ledge: P8 4: P9 3: P10 5: P11 4: P12 5:
P13 5+ - crux: P14 4 - to arrive at the large grassy ramp. Move Rwards to join the descent path.

r52   Li Maye Laya
TD
78
###

J-M and S Cambon, P Chapoutot and O Mansiot, 1994

6a/A0 max: 500m: 6-8hr. The longest route of the Tête de la Maye. Fairly sustained after the first two easy pitches.

Start mid-way along the Rwards sloping grass ledge, by a dark streak.

P1 3: P2 4 - cross the ledge to the overhang: P3 5+, or 6c direct:
P4 A0/4: P5 5: P6 cross the broad ledge, moving slightly to towards the L: P7 5+/5: P8 5/5+: P9 5+/5: P10 4 to the ledge.
Traverse the ledge to the L edge: P11 5+: P12 5: P13 5+:
P14 5+: P15 6a: P16 5+/3: P17 traverse horizontally Lwards:
P18 6a: P19 5+/3: P20 6a+: P21 6a -then easily to the top.

Descent: follow the grassy ramp to join the tourist path.

r53
AD
78
###

Le Gay Pied

Michoud and Michoud, 1991

4+: 300m: 4hr. The easiest route of the crag. A good introduction to multi-pitch climbing and moving quickly over easy rock.

P1 4+: P2 1/3: P3 and P4 3: P5 4+: P6 to P9 all 3: P10 4+: P11 3 - this last pitch arrives adjacent to the grassy ramp and the descent.

Ice Climbing

History

In 1984 Jean-Michel Asselin and Godefroy Perroux produced the first ever book entirely devoted to ice climbing in the modern idiom. It was called simply, *Cascades de Glaces* and contained many evocative pictures and information concerning ice which tumbled from the heights of the the main massif, together with the surrounding lesser known, sub alpine groups. Some of this ice could literally be reached from the car park at which one had fitted crampons and 'tooled up'. The pair created their own theatre, props and all, within the ski area of Alpes d'Huez above Bourg d'Oisans.

Over subsequent winters they extended their interest to cover the Romanche and Vénéon valleys from la Grave and St Christophe (la Bérarde) respectively. Their activity marked a change in attitudes from those associated with traditional alpinism to those of the valley crag rat, almost literally, Llanberis Pass or Tremadog - on ice!

Only three or so years before this pair produced their book, a group of mainly young, gifted guides from around Briançon opened up new climbing possibilities on their own doorsteps. Ceillac (Queyras) tumbled first in 1979/80 when the Troussier brothers with Jacques (Pschitt) Perrier and Christophe Moulin climbed all the earlier lines facing the ski lift below the Fonte Sancte combe. The following winter with Robert Balestra, a Briançon policeman, they moved up into the Fournel valley above l'Argentière la Bessée in the Durance valley. The rest is history.

There are now over eighty ice climbs in Fournel alone, whilst in the parallel valley of Fressinières climbs of over 500m are recorded on the 'Torrent de Gramusat' (V/5+) and 'Au Dela les Ombres' (V/5) which is 600m in length and was put up in 1991. A direct to Gramusat was completed in the same year by

François Damilano and Robin Clothier (VI/6+). Standards have rocketed. It remains to list some of the major concentrations of activity but before doing so it leaves me to point out that developments have also taken place in the high mountains. Above Ailefroide, reached by ski or snow shoes, the valleys leading to Pré de Mme Carle and the Sélé/Pelvoux huts contain their share of ice for climbing. Finally, on the N face of the Pic Sans Nom is the superbly situated *Raie des Fesses*, translated literally as 'Bum Cleavage' and which splits the two distinctive buttresses in one simple, direct line. This was created by the one and only Jean-Marc Boivin in 1976 and still carries a grade of alpine ED3!

Technical note

From the foregoing paragraph it is obvious that access is resolved either very easily or by ski or snow shoes, which can involve serious commitment. The Fournel valley is a case in point. If the commune have cleared the road to la Salce, some 8km up the valley, then all one requires is a set of good winter (contact) tyres or chains. If the snow plough has not been in, then 1½hr on ski must be added to the schedule simply in order to reach the beginning of the real climbing potential.

Whilst the climbs throughout the region may be low down in the valleys, never forget that poised above may be 500m high, snow-packed slopes. Thus, the greatest single danger is that of avalanche. Following long, dry spells of weather, both wind slab and powder accumulate. They are deadly and the avalanches from them follow natural (ie gully) lines. Periods following heavy, recent snowfalls should also be avoided. The newcomer is strongly advised to consult not only the appropriate local guide book/topo but to seek advice from the local guides or gendarmerie (most of whom are guides or knowledgeable about snow conditions). Avalanche conditions are reported by *Meteo France* (see Weather in the General Information section of this guide). Snow can fall to depths of several m at a time, even as early as November, and no general rule or advice can possibly be given.

Temperatures of minus 20° are normal at 1,500 m and above. Many people have temporarily lost their cars, which they have inadvertently parked in remote positions and been caught in heavy, sudden snow falls, buried beyond hope of recovery. Most of the victim have been ski-mountaineers staying at huts, travelling between valleys.

The risk of detached ice is ever present, check all *in situ* equipment and treat the medium with the respect it deserves because very often, help is a long way away. The scale of things is often several times greater than in Scotland. Be cautious if a warm, Föhn wind has been or is blowing. Vertical columns of ice (cigars) are particularly prone to detachment in these circumstances.

Equipment

This is much as required for technical winter climbing in Britain, with additional ski gear where appropriate. Modern ice tools (called 'engins' by the French) are essential as are screws and a selection of rock gear. If travelling on ski or climbing in avalanche prone terrain, an avalanche shovel is advisable as is a transceiver (Pieps, Barryvox, Ortovox, Tracker, etc). Generally, only belay bolts are found in place and these are often encased in ice! Crampons need to be up to the standard dictated by the climbs. Grades on modern ice are much, much higher than for classic alpinism.

Grading of ice climbs

There are two elements in the grading system.

(a) The overall standard of the undertaking: I, II, III, IV, V, VI, VII. This takes into account the length, continuity, remoteness and difficulties of descent.

(b) The technical difficulty: 1,2,3,4,5,6,7... which relates to the hardest pitch, taking account of continuity, thickness and formation of the ice columns, curtains, mushroom and so on. Examples of grades are given in all the regional guide books of which that by Robert Balestra is essential. As a comparison, Grade 2 is a pitch of 60° with short sections of steeper ground, on good ice, protection and belays. In alpine terms this would equate to D or even D+. Grade 4 gives sustained, generally sound ice at 75°-80°, with good belay/stances but with vertical sections and satisfactory protection. In the author's view this is close to Scottish grade 5 and alpine TD+

It is advised that new visitors err on the cautious side until the standards have been experienced. The sector giving both easy access and a reliable introduction to the style of climbing is Ceillac.

Ceillac

The village is suspended above the Guil valley which, in its turn, descends via a steep and impressive gorge before flowing into the Durance river at Eygliers/Mont Dauphin on the RN94.

From the main road, take the D902 towards Chateau Queyras and Guillestre and after the second tunnel, turn R at the signpost (D60), facing the 'Maison du Roy' hotel. The road climbs in short, steep zigzags for 8km before levelling out into broad alpine meadows at c1,600 m. The valley is dominated by the summit ridge and combe of la Fonte Sancte 3,385m. Skiing here is of the highest quality and caters for all styles. The upper combe is of exceptional beauty and ambience.

Accomodation, varying from weekend facilities offered by the Commune (which is unusual) to family run gîtes and hotels, may be booked through the Office de Tourisme, Place Philippe Lamour, 05600 Ceillac. Tel: 04 92 45 05 74 Fax: 04 92 45 47 05.

Access to the ice climbs is some 2km beyond the village, facing the ski-lifts and ticket office.

There are seven climbs in this sector, equipped at stances by bolts. They vary between 70m and 250m in length and the

Typical Fournel valley ice Lindsay Griffin

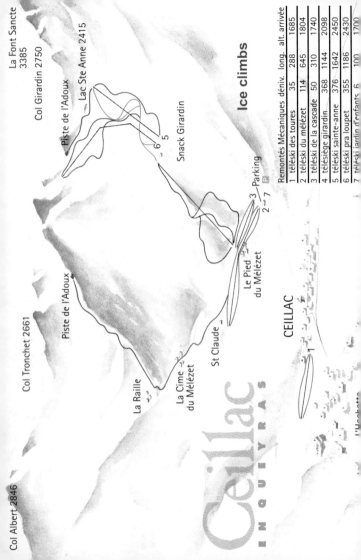

Col Albert 2846

Col Tronchet 2661

Col Girardin 2750

La Font Sancte 3385

Piste de l'Adoux

Piste de l'Adoux

La Raille

La Cime du Mélézet

St Claude

Le Pied du Mélézet

Lac Ste Anne 2415

Snack Girardin

Parking
P

5

6

3
2 7

CEILLAC

E N Q U E Y R A S

Ice climbs

Remontés Mécaniques	déniv.	long.	alt. arrivée
1 téléski des toures	35	288	1685
2 téléski du mélézet	114	645	1804
3 téléski de la cascade	50	310	1740
4 télésiège girardin	368	1144	2098
5 téléski sainte-anne	376	1642	2450
6 téléski pra loupet	355	1186	2430
7 téléski jardin d'enfants	6	100	1700

approach is a mere 10min from the parking area. There are other, short climbs in the valley but they do not merit inclusion here.

Descent from climbs is either by rappel, if there are no other parties beneath, or by the GR5 footpath, which is a sure way off. The climbs are listed L to R.

i1
lll/4
79

Les Formes de Chaos

N Faysse and H Jaillet, 1980

300m: 3hr

Because of the amount of water normally in the gully, a substantial period of freezing is needed for the route to come into condition. The climbing is interesting and varied, sustained but without great technical difficulty. The caves give comfortable and secure stances.

Descent: walk off on the GR 5

i2
ll/5
79

Sombre Heros

J Perrier and J-M Troussier, 1980

100m: 2-3hr

This is a very fine climb on which the second pitch is a characteristic, vertical cigar of c15m supporting the arch - impressive! The ice is generally abundant and sound.

Descent: walk off on the GR5

i3
+/3+
79

Y Gully - Left Branch (Holiday on Ice)

A Coccoz, J Perrier and J-M Troussier, 1980

250m: 1½hr

The climb takes two steps, 10m and 20m respectively, neither exceeding 85°, with belays on large larch trees. The ice is generally good and in abundance.

Watercolour of Ceillac skiing and ice climbing areas Artist unknown

Descent: walk off on the GR 5

i4   **Y Gully - Right Branch**
II+/3+   F Chartin and C Moulin, 1979

79

250m: 1½hr

Descent: walk off on the GR 5

i5   **Easy Rider**
II/3   S and J-M Troussier, 1980

70m: 1hr

The climb follows a deep, narrow gully situated above the large avalanche runnel. The angle is on average 70° with two very short sections of 80°. Due to the tightness of the gully it is not recommended for more than one climbing party at a time!

Descent: Walk L to join the GR5

i6   **Vermicelle**
II/5+

50m: 2hr

This route is the sliver of ice R of Route i5. It gives hard and sustained, technical climbing with c20m vertical. It finishes in a narrow gully of good ice at an angle of 65°.

Descent: a single rappel.

Fournel valley - l'Argentière la Bessée

More than 80 routes are available in Fournel. They descend from both flanks of the valley and climbing begins at its very entrance with *Miss Patata* (II/4: not described here). The climbing area extends generally Wwards towards the Pas de Cavale with the 'Palais des Glaces' and 'Monde des Glaces' sectors some 4-5km up valley. Avalanche danger needs no stressing, it is ever present, particularly on the N facing slope holding deep powder and the S facing aspect affected by direct sun. Wind slab is a frequent feature and many of the descent lines adjacent to climbs lie on steep grass or slate. It is therefore safer to descend directly by the line of ascent, taking careful consideration of parties below. The character of the valley has changed with its growing popularity and importance but it remains a serious winter challenge with almost all of the climbs in the modern idiom. The author has selected only those climbs which form reliably every season. Total coverage is given in Robert Balestra's guide book of 1996 *Les Cascades de Glace*. It is being updated and is readily available locally. There have been several articles written over recent years in all the major magazines such as *Montagne* and *Vertical* in France and *High* in the UK. Modern equipment is absolutely essential.

Access

From l'Argentière la Bessée the valley is well signposted and the road (D423) is tarmaced up to the junction leading to the Col de la Pousterle. Continue easily up the wide track to the chalets of Basse Salce, clearly marked on the sketch map (ample parking). In a normal, early season, the road is drivable using either chains or winter tyres. Later, as the snow arrives, the road is cleared to the l'Eychaillon (parking is limited). The Commune may have ploughed to Basse Salce to give access for the International Rassemblement held in Jan. However, there is no guarantee that the road will remain open and it is wise to contact the Mairie in advance: Tel: 04 92 23 10 03:

email: mairie.argentiere.les.ecrins@wanadoo.fr

The Commune holds the key to the shepherd's hut, 'Chalet du Berger' at Basse Salce and it is available to visitors, upon application. There is no general access to this facility. Basic equipment exists (stove and mattresses). Wood for the stove is available and is provided by the Mairie at the hut. Water is taken from the river. A returnable deposit is made for the key. Early application is advised.

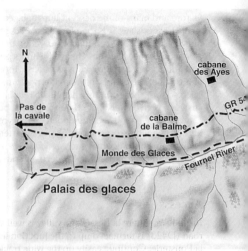

Hiroshima Sector

i7
III/5
1

Hiroshima
J Perrier and companion, winter 1981

150m: 3hr. The climb is justly popular with the crux formed by a hanging curtain of ice, 8-10m high and 90°. The third rope length remains interesting and delicate.

Approach by the road towards Basse Salce. Close to the entrance of the valley you pass the crag, which lies above the true R bank of the Fournel river. Look out for the 'Ecole d'Escalade' sign. Park at the first hairpin bend after crossing the river. Follow the canal above the river to below the climb. The ice is clearly visible through a clearing in the wood. It follows the line of the second major gully line. 20 min from the road.

Descent: by three rappels.

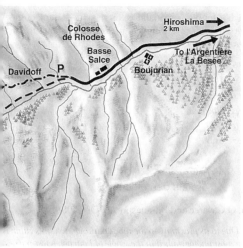

Colosses de Rhodes Sector

i8

V/4+

2

Colosses de Rhodes

R Balestra, G Cavarec and P Pellet, 23 Dec 1988

700m: 7-9hr. The climb falls between a high mountain route and a valley ice-fall. It is fairly sustained, with several sections between 70°/80° and a crux of c8m of vertical ice quite low on the route. These steep sections are interspersed by easier (snow) pitches.

Beware of the 800m of snow slopes above the climb which can be of windslab. They lie above both 'Colosses' and the next climb 'Nains des Ravines'.

Approach in 25min up valley from the parking/refuge at Basse Salce.

Descent: take the wooded slope on the L (W), with great care, to its extremity to reach the top of a three pitch climb (*Ecole des Fans* - not included here). Descend this by way of a 30m *in situ* rappel, which is found by a small tree on the true L bank of the gully. Traverse R along a ledge, then go down easy slopes to the valley. Allow 1hr for the descent

i9 **Les Nains des Ravines**
IV/4 R Balestra with G Cavarec, 29 Dec 1988
2

300m: 4hr. A varied climb which is already a classic. The best pitches are at the top of the route.

Approach as for the previous route in 25min. Descent: by rappel R (E) of the climb.

Davidoff Sector

i10 **Davidoff**
III/5 R Balestra, G Cavarec and B Lanaspre, 27 Dec 1988
3

300m: 4hr. Due to its proximity to the main parking area, this climb is probably the most photographed in the whole of Fournel. Most parties climb the initial pitches only - for the striking 'cigar' - but the full ascent is worthwhile.

Approach: just beyond the parking. 5min

Descent: from to top of the first section, follow the easy series of ramps R of the climb. From the top of the climb descend the true R bank (mixed terrain, delicate) from the upper tiers, then the ice itself, to reach the ramps described above.

Le Monde des Glaces Sector

i11 **Le Monde des Glaces**
IV/5 R Balestra and G Cavarec, 12 Jan 1989
4

200m: 4hr. This is one of the best climbs in the valley, good ice and varied in style. There are several sections of 80°/85° with a final pitch of 30m, 15m of which are vertical.

Approach in 1½hr walking up valley from Basse Salce.

Descent: traverse 100m L to reach the top of a 20m rocky barrier. Rappel this and continue easily to the foot of the face. The rappel point is considered by many local climbers to be a bit 'iffy' and care is required. ½hr

Palais des Glaces Sector

Situated at the head of the Fournel: there are still possibilities for new routes and variants. Depending upon the season, 'cigars' appear, lines present themselves - it's all there for the taking. The chosen climb is one of the best of its standard. It can be picked out from well down the approach track. c2hr from the car park.

i12
IV+/5+
5

Delicados

F Huteau and P Pellet, 15 Jan 1989

250m: 6hr. The climb is R of the cirque and is clearly distinguishable. The climbing is sustained at a high technical level, with the final curtain giving 50m of verticality - without a rest.

Descent: by rappels down the climb.

Freissinières Valley

This hanging valley runs parallel to the Fournel and is reached from the Durance valley road (RN94) some 5km S of l'Argentière la Bessée. 500m before la Roche de Râme fork R to pass beneath the railway bridge on to the D38, signposted to Freissinières. Pass through this village towards les Violins and, if clear of snow, reach the Dormillouse parking area at the head of the valley. Normally, park just beyond les Violins, but space is limited. Avoid becoming trapped in the upper valley in times of snowfall or warm conditions, since huge avalanches and rockfall often cut the road completely beyond les Violins!

The Tête de Gramusat, where climbing only began in 1991, must provide some of the most serious climbing of its style in the Alps. Climbs attain 650m in length and the whole structure varies almost daily. The composite photographs show a typical Gramusat formation.

There are several outlying, relatively minor, formations which are described in the 1996 guidebook *Cascades de Glace*. Of the three areas chosen, Gramusat is the most serious, although easier climbing abounds in the valley.

i13   **Cascades des Violins**

III/6   G Chantiaux, 1982 solo

80

150m: 3hr. Located immediately beyond and L of the last building of les Viollins is an obvious ice formation in the form of a superb 'cigar', vertical for 30m and reached by two 40m pitches of 80°/85°. Two shorter sections complete the climb.

Descent: three rappels.

Also in this sector, before the wide gully known as the 'Torrent de Naval', which is on the S side of the river just beyond the hamlet of les Violins (see IGN map - 3437ET), are two other recommended climbs:

Fine et Delicatesse: III/5: 220m: 6hr

Arc de Cercle III/5: 150m: 2hr. This is the last cascade before the Torrent de Naval.

Descent: down the climb by 3 rappels utilising trees where possible but it is normal to have to equip at least one rappel point.

Main cliff - Tête du Gramusat

The approach to the foot of the routes is left to the judgement of each climbing party. These approaches can be complex and will vary with the conditions underfoot. Allow a minimum of 1hr but it can take up to 2½hr.

i14   **Blow Job**

V/5+   S Angeluccci, F Damilano and C Moulin, 27 Feb 1991

300m: 4-5hr. This is the first large cascade after the Torrent de Naval. It is recognisable by a narrow gutter, followed by a rock wall, giving access to a long tongue of vertical ice.

The gutter gives four pitches at 75°/80° of which the first section is mixed. The 5th pitch is rock (V+), ending in a Lwards pendule, giving access to the last two vertical ice pitches.

Descent: rappel back down the climb on bolts and pegs, except on pitch 6, which is from ice columns in the cave in the middle of the top section.

i15
IV/6

Cascade Serge Rosso

P Clavan and S Rosso, 18 Jan 1992

160m: 5hr. This climb, also known as Esmeralda, takes the cascade at the top of the first ramp (climbing from L to R) beyond the Torrent de Naval.

Four pitches come quickly into condition and remain so. They are steep (90°) with a 95° section on pitch 2.

Descent: traverse R to a large larch tree, thence by four rappels.

i16
V/4

Torrent de Gramusat

400m: 5hr. The climb is 'bitty' but with a good atmosphere. Keep an eye on suspended ice at the start of the route. The foot of the torrent is marked by an avalanche debris cone which often spills over the road and closes access to the upper part of the valley.

The Torrent de Gramusat is clearly marked on the map (3437ET). The climb starts with a Rwards leaning dièdre and a succession of walls of varying steepness leading to a system of curtains and 'cigars', with two possible finishes at the same height.

Descent: rappels down the climb.

i17
III/4
81

Ice Apocalypse / Happy Together

150m. The two climbs take the L and R branches of the Y gully respectively.

Ice Apocalypse gives three pitches with the first pitch at 85° for 4m followed by an easy section to the second steep and final part, which gives 15m at 85°/90°.

Happy Together follows the same first pitch, then climbs directly by two steep sections (70°/80° with 6m vertical). The vertical section is avoidable.

Descend *Apocalypse* by rappelling the route. Descend *Happy Together* by climbing down to the L via a wooded crest, to the L branch and rappel down *Apocalypse*.

i18   **Directe des Ombres**
IV/5
81

C Moulin and Weiss, 2 Jan 1992

200m: 4hr. The climb starts in the Lmost (E) corner of the N face of Gramusat and R of the previous climb.

Take the curtain of ice directly, then traverse Rwards towards the long, continuous section above, which is flanked on either side by rock spurs. There are five pitches with several vertical sections.

Descent: slant down to the top of the previous climb and descend as for that route.

i19   **Geronimo**
V/5
81

S Angelucci and C Moulin, 25 Feb 1991

650m: 7-9hr. It is the longest climb on Gramusat. There are several pitches of 70°-85°and a vertical 'cigar' on the penultimate pitch.

Start as for the previous climb but fork R for c10 rope lengths up an immense build-up of ice.

Descent: from the top, traverse L (E) to a wooded ridge, which runs down the face. Rappel from tree to tree, avoiding moving too far L, to the top of *Direct des Ombres* then descend as for that route. 2hr

i20   **Blind Faith**
VI/6+
82

J Lowe and T Renault, 13 Jan 1992

320m: 7hr

The first pitch shares the same ice curtain as *Gramusat Directe*. It continues by a line L of and parallel to it, climbing the barrier of little roofs directly (A1). The key pitch is the set of two hanging icicles.

Descent: climb directly R towards the spur on the R-hand side of the face. The descent is equipped for 6 rappels. 2hr

i21
VI/6+

Gramusat Directe

R Clothier and F Damilano, 10 Feb 1991

420m: 10hr. This was the first route to penetrate the central ice formations of Gramusat. There are eleven pitches, of which nine are very difficult (90°) with some overhanging sections.

The climb starts in the centre of the face where a system of draped ice gives access to the upper section.

Descend as for Route i20

i22
V/6

Joe's Garage

S Angelucci and Gégé, 2 Jan 1994

400m: 5hr

Start at the R-hand end of a short rock wall situated below the R edge of the central ice curtain. Climb icy steps then traverse L along a ledge, to point directly below the R edge of the same curtain. Climb a series of steep, fragile curtains to reach the main section of ice R of *Gramusat Directe*. Follow an obvious line, normally holding an abundance of ice.

Descend as for Route i20

i23
VI/6
82

Juste Une Illusion

F Damilano and P Allardin, 20 Jan 1991

380m: 8hr. The second 'cigar' gives the crux of the route. Climbing is very sustained.

Start R of *Joe's Garage* by a 40m high column, then take a more or less direct line for seven rope lengths

Descent: as for Route i20

i24   **Lacelle Qui Reste**

V/6+

82

G Lacelle and J-P Mottin, 21 Jan 1994

300m: 8hr. A good climb which is not sustained but has two hard sections.

Pitch 5 gives a section of 90°, an A3 artificial traverse and a 30m vertical column. The next pitch (6) also has a 45m long, vertical challenge.

Descent: traverse R and rappel down a tree covered ridge.

i25   **Jeux Qui Quilles**

V/6+

82

P Isoard and C Laffaille, 17 Jan 1994

300m: 7hr. There are sustained vertical passages.

After two easy rope lengths, the climb steepens and ascends the big gorge, the R edge of the NW facet. The crux pitch is a free standing section on the penultimate rope length.

Descent: as for Route i24

Diable Valley

The Diable Valley lies above and E of the village of St Christophe en Oisan in the Vénéon valley. It is named on the IGN map (3336 ET) as the Vallée de la Selle, rising to the hut and glacier of that name.

The 'Auberge la Cordée' in the village offers gîte or hotel accommodation and good food.

The climbs here are ideal for a day visit, none of them being excessively long or difficult. No times are quoted for the climbs themselves but, given an early start it should be possible to walk in, climb the route and walk out again before dark.

In a normal winter, from Nov to mid-Jan, it is possible to drive almost to the EDF turbine hut, which is fed by a small reservoir clearly marked on the map.

c300m beyond the village a narrow road with continuous,

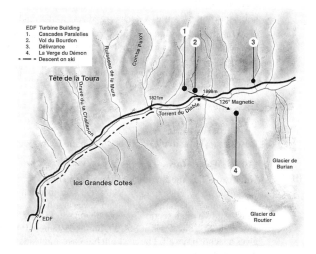

tight hairpin bends climbs up L, via the chálets of les Prés, to reach a parking area and waymarkings to the Refuge de la Selle. The upper section of the road may be very icy and chains may be needed. Take the broad (EDF vehicle access) track, on the true L bank of the Torrent de Diable, to reach the EDF building. Cross the stream and follow the R bank of the torrent to below le Jandri 3,288m, L (W) of which is an obvious, funnel-shaped gully which descends to Pt 1,821m. The ice on both flanks of the valley is clearly seen from this point. 1hr from the parking

Basically 'you pays your money and takes your pick'. Two of the classics, on the Jandri flank, which are always feasible, are shown on photo 84 *Vol du Bourdon* and *Délivrance*.

Avoid the valley during and immediately following heavy snowfall, as the avalanche danger is very high.

Jandri flank

The climbs below the Jandri, on the N side of the Diable valley, are S facing and tend to be short (c200m), reminiscent of the northern corries of Cairngorm. The ambience is superb. The twin 'cigars', *Cascades Parallèles* (photo 83), directly below the Jandri, mark the start of the main interest and a base for camping is possible between the boulders.

i26 Cascades Parallèles

IV/4+
IV/3
83

Both are 40m

Descent: take the true R bank of the L-hand route. Easy.

i27 Vol du Bourdon

III/IV+
84

G Perroux, T Renault and J Carton, 13 Jan 1982

280m

The first, five pitch section is generally on sound ice. P1 and P2 give ice at 80°/85°. P3 is at 85°/90° and is sustained. P4 (40m) gives a steep, 6m wall. The next pitch is easy and leads to the final 'cigar' of c12m.

Descent: rappel down the climb.

i28 Deliverance

III/IV+
84

A Parkin, G Perroux and T Renault, 24 Jan 1983

180m

Pitch1 may be climbed by the cigar (10m: 90°) or, easier, the gully on the L. A further three pitches followed by short walls lead to the top of the shelf.

Descent: rappel down the climb.

Aiguille Plat de la Selle

Low on the N flank of this peak, effectively the S side of the Diable valley, are N facing climbs. They can be located from the

Cascades Parallèles route. On a bearing of 126° magnetic from the base of the 'cigars' is an obvious steep couloir, this is 'La Verge du Démon'. Before this is a steep, easily identifiable wall of red rock on the N facing flank. It hides three more classic climbs - *Autisme*, *Repulsion* and *Cristal Palace*.

i29
IV/6
85

La Verge de la Demon

F Damilano, M Haran, M Legeais J-J Loison, and J Sanavoine, 29 Jan 1991

100m

The first pitch varies in its formation and leads to the 'cigar', which is the main pitch of the route. The third pitch leads Rwards to a stance and rappel point.

Descent: by rappel down the adjacent wall on the R.

i30
IV/5
85

Repulsion

G Perroux, P and H Ranville, 13 Feb 1982

150m

A five pitch climb, the first two being relatively accommodating (70°/80°). P3 gives the crux, with two vertical sections. P4 is easy and the last pitch follows a tunnel of ice on the L.

Descent: by rappel down the climb.

i31
IV/4
85

L'Autisme

G Perroux, S Cattelli, P Castres and A Dakari, 6 Feb 1982

180m

L of the previous climb, P1 gives short sections of 80°. P2 is easy. P3 (50m) starts at 75° then traverses easily L for 30m. P4 (30m) 70° then 85° to a stance.

Descent: rappel to the 3rd pitch then take the rock wall direct to the first stance, followed by a 50m rappel to the base.

i32   **Cristal Palace**

IV/6+   F Damilano and C Blazy, Dec 1991

85

150m. A highly technical climb which is not always formed…

Follow the first two pitches of the previous climb. Take a stance in a small cave a few m higher than the classic position on *Autisme*. Climb the overhanging curtain and stalactites directly (50m: acrobatic). Take a stance in a cave below a roof (2 pegs in place).

Descent: rappel down the curtain then via Route ice31

There are several other short climbs on this flank of the valley. Continue up the valley for a few hundred m from where the classic lines are obvious They are about grade IV/4.

An alternative (ski) approach exists when the snow cover is adequate.

From la Grave take the téléférique to the Col de Ruillans, traverse the Girose glacier and descend via the Col de la Lauze to the Selle glacier. (Note: avoid the Col de Girose, which is steep and leads away from the Selle valley). The descent below the col is relatively easy angled. La Grave is regained by descending to St Christophe, take the ski-navette (free bus connection) to the ski-lift at Venosc which rises to les Deux Alpes. From there, the lift system enables the Col de Ruillans to be reached by an easy, traversing link (often well marked) which takes a line slightly below the original route to the Col de la Lauze.

Via Ferrata

The *via ferrata* offer the opportunity for some entertainment on an off-day. For some of these there is a small charge (3-4€) but most are free of charge. It is important to use the correct protection equipment when climbing *via ferrata* since they can instil a false sense of security. This consists of a helmet, harness and two slings with an appropriate energy absorbing device. Some local sports shops will hire out appropriate gear. Always use both slings when passing a cable anchor. It is always better to move roped up and to belay. Both the rock and the cables can be slippy when they are wet. Wear appropriate footwear; this is particularly important for the footpath descents. All the routes can be accomplished in 4-6 hours

vf1
68

Aiguillette de Lauzet

The approach is from Pont de l'Alpe on the Col de Lautaret - Briançon road. The 'walk in' is an obvious, wide footpath passing the Chalets de Lauzet. Otherwise it is clearly waymarked.

The route itself traverses the Aiguillette from L to R and finishes at the summit, which is one of the finest positions in the Massif des Cerces from which to view the Ecrins group. There is a choice of descent (see photo 68).

vf2

Mines du Grand Clot

Descend W along the RN91 from la Grave. Pass through les Fréaux and continue for 1½km to an obvious industrialised site on the R side of the road. Park below the site where there are several lay-byes and a signpost marking the access path to the *ferrata* which is reached in 10min.

The main attraction of this route, which is most interesting in the first half, lies in the stunning panorama of the N faces of the Râteau and Meije. There is 750m of direct ascent.

Follow the line of old mine workings and the obvious, natural cleft which gave access to the mines themselves. Above the mines the technical climbing gives way to a steep, rocky path which scrambles its way upwards to the Plateau d'Emparis (also known as the Plateau de Paris). The descent is reached by heading E to the GR54. Follow this to the chairlift above Chazelet and continue down to the village, where a signpost indicates the path to les Fréaux. Pass the little chapel of Notre Dame de Bon Repos on the way.

vf3 Croix de Toulouse

From the huge car park, Champ de Mars, above the old town in Briançon, turn up the steep hill opposite marked 'Fort des Sellettes'.

The route is approached by a comfortable path through the trees in c30min. At the summit is a triangulation point and observation table. The views are stunning! The descent is a delightful path through the woods passing the Fort des Sellettes just above the car park area.

vf4 Grande Fallaise

Enter the Fressinières valley via Pallon, cross the bridge by the EDF barrage and continue along the almost straight road for c1½km to a R turn towards Hodoul. Parking is available and a large sign giving detail of the *ferrata* is prominently displayed. The route is in two sections and traverses the cliff from L to R. The positions are often spectacular but the difficulties are not sustained. The easy descent is clearly marked.

vf5 Les Vigneaux

Les Vigneaux is in the Gyronde valley N of l'Argentière la Bessée. At the edge of the village, both parking and detail of the routes are obvious. There is a choice between two lines at mid-height, one easy, one more strenuous. The positions are good and the climb depends almost entirely on fixtures. The descent is steep and requires caution if wet.

vf6 St Christophe en Oisans (Vénéon valley)

The village of St Christophe en Oisans lies between Venosc and la Bérarde. The route is in two sections. The first is situated below the village and follows the river gorge on its true R bank. Access is from the Plan du Lac watersport site, where there is parking. The start is clearly marked. The route is in the same style as that of vf7, steep and impressive above the torrent. The second section is relatively short and finishes by a statue of the Virgin, on a boss known as 'le Collet'. The descent is via the village from the summit, then by a footpath to the Pont du Diable to reach the Plan du Lac. The first section in not recommended for young children.

vf7   Durance Gorges

Situated just N of Argentière la Bessée, access to the route is by the 'Lottissment du Barry' in la Batie des Vigneaux, where there is a huge sign post marked *'Via Ferrata'*. From the bridge over the Durance, a track leads up and along the L bank of the river to a small hut, at which one pays a small fee. The climb itself is in two parts, crossing and re-crossing the gorge on ground which is often steep beyond the vertical. The style of equipment is different from the other *ferratas* and is more a 'climbers' outing. The final slab and wall are exhilarating. The whole route, which is strenuous in places, is beneath the huge pipe/siphon spanning the gorge which can be seen for miles.

All these facilities are regularly upgraded by the respective communes. A mini *via ferrata* has been created below the clock tower which is in a dominant position above the station of Argentière - les Ecrins. It is suitable for children.

A second 'mini' route lies on the track between the Col de la Pousterle and the ski-station of Puy St Vincent. This *ferrata* is short, steep and (at the time of writing) somewhat loose and dirty. The lines of the approach and descent are clearly marked.

List of Mountain Routes

The following table of routes in numerical sequence is designed to provide a quick reference to climbers who, from a particular valley base, want to know which routes are available to them in terms of grade, style of climbing and overall length. Style (such as Rock, Mixed etc) generally refers to the type of ground predominant on the route and more detailed description will again be found in the text. Length is termed either Short, Medium or Long, attempting to give an idea of the length of day one should expect when climbing the route from the usual starting point (hut, valley etc). On Short days the ascent times will normally be 4hr or less. Long days will generally have an ascent time of 8hr or more.

Some routes described in the text appear to be short according to the times quoted but are classified Medium or Long in this index. This implies that these routes can only be climbed in combination with another route.

Mountain	Route No.	Route	Valley base	Grade	Style length	Route length	Page
North-West Sector							
Tête de Rouget	1a	Voie des Plaques	la Bérarde	PD+	rock	short	47
	1b	Eperon Girod	la Bérarde	TD-	rock	medium	48
	1c	le Tresor de Rackham le Rouget	la Bérarde	ED1	rock	medium	50
	1d	S Face Direct	la Bérarde	TD	rock	medium	50
	1e	S Pillar and SW Ridge	la Bérarde	D-	rock	short	51
Le Plaret	2a	N Face	la Bérarde	TD	rock/mixed	medium	52
	2b	Descent by E flank	la Bérarde	F	rock	medium	53
Aiguille Dibona	3a	Boell Route	la Bérarde	AD	rock	short	54
	3b	E Face Direct	la Bérarde	TD	rock	medium	55
	3c	Martine is on the Rocks	la Bérarde	TD+	rock	medium	56
	3d	S Face Direct	la Bérarde	TD	rock	medium	56
	3e	Visite Obligatoire	la Bérarde	TD+	rock	medium	58

3f	Voie des Savoyardes	la Bérarde	TD+	rock	medium	58
3g	W Face - Madier Route	la Bérarde	TD	rock	short	60
3h	Descent via N Ridge	la Bérarde	PD	rock	medium	60
Massif du Soreiller						
Pointe d'Amont						
4a	N Ridge	la Bérarde	D	rock	medium	62
Aiguille Orientale du Soreiller						
4b	N Face	la Bérarde	TD	mixed	medium	63
4c	N Ridge	la Bérarde	TD	rock	long	64
4d	Soreiller Ridge Traverse	la Bérarde	AD-	rock	long	65
Tête de la Gandolière	Traverse by the Dôme de la Gandolière	la Bérarde	AD	rock/snow	long	66
Aiguille de la Gandolière	N Pillar	la Bérarde	TD	rock	medium	68
Le Râteau						
East summit						
7a	S Ridge - W Flank	la Bérarde	PD	snow	medium	70
7b	S Ridge - W Pillar /le Silence de la Mer	la Bérarde	D	rock	medium	71
North Face						
7c	Arêtes Route	la Grave	TD+	rock/mixed	long	72
7d	Fournastier-Madier Route	la Grave	ED2	mixed	long	73
7e	NW Couloir	la Grave	D	snow/ice	long	74
7f	SE Flank	la Bérarde	PD	snow	short	75
Enfetchores de Droite						
7g	Pilier O Sol E Mio	la Grave	TD+	rock	medium	76
7h	Brèche de St Antoine - Grand Couloir	la Grave	PD	snow	short	77
7i	Voie Candau	la Grave	D	rock	short	77
Râteau West Summit						
7j	S Pillar (Pilier Candau)	la Bérarde	D+	rock	medium	78
7k	W Ridge	la Grave	PD	snow/rock	short	79
Col de la Girose						
8a	S Flank	la Bérarde	F	snow	short	80
8b	N Flank	la Grave	F	snow	short	80

301

	No.	Route	Area	Grade	Terrain	Length	Page
Pic Stépané	15a	S-E Ridge	la Grave	TD	rock	long	112
	15b	E Face Descent	la grave	PD	snow/rock	medium	113
Pointe des Aigles	16a	W Ridge	la Bérarde	D	rock	medium	114
	16b	SE Ridge Descent	la Bérarde	F	rock	medium	115
Pic Nord des Cavales	17a	S Ridge	la Grave/	PD	rock	short/med	116
	17b	W Ridge	la Bérarde	D+	rock	medium	116
East Face	17c	Voie Tormoz	la Bérarde	TD	rock	medium	117
	17d	Voie du Genepi	la Grave	TD	rock	medium	118
Col du Clot des Cavales	18a	E-W Traverse	la Grave	F	path/snow	long	119
Col du Diable	19a	N Couloir	la Grave	D/D+	ice	medium	120
Tour Carrée de Roche Méane	20a	S Face	la Grave	AD	rock	short	121
La Grande Ruine							
Pointe Brevoort	21a	E Ridge	la Grave	F	snow/rock	short	122
Pic Maître	21b	W Pillar and WNW Ridge	la Bérarde	TD	rock	long	122
	21c	N Face - Voie Diagonale	la Grave	D+	ice	med/long	123
Pic Bourcet and Tour Choisy	22a	Tour Choisy E Face/traverse to Pic Bourcet	la Grave	D	rock	medium	124
	22b	E Flank Descent	la Grave	D	rock	medium	125
Roche Faurio	23a	SE Flank	Ailefroide	F	snow	short	126
Brèche de la Tombe Murée	24a	N Couloir	la Grave	TD+	ice	medium/long	126
Pointe Louise	25a	SE Ridge	Ailefroide	AD	rock	short	127
	25b	NW Face (Louise Fine)	Ailefroide	TD+	ice/mixed	long	128
Col de la Roche Faurio	26a	N Flank Direct	la Grave	AD	snow/ice	medium	129
Pic de Neige Cordier	27a	SW Flank and Ridge	Ailefroide	F	snow/rock	short	130
	27b	N-S Traverse	la Grave	PD	snow/rock	medium	130
Pic du Glacier Blanc	28a	S Ridge	Ailefroide	AD	rock	short	131

	Code	Route	Area	Grade	Terrain	Length	Page
	38c	N Couloir	Ailefroide	D-	ice	medium	156
	38d	Couloir Ritchie	Ailefroide	TD-/TD+	ice	medium	157
	38e	Couloir Deweze	Ailefroide	D	ice	medium	157
Col la Temple	39a	E-W Traverse	Ailefroide	F	path/snow	medium	158
l'Ailefroide	40a	SE Spur	Ailefroide	F	snow/rock	medium	159
	40b	Col de l'Ailefroide	la Bérarde	F	rock	medium	160
	40c	W Face and S Flank	la Bérarde	PD	snow/rock	medium	160
	40d	NW Face via Glacier Long	la Bérarde	D	ice/rock	long	161
	40e	NW Wall	la Bérarde	ED2	rock/mixed	long	162
	40f	N (Coste Rouge) Ridge	Ailefroide	D	rock	medium	165
	40g	Descent by the S Face	Ailefroide	PD	rock/snow	medium	166
North Face	40h	Pilier des Seracs	Ailefroide	TD+	rock/ice	long	167
	40i	N Face of Pointe Fourastiere /Y Couloir	Ailefroide	TD-	ice/mixed	long	167
	40j	S Ridge	Ailefroide	PD	snow	medium	168
East Summit	40k	SW Flank	Ailefroide	F	rock/snow	medium	170
	40l	N Face of Brèche du Glacier Noire	Ailefroide	ED1	ice/mixed	long	170
Pic du Coup de Sabre	41a	NW Buttress	Ailefroide	D	rock	medium	171
	41b	Descent by S Face	Ailefroide	PD	rock/snow	medium	172
Le Coup de Sabre	42a	N-S Traverse	Ailefroide	D	snow/ice	medium	172
Pic Sans Nom	43a	W Ridge	Ailefroide	TD	rock	long	174
	43b	NW Couloir	Ailefroide	AD	snow/ice	long	175
North Face	43c	Original Route	Ailefroide	ED2	rock/mixed	long	176
	43d	Raie des Fesses	Ailefroide	ED2	ice	long	178
	43e	Pilier Chapoutot	Ailefroide	TD	rock	long	179
	43f	Magic Stones	Ailefroide	TD+	rock	medium	180

	430	Diable Par le Queue	Ailefroide	TD-	rock	medium	203
Les Bans	50a	ENE Ridge	Ailefroide	PD	rock	medium	203
	50b	SE Flank and S Ridge	Ailefroide	PD	rock	medium	204
	50c	NE Couloir	Ailefroide	D	rock	medium	206
	50d	NE Pillar	Ailefroide	D	ice	long	207
	50e	SE Face direct - Voie Giraud	Ailefroide	TD+	rock	medium	208
Contrefort Médian	50f	Original Route	Ailefroide	D	rock	long	208
	50g	Pas d'Asile Pour Pazazu	Ailefroide	ED1	rock	medium	210
	50h	Sous le Soleil du Satan	Ailefroide	TD+	rock	medium	211
Pic Jocelme	51a	NE Couloir	Ailefroide	D	snow/rock	medium	212
	51b	Descent by the Bonvoisin Glacier	Ailefroide	PD	rock/snow	medium	212
Mont Gioberney	52a	NE Flank	la Bérarde	F	snow	short	213
	52b	NE Ridge	la Bérarde	PD	snow/rock	short	214
Les Rouies	53a	NE Flank	la Bérarde	F	snow/rock	medium	214
	53b	SE Ridge - Voie Rébuffat	Valgaudémar	AD+	rock	medium	215
	53c	SE Face - Original Route	Valgaudémar	AD	rock	medium	216
	53d	Voie de la Rampe	Valgaudémar	D+	rock	long	216
	53e	La Mafia	Valgaudémar	ED2	rock	long	217
Pointe du Vallon des Erages	54a	NE Ridge	la Bérarde	PD	snow/rock	medium	218
	54b	Voie du Grand Dièdre	la Bérarde	TD	rock	long	218
	54c	N Face	la Bérarde	TD	rock	med/long	220
Tête de l'Etret	55a	NE Face Direct	la Bérarde	TD	ice/mixed	med/long	221
	55b	N Face Direct	la Bérarde	D-	rock	medium	222
Tête des Fétoules	56a	S Pillar	la Bérarde	TD	rock	long	223
	56b	Descent by the SE Ridge	la Bérarde	F	rock/snow	medium	224
L'Olan	57a	N Ridge	Valjouffrey	PD	rock	medium	225

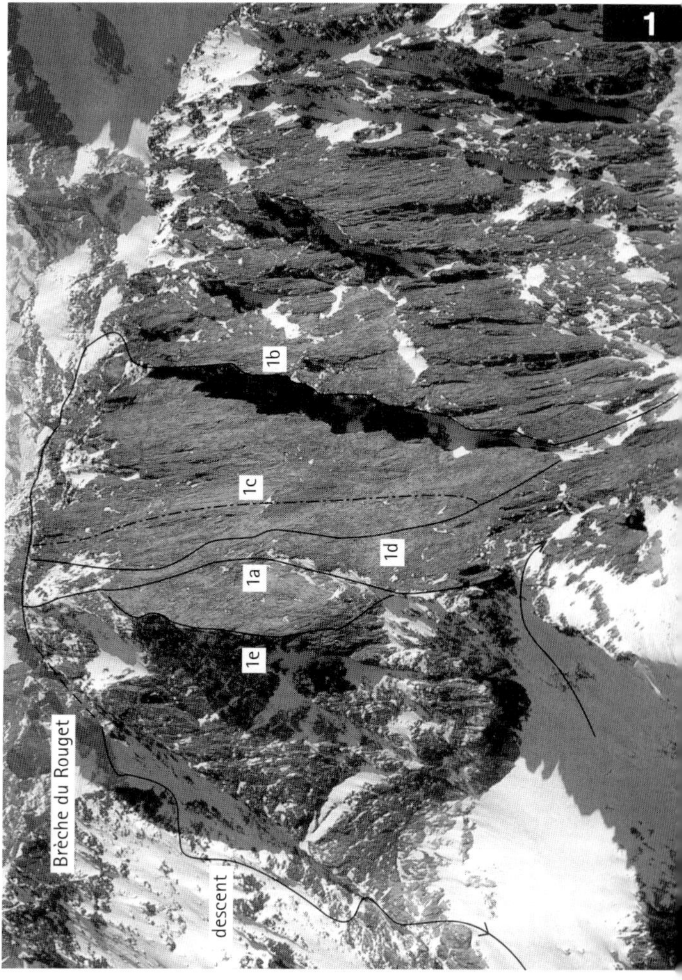

Tête du Rouget SW ridge and S face

1

1b

1c

1d

1a

1e

Brèche du Rouget

descent

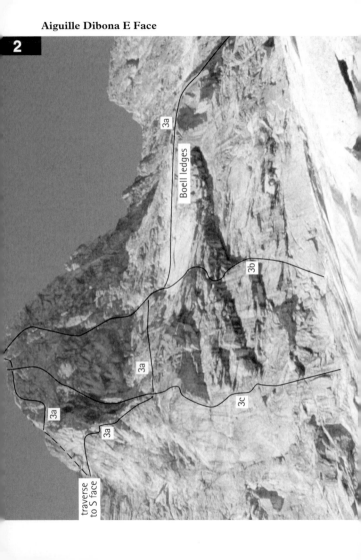

3a

Boell ledges

3b

3a

3c

3a

3a

traverse
to S face

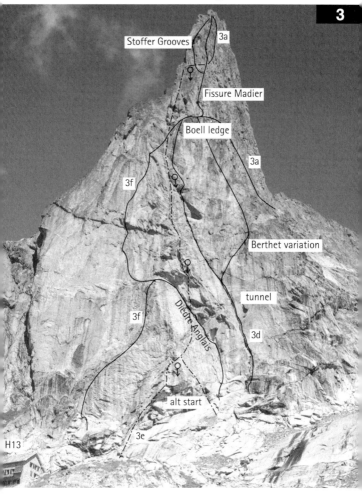

Stoffer Grooves

3a

Fissure Madier

Boell ledge

3a

3f

Berthet variation

tunnel

3f

Diédre Anglais

3d

alt start

3e

H13

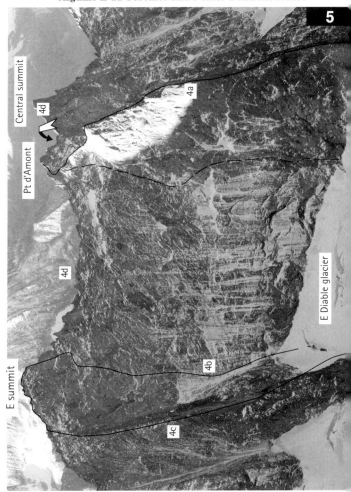

Tête de la Gandolière

le Plaret

5a

2b

6a

Gandolière glacier

5a

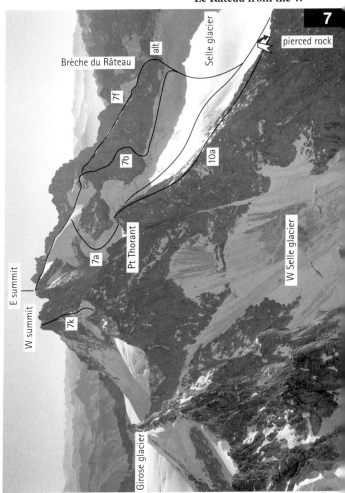

pierced rock

Selle glacier

Brèche du Râteau

alt

7f

7b

10a

7a

Pt Thorant

W Selle glacier

E summit

W summit

7k

Girose glacier

Etançons glacier

7f

E summit

W summit

7f descent

7j

Col de la Girose

8a

Pt Dosia

Selle glacier

9a

9b

Tête N de Replat

Brèche du Râteau

Pt Thorant

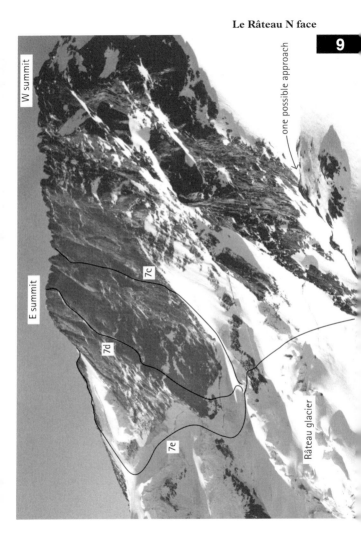

W summit

E summit

one possible approach

7c

7d

7e

Râteau glacier

Rateau E

7i

alt

Pt St Antoine

gros rognon

7g

7h

7i

Entrechores R

Brèche de la Meije

13h

13i

13j

12a

Grand Pic

13k

13l

Entrechores L

13m

13n

Meije glacier

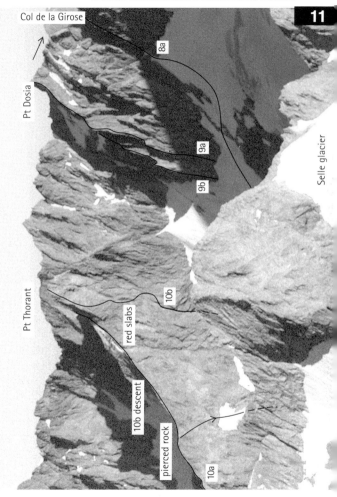

Col de la Girose

Pt Dosia

Pt Thorant

Selle glacier

8a

9a

9b

10b

red slabs

10b descent

pierced rock

10a

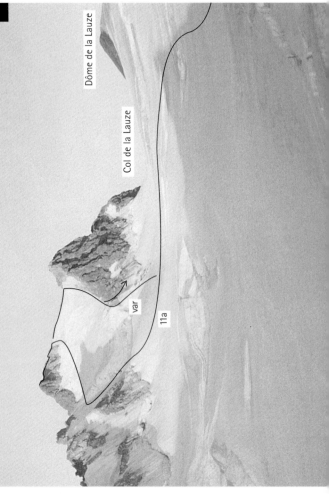

Dôme de la Lauze

Col de la Lauze

var

11a

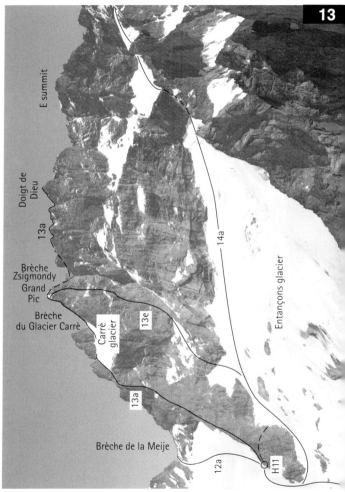

E summit

Doigt de Dieu

13a

Brèche Zsigmondy Grand Pic

Brèche du Glacier Carrè

Carrè glacier

13e

13a

Brèche de la Meije

12a

H11

14a

Entançons glacier

La Meije S face - Central buttress

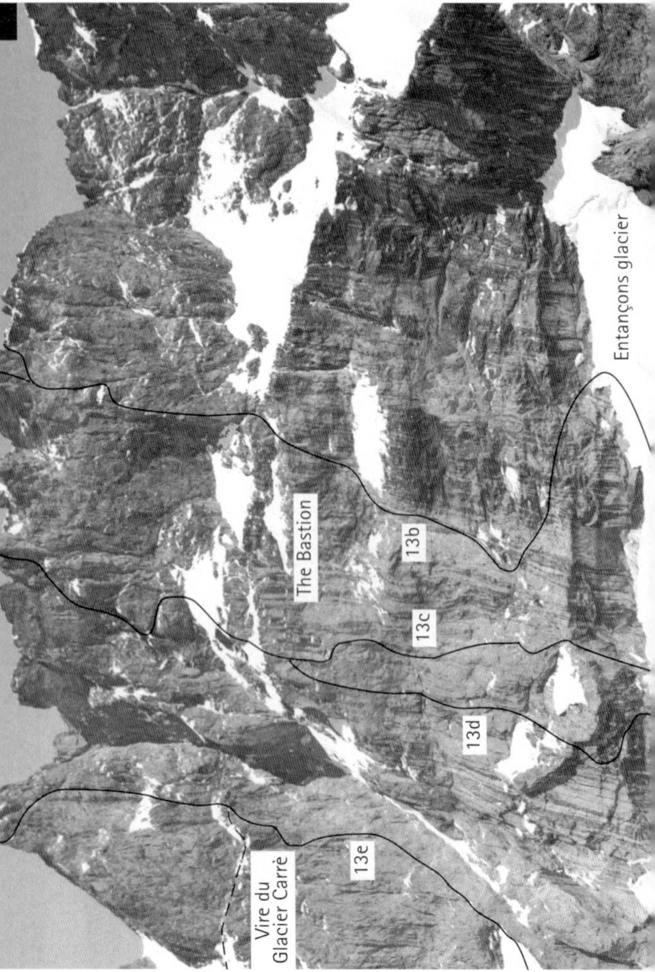
Doigt de Dieu
Entançons glacier
The Bastion
13b
13c
13d
13e
Vire du
Glacier Carrè

Grand Pic

Pic du Glacier Carré

Brèche Zsigmondy

Doigts de Dieu

Carrè glacier

13e

13a

8m wall

13g   13f

Brèche de la Meije

12a

Brèche du Crapaud

H11

La Meije E summit and Doigt de Dieu N flank

16

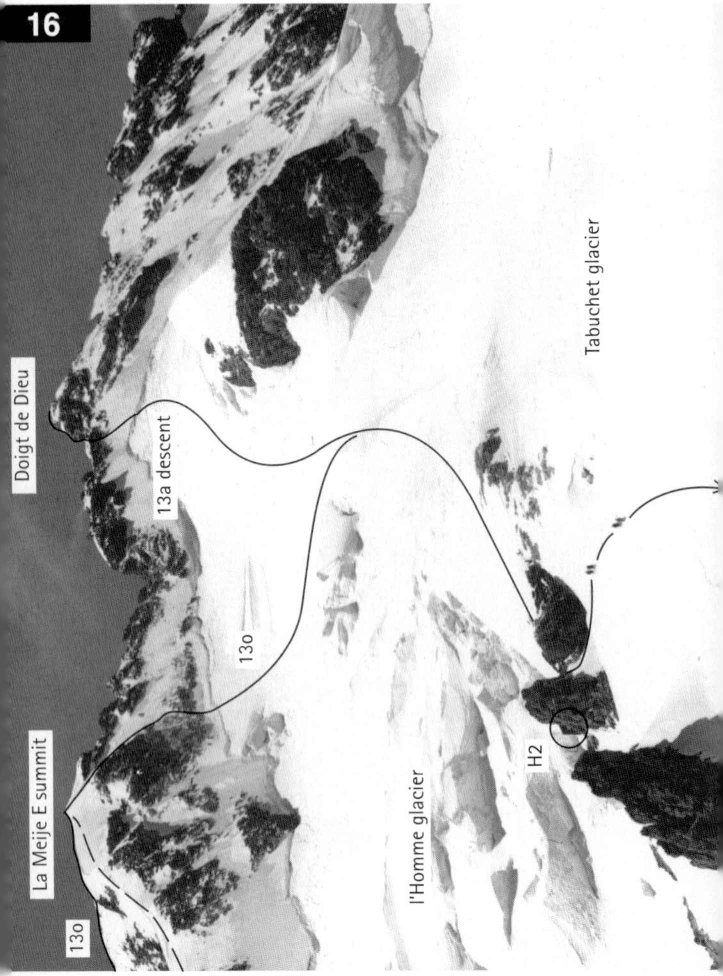

Doigt de Dieu

13a descent

13o

La Meije E summit

13o

Tabuchet glacier

l'Homme glacier

H2

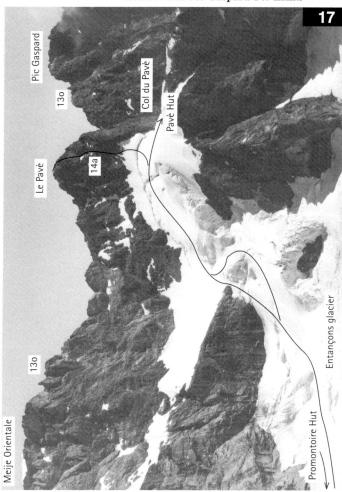

Meije Orientale

Le Pavé

Pic Gaspard

130

14a

130

Col du Pavè

Pavè Hut

Entançons glacier

Promontoire Hut

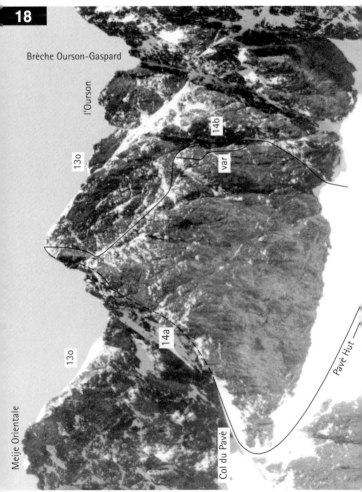

Brèche Ourson-Gaspard

l'Ourson

13o

14b

var

Meije Orientale

13o

14a

Col du Pavé

Pavé Hut

Clot des Cavales glacier

17c

17d

Pavé hut

17a

Col des Clot
de Cavales

Pic Bourcet

22a

Tour Choisy

Col de la Casse Déserte

21a descent

Grande Ruine Glacier

Chatelleret hut

Pt
Brevoort

21b

Pic
Maître

Col du Diable

Roche Méane

Col Clot des Cavales

19a

18a

17b

Pic N de Cavales

Roche Méane and Grande Ruine N faces

21

Pic Maître

Clot des Cavales glacier

21c

Col du Diable

19a

Roche Méane

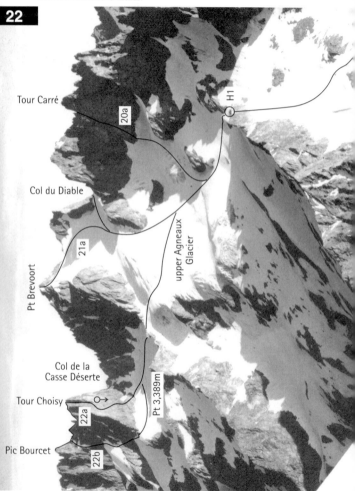

Tour Carré

20a

Col du Diable

H1

upper Agneaux Glacier

21a

Pt Brevoort

Col de la Casse Déserte

Tour Choisy

Pt 3,389m

22a

Pic Bourcet

22b

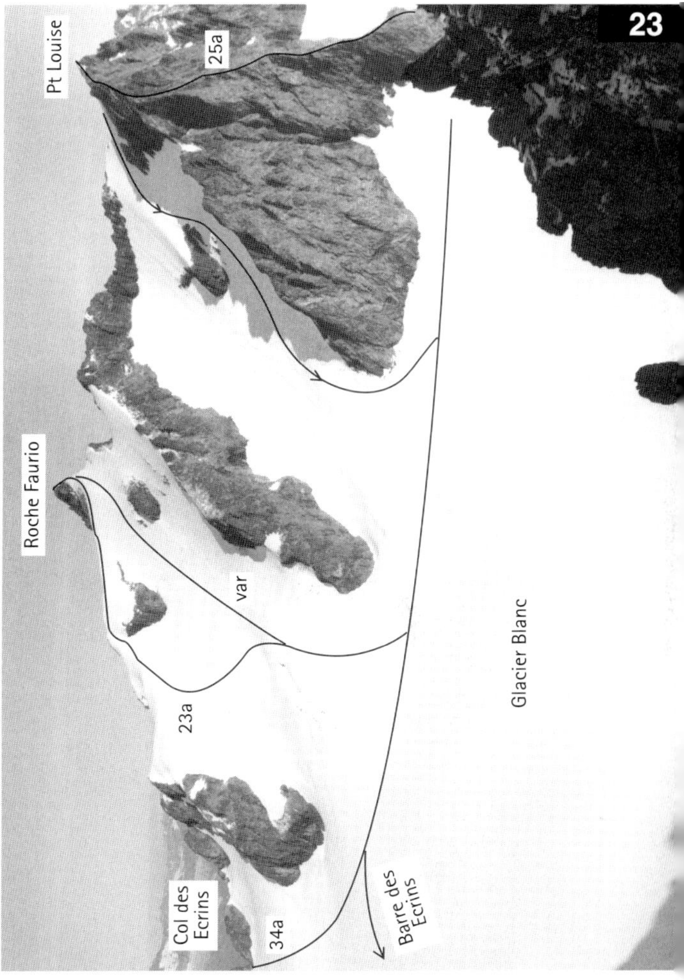

Pt Louise

25a

Roche Faurio

var

23a

Col des Ecrins

34a

Glacier Blanc

Barre des Ecrins

Brèche de la
Roche Faurio

twin gendarmes

Pt Loiuse

24a

26a

25b

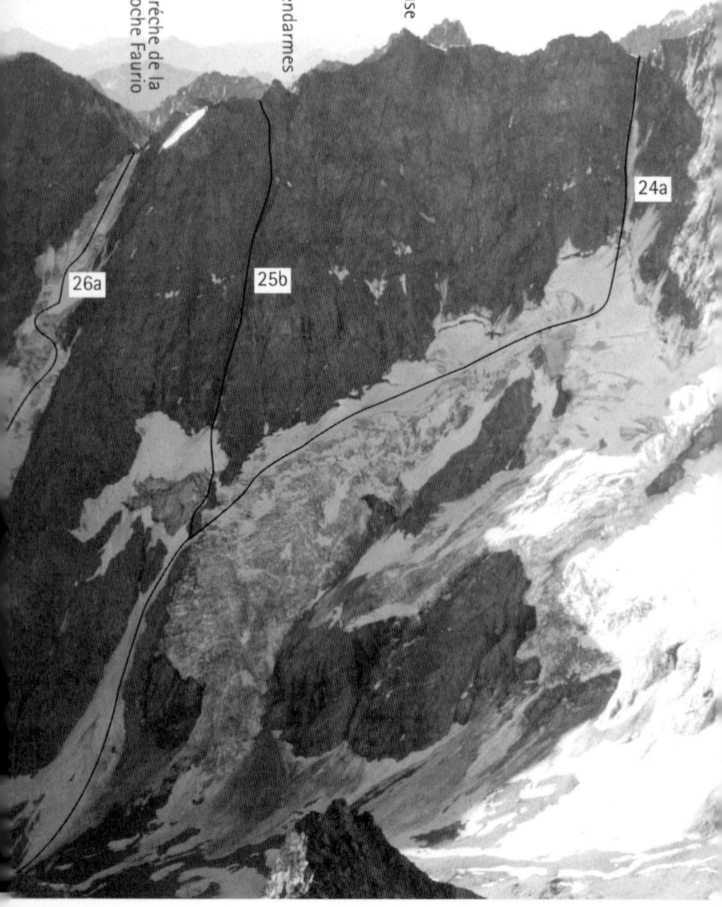

Roche Paillon

Col Emil Pic

Pic de Neige Cordier

Pic du Glacier Blanc

to Pic de
la Glacier d'Arsine

28a

29a

27a

H16

Pic de Neige Cordier E flank

26

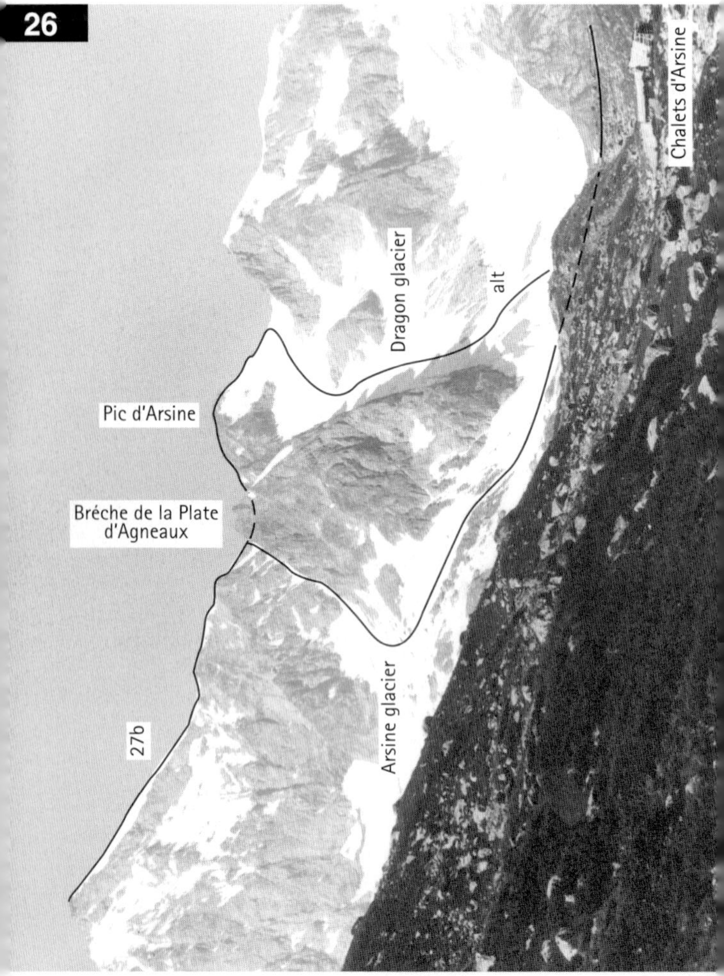
Chalets d'Arsine
Dragon glacier
alt
Pic d'Arsine
Bréche de la Plate d'Agneaux
Arsine glacier
27b

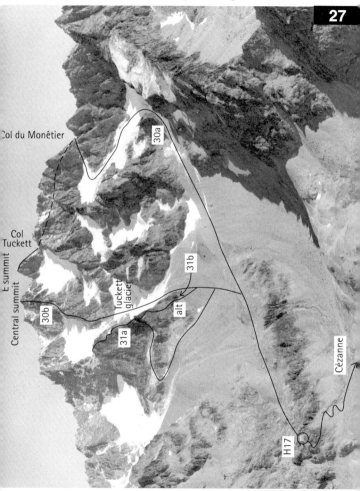

Col du Monêtier

30a

Col Tuckett

E summit

Central summit

31b

30b

Tuckett glacier

alt

31a

Cézanne

H17

Roche du Jabel

Col des Prét des Fonts

Col du Casset

32a

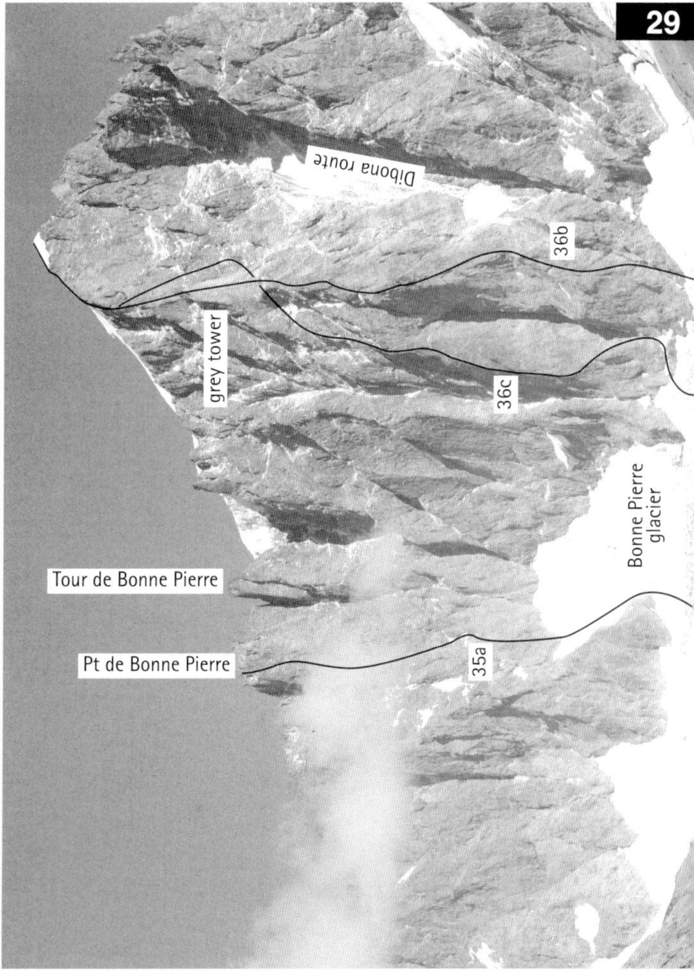

Dibona route

36b

grey tower

36c

Bonne Pierre glacier

Tour de Bonne Pierre

Pt de Bonne Pierre

35a

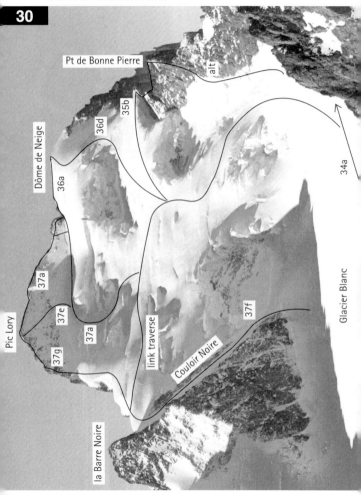

Pt de Bonne Pierre

alt

35b

36d

Dôme de Neige

36a

34a

Pic Lory

37a

37e

37a

37g

37a

link traverse

Couloir Noire

37f

Glacier Blanc

la Barre Noire

Col des Avalanches

ifre

Brèche des Ecrins

37g

37c

Arête Rouge

37b

var

Glacier Noire

Pic Coolidge

38a

Col de la Temple

39a

Le Fifre

Pic Lorry

37a

37d

36a

Dôme de Neige des Ecrins

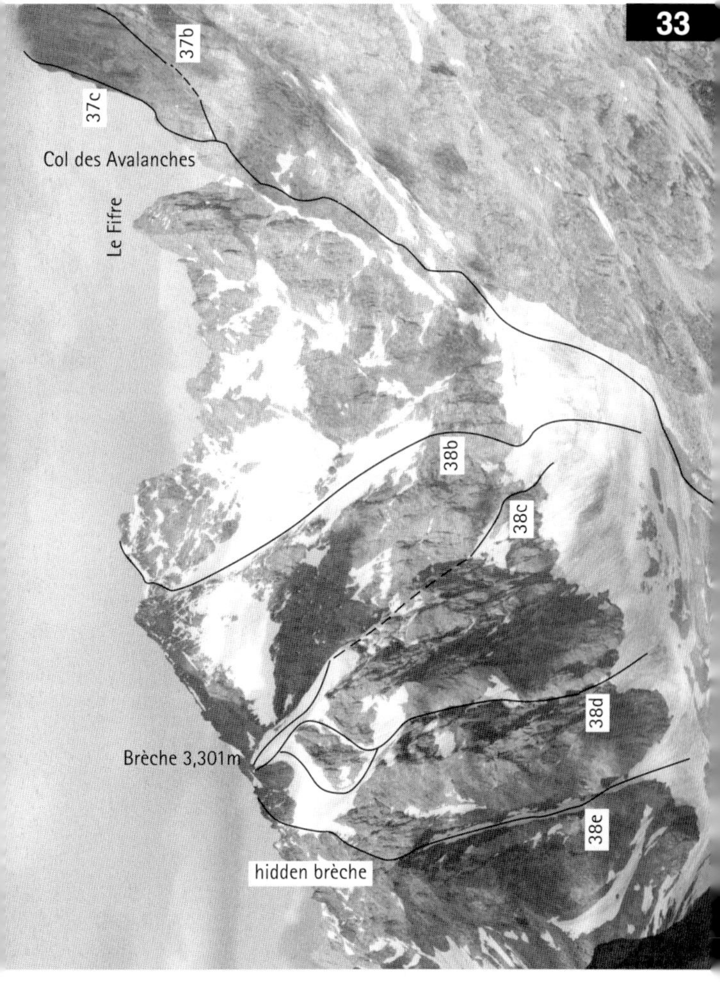

37b

37c

Col des Avalanches

Le Fifre

38b

38c

38d

38e

Brèche 3,301m

hidden brèche

Pic du Coup de Sabre

41b

var

E summit

40j

Central summit

Ailefroide glacier

40k

40g

40a

40e

40a

W summit

40c

to 40b

Ailefroide glacier

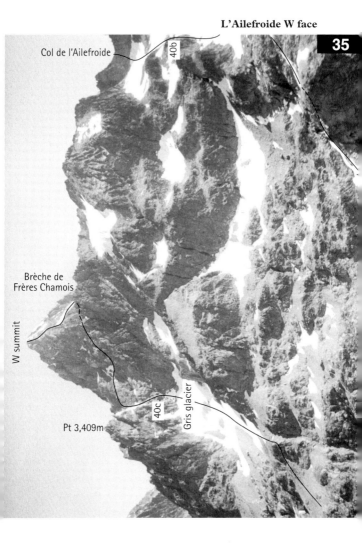

L'Ailefroide W face

Col de l'Ailefroide

40b

35

Brèche de
Frères Chamois

W summit

40c

Gris glacier

Pt 3,409m

Central summit

hanging
glacier

zone of slabs

top of pillar

Les Bans

50c

40f

40e

Glacier Long

40d

Central summit

Pt Fourastier

Brèche du Glacier Noire

40l

40i

40h

40f

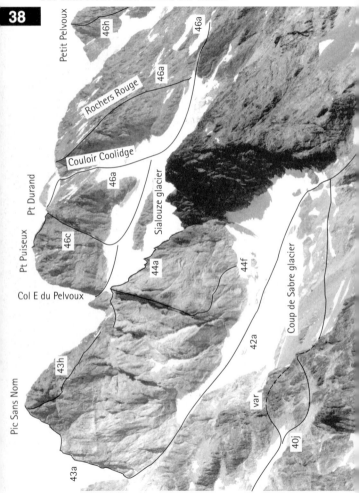

Petit Pelvoux

46h

46a

Rochers Rouge

46a

Couloir Coolidge

Pt Durand

46a

Sialouze glacier

Pt Puiseux

46c

44a

Col E du Pelvoux

44f

Coup de Sabre glacier

42a

43h

var

Pic Sans Nom

40j

43a

Pelvoux, Pic Sans Nom and Pic du Coup de Sabre N faces

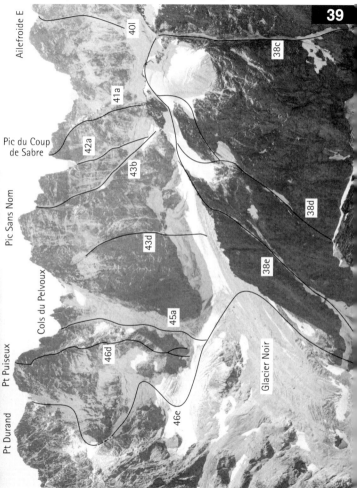

39

Ailefroide E

Pic du Coup de Sabre

Pic Sans Nom

Cols du Pelvoux

Pt Puiseux

Pt Durand

40l

38c

41a

42a

43b

38d

43d

38e

45a

46d

Glacier Noir

46e

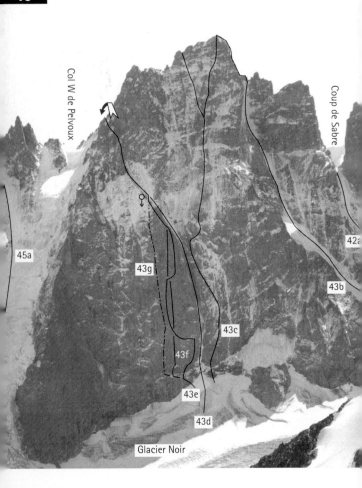

Col W de Pelvoux

Coup de Sabre

45a

43g

42a

43b

43c

43f

43e

43d

Glacier Noir

crux 7b

44g

44h

44a

Sialouze glacier

Aiguille de Sailouze SW face

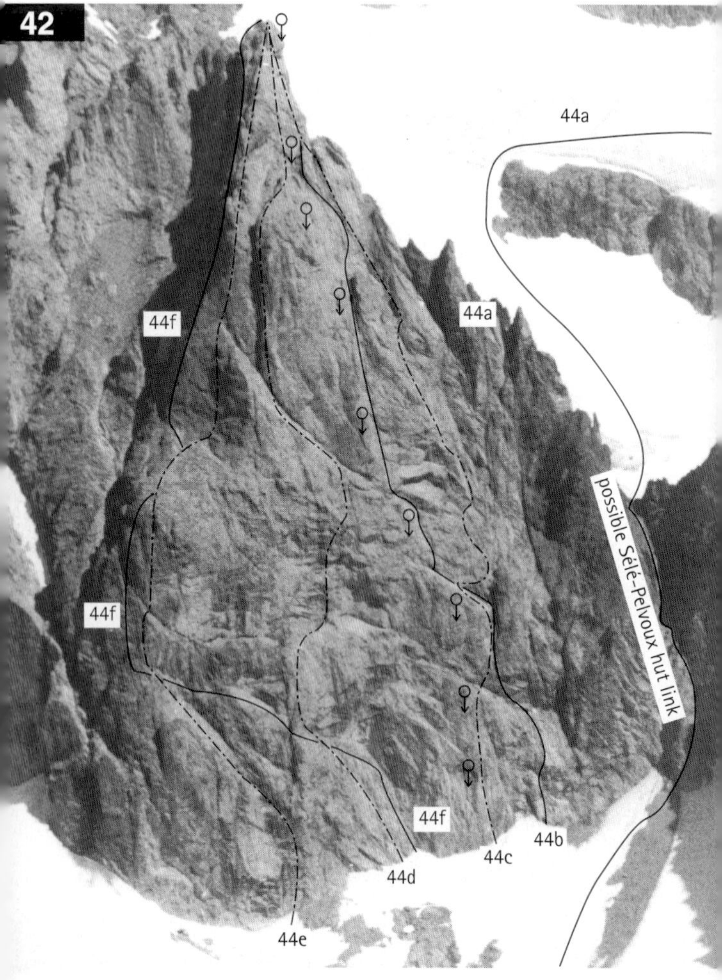
42
44a
44a
44f
44f
44f
possible Sélé-Pelvoux hut link
44b
44c
44d
44e

Pt Durand Pt Puiseux

l'Ailefroide

Voilettes glacier

46b

Glacier
Noire

46f

Momie
glacier

Col E de Pelvoux

45a

46d

Pt Puiseux

Pt Durand

46d

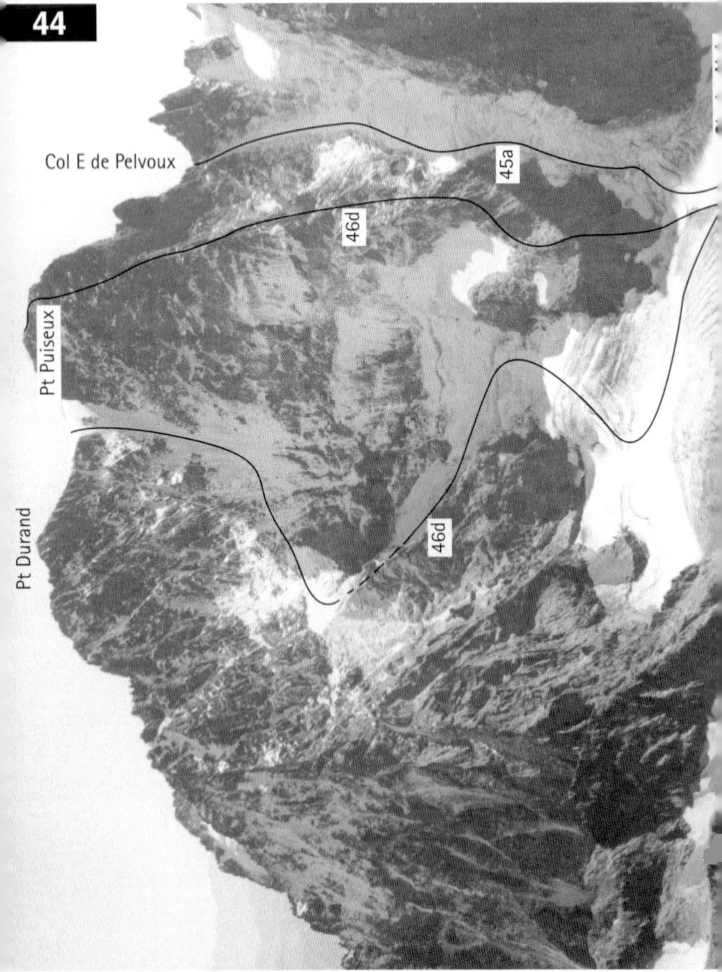

46g

Voilettes glacier

bivouacs

Dents du Coste Counier

49a

49b

50e

49a

Brèche des Bans

50b

Pas d'Aupillous

51a

Mont Gioberney

52b

La Bérarde

52a

H10

Cols des Bans

50c

50d

Pilatte glacier

50a

47a

Pt de la Pilatte

S summit

Coste Counier arête

Névé Ovale

Brèche Carrée

49b

50e

50f

50g

50h

50b

Col du Sellar

Col du Bonvoisin

51a

51b

Bonvoisin glacier

Mont Gioberney SE flank

50

Les Rouies
Col de Gioberney
Rouies glacier
Mont Gioberney
53a
52a
52b
Pilatte glacier

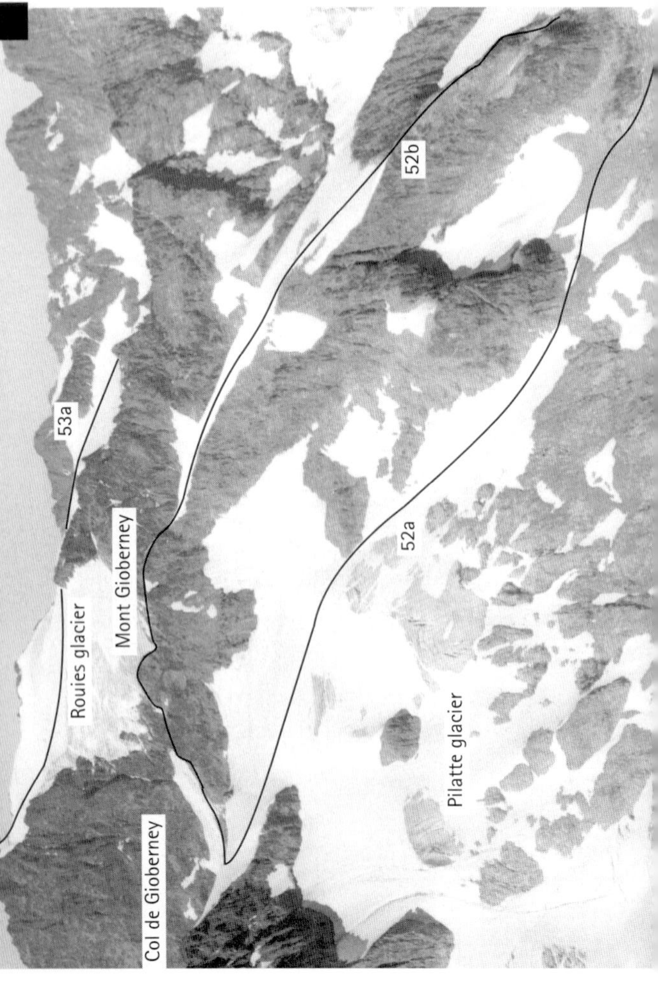

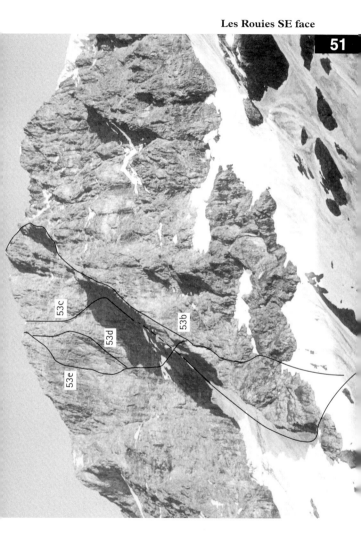

Pointe du Vallon des Etages N face

52

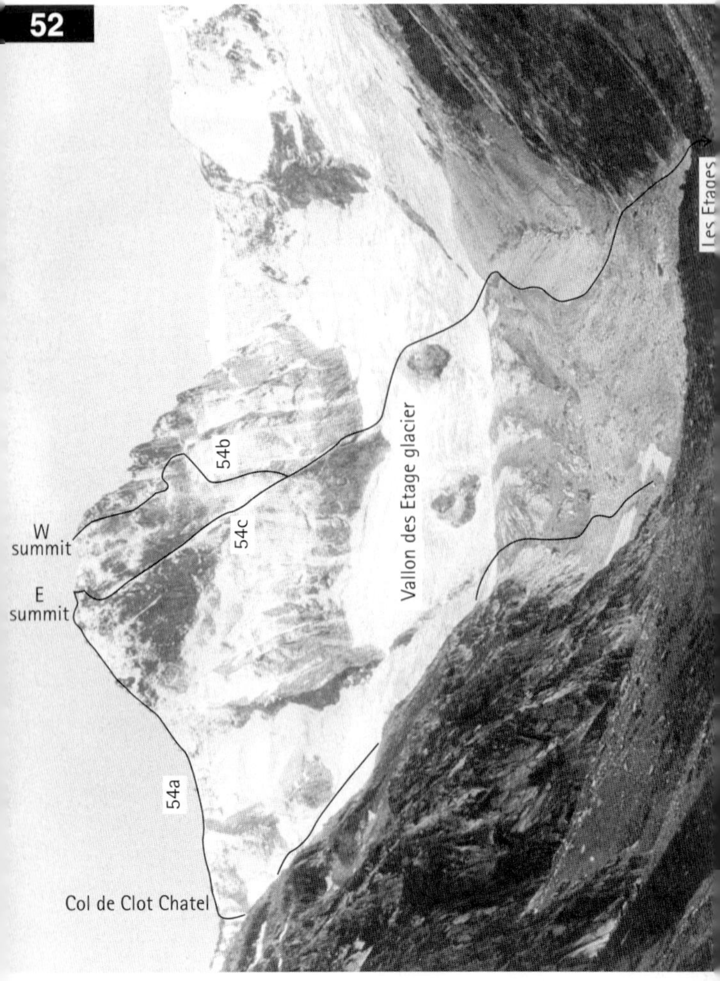
Les Etages
54b
W summit
54c
E summit
Vallon des Etage glacier
54a
Col de Clot Chatel

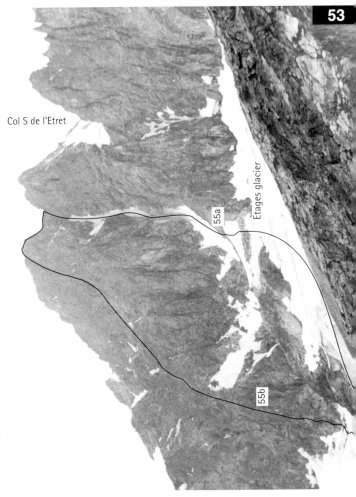

Col S de l'Etret

Étages glacier

55a

55b

Pt 3,311m

S shoulder

Central summit

N summit

57c

57a

57d

57b

Pilier Candau

Pt 3,228m

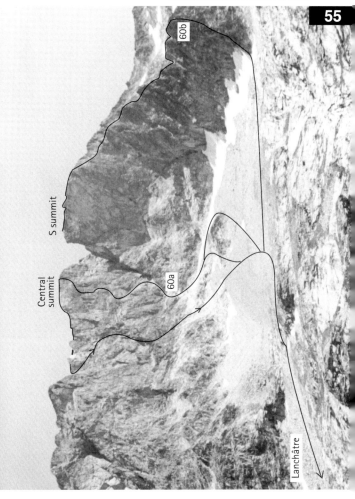

Vallonpierre glacier

62d

62a

62b

Banc des Aiguilles

62c

var

Sirac glacier

62b

62a

Descent

detached gendarme

63a

63b

descent path

practise slabs

r2

r1

gully

r3

6a

5/5+

gully

r4

r5

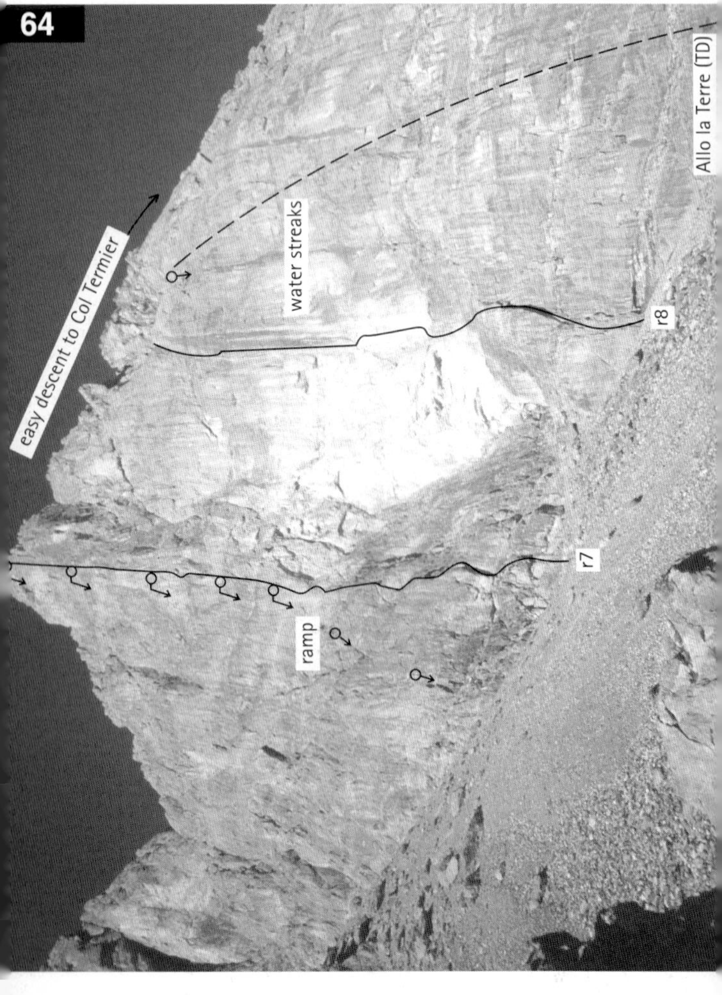

Allo la Terre (TD)

easy descent to Col Termier

water streaks

r8

r7

ramp

walk off

r9

approach

Briançon → N94

Col du Lautaret

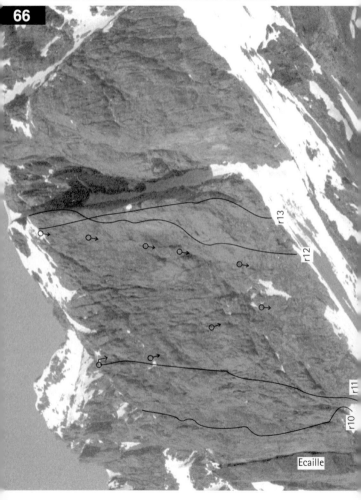

r13

r12

r11

r10

Ecaille

summit

letter box

leap

5

4

r14

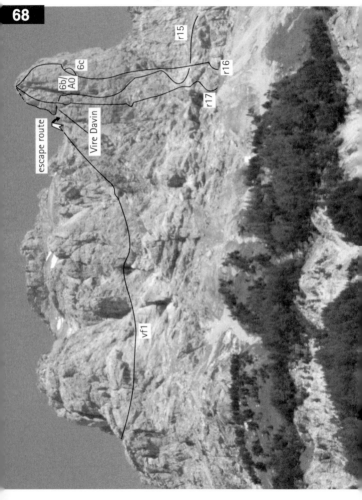

first tower

r20

r19

r18

to descent path

r21

second tower

r22

Pear Buttress

Pavé du
Chardonnet

way off

r24

second tower

r25

descent via Col du Roche Noire
cairn

white slab

r27

r26

direct
variation

r28

rappel W side

descent behind
tower

45m

r30

r29

r34

huge block

linking path

r31

r32

r33

fixed rope for descent

r35

walk off

Encoula glacier

Cima de l'Encoula

r39

r38

r37

r36

r40

r41

r42

r43

fixed rope

from La Bérarde

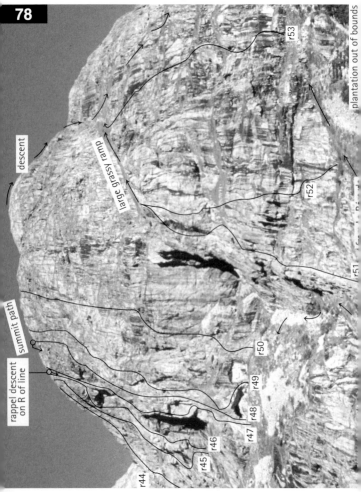

descent

large grassy ramp

summit path

rappel descent
on R of line

plantation out of bounds

r53

r52

r51

r50

r49

r48

r47

r46

r45

r44

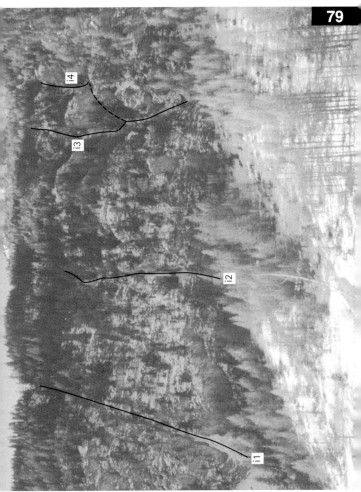

i13

i19

i18

i17

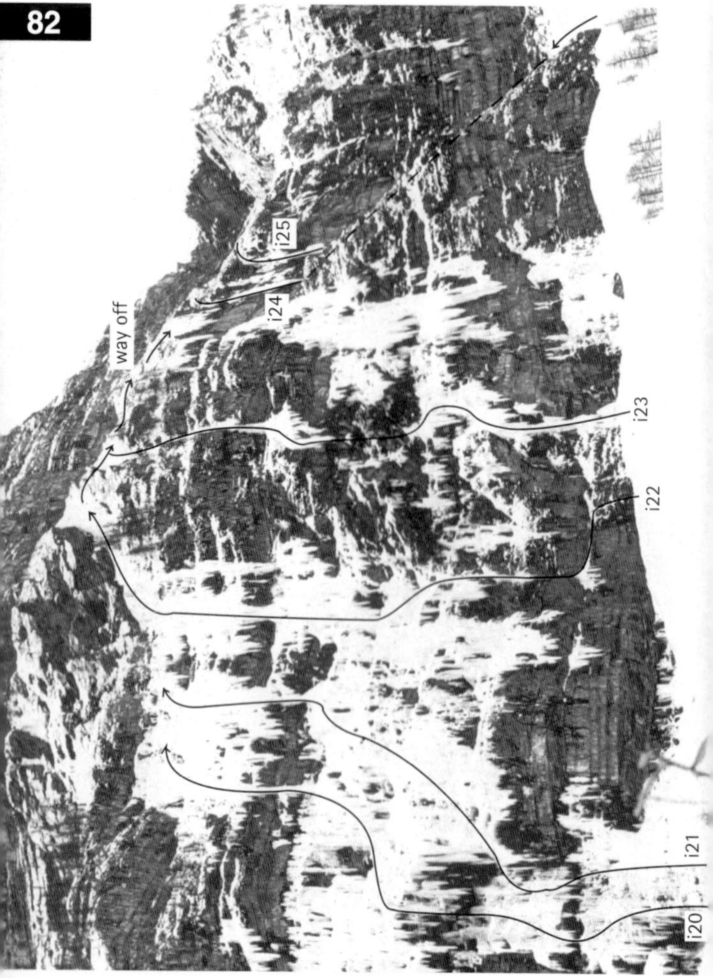
way off
i25
i24
i23
i22
i21
i20

i26

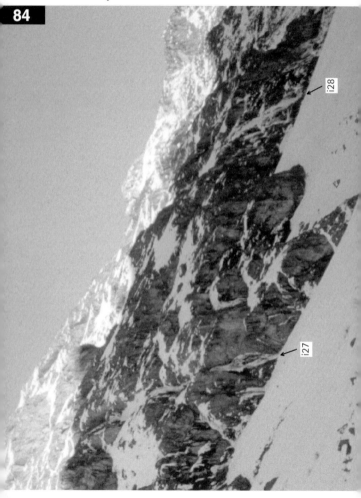

Aig de la Plat de la Selle

red
wall

i29

i30
i31
i32

90°

45°

90°

80/85°

i7

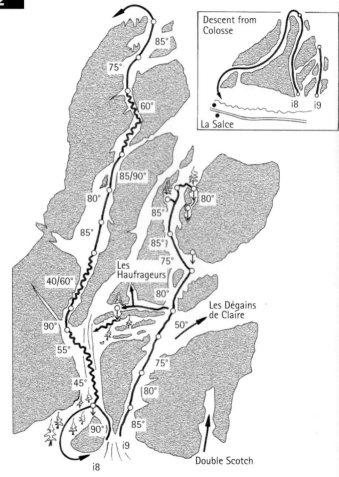

Descent from Colosse

La Salce

i8 i9

85°
75°
60°
85/90°
80°
85°
40/60°
90°
55°
45°
90°
i8
i9

80°
85°
85°
75°

Les Haufrageurs
80°

Les Dégains de Claire
50°

75°
80°
85°

Double Scotch

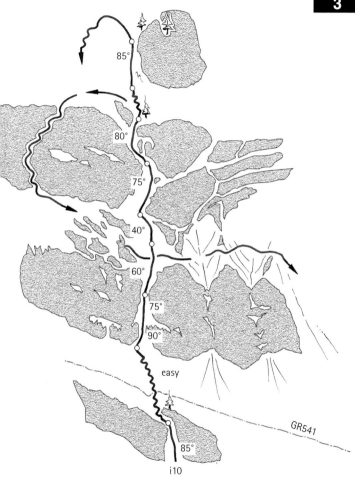

85°

80°

75°

40°

60°

75°

90°

easy

GR541

85°

i10

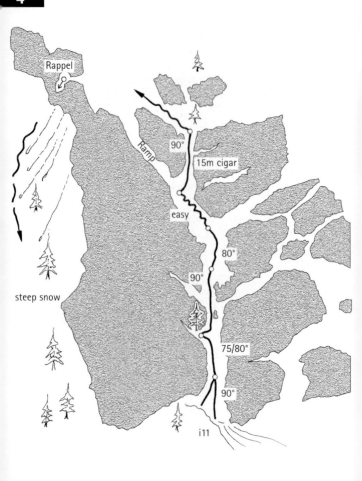

Rappel

Ramp

90°

15m cigar

easy

80°

steep snow

90°

75/80°

90°

i11

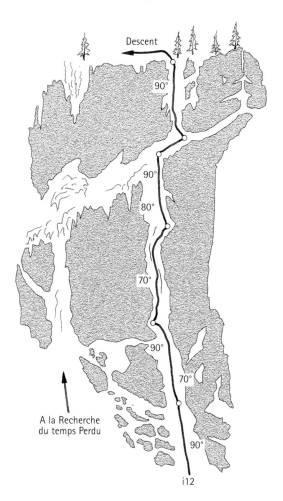

Descent

90°

90°

80°

70°

90°

70°

A la Recherche
du temps Perdu

90°

i12

The Alpine Club

The Alpine Club welcomes new members.

This guidebook is one of the many services which the Alpine Club offers to the mountaineering community and to its membership in particular. The Alpine Club is the only UK-based mountaineering club catering specifically for those who climb in the Alps and the Greater Ranges of the world. It is an active club, with regular a programme of events and meets.

The Alpine Club was founded in 1857 for "the promotion of good fellowship among mountaineers, of mountain climbing and mountain exploration throughout the world, and of better knowledge of mountains through literature, science and art." Throughout its existence, the Club has included in its membership many of the leading mountaineers of each generation, and now has members in more than 30 countries worldwide.

The Alpine Club Library has one of the foremost collections of mountaineering literature in the world, and is located at the Club premises in London. The Himalayan Index, owned and maintained by the Club, is a unique computerised record of climbing activity in the Himalaya.

The membership includes climbers of all abilities, and most active alpine climbers are qualified to join. There are three categories of membership, each with its own entrance requirements, benefits and subscription rates. Full Members are expected to have a record of at least 20 reasonable Alpine routes (or equivalent) over a minimum of three years. Aspirant Members status is for climbers who have some experience of Alpine climbing, and who expect to qualify as Full Members within 5 years. The third category is the Alpine Climbing Group (ACG). Members belonging to the ACG are expected to be active climbers with a record of hard climbs in the Alps and/or Greater Ranges.

Benefits of membership include:

* Climbing meets in the UK, Alps and the Greater Ranges
* Reduced rates in many Alpine huts
* BMC affiliation
* Discount on Alpine Club publications, including guidebooks
* Premises in London
* Free access to the Library and Himalayan Index
* Free Alpine Journal
* Regular lectures and symposia

A brochure outlining Club activities and how to join is available from the Assistant Secretary. If you have any queries about the Club, please contact the Assistant Secretary at the Club during office hours, or check out the Alpine Club web site.

The Assistant Secretary,   Tel. & Fax: 020 7613 0755

Alpine Club,   e-mail: asst-sec@alpine-club.org.uk

55 Charlotte Road   http://www.alpine-club.org.uk

London EC2A 3QF